GREAT WALDINGFIELD VILLAGE SCRAP BOOK 1951-2011

compiled by
EDNA ALLEN

DESERT ISLAND BOOKS

Index

Introduction

Foreword.

To those who find interest in the simple annals of the history of their native soil, which has passed from a simple agricultural community, with an overlord claiming serfs, to the age of complete freedom for the individual and the claims of modern development, this Scrap Book of 1951 may afford an interesting retrospect.

History

Great Waldingfield

A Glimpse into the past.

There is no doubting the antiquity of East Anglia and that most of its small communities are proud of some relic of the past. In this very short survey, we are particularly interested in our village of Great Waldingfield.

This village lies about three miles N.E. of the town of Sudbury. Although it has no claim to historical importance, we have some proof that the people of this village, down the ages, knew of and shared in passing events.

Research proves that Great Waldingfield was mentioned in the Domesday book of 1087; that proves it must have existed in Saxon times, for in 1066 the Normans conquered England, and later, made a survey of what they found.

The fierce German tribes, Angles and Saxons, attacked this Island after the recall of the Romans in 410 A.D.

Sailing up the Suffolk rivers, hordes of Angles burnt and plundered the homes of the helpless Britons. Here they had come to settle. They made clearances in the forests and formed little communities and for a time settled down comfortably.

Now these people spoke the German language. A forest to them was a "Wald" or "Vald". They made clearances to cultivate their crops and this is how the name of the village originated. Great Waldingfield — (Big field in Forest) and Little Waldingfield — (Small field in Forest). It might be stated here that Great Waldingfield appears as Waldingfield Magna and Little Waldingfield as Waldingfield Parva in the Domesday Book, Eight hundred and Sixty Four years ago.

There is authoritative evidence that the Romans passed this way, for a portion of a Roman subsidiary road crosses Waldingfield Road, south of Washmere Green.

This can be traced from Clare, which was a Roman Camp, to a main Roman road northwards.

When William the Norman caused the Domesday Book to be compiled, the Saxons (Angles) had three Manors in Waldingfield.

Here is an Extract of one :—

2 Carncates of land with soc and sac.
4 Villeins – 10 Borders – 4 Slaves – 2 Plough Teams
4 Acres of Meadow – 1 Horse at Hall – 3 Beasts
16 Hogs – 100 Sheep (Value £5)

Another proof of Great Waldingfield's long existence mentioned in the Domesday Book, is that one, Earl Gislebert, was appointed Tenent-in-Chief for the Parish, with two Freemen, one under Robert, son of Wimarc.

It is very interesting to note that the name of Whymark is still in the village after a period of more than Eight hundred years.

The land had long existed in Hundreds or Divisions. Waldingfield came within the Babergh Hundred. It held three Parishes and one hundred and Eighteen Manors — Great Waldingfield had six Manors :—

Carbonnel or Butler — Badley – Moreves
Sandesford – Brandeston Hall — Dowres.

Carbonnel's Manor was the chief one in Great Waldingfield. In the Domesday Book it was held by Aubrey de Vere. In 1277 Robert Carbonnel received for his homage and service, three Marks of Silver and three and a half acres of land plus the Manor in Waldingfield.

In 1333 it passed to James Butler Earl of Wiltshire. In 1461 it was held by the family of Botcher and finally passed to the family of Crane.

Badley's Manor was first held by Badele Baddeless a Norman Knight in 1240, hence the name of Badley's. Brandeston Hall has a special mention in the Domesday Book. In 1360 it was a Convent for the Nuns of Deptford.

Moreves included Babergh Hall.

Sandesford Manor is mentioned as belonging to James Goodene Sparrow in 1800.

Of Dowres Manor there appears to be no trace.

Up to the year 1800, Waldingfield was open Heath, with just tracks and paths crossing it. It was known as Babergh Heath. Annual fairs were held, stalls and tents were erected round the "White Horse" Inn and merrymaking continued for two or three days.

Passing events lightly touched this East Anglian village. It is said that Cromwell quartered some of his soldiers in a cul-de-sac, called The Garrison, before his attack on Colchester on the 27th August 1648.

Also in the Garrison is reputed to be the oldest house in the village, called "Malting Farm" It was formerly an Inn, known as "The Bottle". To-day can be seen the large old kitchen with a huge oak beam across the fireplace, with a central carving of the Tudor Rose.

In the 14th Century flourished the weaving of the Flemish settlers. Lying between Lavenham and

Sudbury, this village came in for a big share of the work and returns shew that Waldingfield played an important part in this industry. There is a reminder of this period in a row of charming cottages, which are distincly Flemish in design.

There is a land mark about which we should like to know more. For generations it has been called "The Great Tree". It stands at the junction of the main road and the road leading to the Church and School. In its day it was a mighty   Hence the name "Great". Today it shews signs of age.

Leaving the Great Tree behind and continuing a short distance, the church of St. Lawrence comes into view.

This Church, with the exception of the Chancel, dates from the end of the 14th century. The greatest change made within its precincts, was in 1869, when the Rector was the Rev. W. D. Bailey, who, with his three sisters made a pilgrimage to The Holy Land and visiting places en route, brought home many reminders. The Reredos contains mosaics made from the fragments of marble found among some ancient Roman ruins. The alabaster from which the Cross is made came from a small temple near the Sphinx; the granite slabs over the Credence from Mount Sinai, and the Syenite from a fragment of the statue of Rameses II at Thebes. A National School for the village was established in 1842 by the then Rector, the Rev. Henry Kirby. In 1852 the present school was erected at a cost of £500.

It was to accomodate about 120 children. It was open to Government inspection and was maintained by a Government Grant, subscriptions and the Scholars' pence. The average number of scholars between 1852 and 1866 was 123. Of this number, only just over half attended regularly, owing to child labour.

In 1869 the Rev. W. D. Bailey gave the school his impressions of his journey to the Holy Land. Thorns were shewn the children like those which made up Christ's Crown of Thorns. They were shewn gold, franckincense and myrrh, and the latter was burnt before them. Each teacher received a beautiful shawl. Today the old school still exists, and under the new order of things is now a school for children under the age of eleven, from surrounding villages.

Before taking leave of the village, it is interesting to note the names of the families which have been handed down. Nearly all of them relate to rural life. There are Sparrow, Finch, Partridge, Steed, Bowers, Diggins, Bird, Martin, Starling etc.

Norman French gave the name of Theobald. For many years the name was referred to locally as "Tebble". When one recalls that this is a very good imitation of the French pronunciation of Theobald, the explanation is clear.

So, in conclusion, Waldingfield has heard through the ages, the tramp of Roman soldiers, Norman French, Cromwell's Ironsides, and up to date, those of America.

From our files

Over the years, many readers have supplied us with pictures of the past — showing local life as it was earlier this century. As 1978 dawns, we show four views of yesterday...

Readers are invited to send old pictures to us with a view to publication but they must be clearly marked with your name and address on the back of each photograph.

Down Memory Lane

Men of Great Waldingfield who served in the forces during the First World War.

A pre-war postcard view of Melford Road, Sudbury. There are more cars nowadays, but the scene has otherwise changed very little.

North Street, Sudbury — and not a supermarket in sight.

THIS week's Memory Lane photograph comes from Ernest Shaw, of Hillside Cottages, Newton Road, Sudbury.

The former International Stores shop on Market Hill in Sudbury is occupied today by Sketchley. The figure in the centre is Mr Shaw's father, who was also the steward of the Conservative Club in Sudbury.

Celebration

Free Press, Thursday, September 20, 1990 **13**

● Cheers! The ladies of Great Waldingfield W.I. celebrate with a cup of tea. (0730).

Over at Great Waldingfield the whole village was invited to tea at the Village Hall and at Newton Green nursery rhyme characters teamed up with a host of teddy bears for a tea party celebration at the Jubilee Gardens.

LADIES OUT TO PROVE A POINT

LOCAL WI members are out to quash jokes about women drivers by competing in a national competition to find the WI Driver of the Year.

The competition — staged by car giant Vauxhall — aims to showcase the driving skills of the fairer sex and has attracted 18 competitors from the Sudbury area who are taking part in a local heat organised by Sudbury Vauxhall dealers Solar Garage.

Entrants have to drive a Vauxhall Nova around a ten-and-three-quarter mile route using the least amount of petrol and the winner and two runners-up will win cash prizes and the chance to go forward to regional heats and a grand final designed to test their driving abilities to the full.

by NICK CROWN

Solar Garage general manager, Ron Mansfield, aid: "We've prepared a Nova with a fuel flow meter which will show who drives the most economically and so decide the first three placings."

Among the contestants taking part the competition are Great Waldingfield WI members Ann Holloway and Edna Allen, pictured above right with Mr Mansfield and another prospective competitor Gill Leech of Glemsford WI. (Pic no 0262).

"It sounds great fun and is an ideal opportunity to lay to rest the myth about bad women drivers once and for all," said Mrs Holloway.

Top prizes in the national final include a Vauxhall Nova 1.6I and a weekend for two in Paris.

highlight of our year was being able to meet and entertain Albina, Tonya and Natalya, three representatives from the Soviet Women's Committee.

COMMUNITY AFFAIRS our WI members are not just Institute members we are active members of Great Waldingfield's community too and we have not been idle there either...

We compiled and delivered to every house in the village a short Directory of where to take everything for re-cycling. We have also urged the Parish Council to consider a Bottle Bank. The village boundary signs and telephone box were cleaned by our members and our own Village Hall was our Charity for the Year.

Our members have taken part in and helped with national Surveys on Hedgehogs and Village Greens and our members are involved in voluntary organisations, Parish Council work and charity groups which are far too numerous to mention – but what a busy lot we are.

Surely no-one can truly say we don't do anything – WI should stand for (among other suggestions) Wonderfully Industrious.

Edna Allen, President, Great Waldingfield WI

PARISH COUNCIL —At last month's meeting the first item concerned the recent site meeting with the Highways Dept, at which the remedial work at Chilton Corner was outlines.

This will involve the widening of the junction and the erection of an elongated island with illuminated giveway signs. Further advance warning signs would be supplied as well as some signs at the post office crossroads. Both these junctions have been the scene of fatal accidents in the last year.

JANUARY 6th
Mr H. Butcher. Holiday Slides.
Comp: Holiday Souvenir

FEBRUARY 3rd
Mrs J. Cricklemore.
Electricity in the Home.
Comp: Valentine Novelty.

MARCH 2nd
Mrs J. Howlett. Keeping Fit
in the Middle Years.
Comp: Salad on a Plate.

APRIL 6th
Mrs E. Freeman. Sudbury in the
time of Thomas Gainsborough.
Comp: Easter Bonnet.

MAY 4th
Mr Markham. Pawnbroking.
Comp: Prettiest Vase.

JUNE 1st
Our 70th Birthday.

GREAT WALDINGFIELD

PARISH COUNCIL — The Parish Council held their last meeting of the year on Tuesday 27 November at the Village Hall.

The Girl Guides had approached the Council with a view to siting a hut for storage on the land at Ten Trees Road and this was viewed favourably.

It was unofficially confirmed that the Footpath along Hole Farm Road had been upheld following the Inqiry and a new Circular Footpath Map will be produced in conjunction with Little Waldingfield.

A planning application for an extension at 2 Malting Barn was recommended for approval. The Parish Council considered a request for assistance in fund raising for the Church Roof and a sum of £2,000 was agreed.

The Parish Council then considered the precept amounts which would be required for the year from April 1st 1990. The Council put forward for a grant to the Village hall for repairs to the car park, a further grant to the Church, additional fencing near the pumping station in Folly Road, and together with running expenses of street lights, pavilion and playing field and general administration, a total request for £15,000 was made. A grant for £65 was forwarded to the Citizens Advice Bureau.

A cheque for £100 was received on behalf of the Village Hall funds from the Women's Institute for the purchase of new trestle tables.

The playing field equipment contract had been made to Mr Munson of Folly Road and it is hoped the work would start as soon as possible. The rocking horse is to be repaired and Babergh District Council would be asked to repair once again the fence near Kenyon Drive.

Mr Skinner and Mrs Bates gave a report on the Suffolk Association of Local Councils AGM and the Area Meeting. It was noted the last date for inclusion in the local electoral lists was December 19th.

During the public comment period, it was mentioned that the 40mph limit was very erratic and it was hoped that a total scheme was not far off. Complaints about skips of rubbish on the airfield would be passed to Babergh District Council.

A request for a name to be put forward for a ward naming scheme at Walnuttree Hospital was considered and the name Lawrence Ward was put forward. The Chairman wished all Councillors a Happy Christmas and Prosperous New Year and the next meeting will be held in January 1991.

OUTSIDE THE WHITE HORSE

ACTON AND GREAT WALDINGFIELD FRIENDSHIP CLUB

We meet at Acton Village Hall every other Monday, (avoiding Bank Holidays) at 1.30 pm to 4.00 pm. A Felix bus is hired to take members to and from Acton Village Hall. If you wish to use your own transport there is ample parking space in front of the Hall. The bus is free. New members are always welcome. Subscription is 40p each. Next meetings are 11 and 25 April and 9 and 23 May. Both ladies and gentlemen must be 55 years and over. The meetings consist of playing cards or other games, having a friendly chat, and meeting other people. We also run a raffle. The prizes are gifts from members as and when they feel like supplying a prize. A break midway we have free tea and biscuits finishing with Bingo. We also have during the year, two Jumble Sales and various bring and buy sales. The money raised helps towards four or five outings in the summer, plus a Christmas Dinner and party in December. For further information please ring Harry Blazey 311108, Chairman.

VILLAGE HALL

A most unusual situation had arisen over the hiring of the Village Hall for a party on Saturday 24th November.

The hall had been booked by letter, and when a follow up was made to complete a letting form and secure a deposit it was found to be supplied with a false address.

After several days of enquiries, it was understood that the hall was being booked by school children for a dance, and tickets had already been sold. The major schools in the area were asked to announce that for legal and security reasons the event could not take place and it was pleasing to note that on the evening, no disappointed revellers had to be turned away.

The irony was that three days before the event a letter (without an address) was received together with a £5 deposit. As the Council do not expect anyone to call and claim the money, it will, at the end of the month, be donated to the Children in Need fund.

The regulations for the Hall are strictly adhered to and these are that all bookings must be supported by a letting agreement and a deposit and any dances and discos must have the name and address of two persons over the age of 25.

The incident did cause comment on the sheer audacity and ingenuity of the organisers but it also wasted a lot of time on the part of the Letting Secretary, the Council, Police and Schools and it is hoped it will not be repeated.

GT WALDINGFIELD W.I.

The Festive Season was celebrated in a gaily decorated Village Hall with two Xmas trees. Everyone contributed a savoury or sweet plate, which made an appetising and varied spread. A questionnaire game was played with catch questions relating to Pounds, Shillings and Pence, which, if answered correctly, resulted in a total in old money. Mrs Mary Jackson won a prize with the highest correct answers. Various prizes were won in the Christmas raffle, followed by carols and a sing-song, ending a very happy evening.

A parcel containing a variety of 'English' Teas were sent to the New Zealand link between them and Waldingfield WI, as a token Christmas gift.

PRIMARY SCHOOL — Last Saturday, Dec 1st, a surprise visitor arrived at the school. This was Father Christmas, who attended the Christmas Bazaar, to talk to children and to hand them a 'taster' gift. The Bazaar was very well supported with a wide variety of stalls, including crafts, toys, china and glass, cakes and sweets, white elephants and seasonal raffles. On sale also, were tea towels and notelets featuring a self portrait of all the children, of the staff, a cup of tea or coffee and a mince pie were offered as welcome refreshments. The event organised by the friends of the school, and supported by other parents, staff and governors, raised over £340 towards a third computer.

BOOK FAIR — During the first week of December the school has been running a Book Fair. A large selection of books have been on sale to the children and in the afternoons to parents, friends and children from other schools. Because of the great support for this venture each class was able to have a variety of free books for their classrooms.

GREAT WALDINGFIELD WOMEN'S INSTITUTE

Founded June 1918
Suffolk West Federation

PROGRAMME 1990

OFFICERS

PRESIDENT
Mrs. E. Allen
Newbarn Farm
Valley Road
Newton
Sudbury 72206

SECRETARY
Mrs. Ann Holloway
8 Hollbrook Close
Gt. Waldingfield
Sudbury 79227

TREASURER
Mrs. S. Lester
34 Heath Estate
Gt. Waldingfield
Sudbury 77766

Meetings: First Wednesday each month in the Village Hall.

VISITORS WELCOME

Subscription £7.50

CHRISTMAS WISHES

The Rector and Mrs Pizzey take this opportunity of wishing all a joyous Christmas and a Happy New Year. We shall not be sending Christmas cards this year to friends who live locally; but shall instead donate what we would have spent on cards to the work of the Children's Society.

MR HAROLD DAY — The funeral of Harold Day took place recently at St Laurence Church, Great Waldingfield.

Mr Day died at the West Suffolk Hospital on December 31, aged 89.

The service was conducted by the Rev L. Pizzey, assisted by David Rutherford with organist Mrs J. Musclow.

Immediate mourners were: Mr and Mrs P. Miles, Mr and Mrs F. Cadge (sons-in-law and daughters), Mr and Mrs P. W. Miles, Mr and Mrs D. C. Miles, Mr and Mrs R. Mortlock, Miss S. Cadge (grandchildren), Master B. W. Miles, Miss L. V. Miles (great-grandchildren), Mrs V. Gibbs, Mr R. Simpson, Mrs P. Garrett rep Mr R. Garrett, Mrs J. Edwards (nieces and nephews).

1st ACTON AND WALDINGFIELD SCOUT GROUP NEWS

News from the Beavers

Five new Beavers were invested at the beginning of June and all knew their promise well. Welcome to the colony.

Towards the end of May the Beavers went for a walk around Acton. A first taste of hiking for the boys.

News from the Cubs

Lots of badges have been attained by several cubs recently including probably the only astronomer's badge in the district. Other activities recently have included Swimming, Tent Pitching, Hiking and a visit to 3rd Sudbury 'C' Pack Cubs at Great Cornard.

Over the weekend of 12-14 July, thirteen cubs will be going on the District Cub Camp in Lavenham.

News from the Scouts

At the District Camping Competition our troup did very well coming fourth in the Activities section and came eighth overall. A marvellous result considering two of the boys were cubs and another two very young inexperienced scouts.

News from the Ventures

Recently two teams came 5th and 6th in the Roger Hammond Trophy, and Egg Throwing Competition. The winning team threw well over 90ft and even then some of the missed eggs bounced and didn't break.

13

Crisis in Africa booster

WE WOULD like to thank the generous Sudbury public for contributing £202 to a Crisis in Africa street collection on February 2. This will go to helping give relief to 27 million people who are at starvation point in seven different African countries.

BRIAR SKINNER
Sudbury Group,
Hungry For Change – Oxfam

The village hall was filled with the sound of rattling dice in January. A beetle drive was in progress and laughter echoed round the hall as beetles were drawn and completed with various numbers being thrown by four persons at each table arranged around the room. Tea and coffee with home-made mincepies followed - a very pleasant evening to start the New Year.

An informal and friendly atmosphere was enjoyed at Tye Farm at the kind invitation of member, Mary Stubley, where ideas and useful hints and tips were exchanged by members. Some members indulged in a quiet swim in the adjacent indoor pool. Tea and coffee, accompanied by Mary's home-made rolls and jam completed a perfect afternoon.

The Parish Council has acknowledged the £100 donated by the WI towards new tables in the village hall, and it was a unanimous decision that this coming year's charity will be to help the group's own funds.

On the road again

WITH reference to your report in the edition of January 24, we want to put the record straight on the highway problem near Morris Farm, Great Waldingfield.

Prior to this report we had an on-site discussion with representatives of the parish council on the condition of the road, the reasons for its deterioration with constructive suggestions as to a solution. We were in full agreement to the proposals, which will involve consultation with the Sufolk County Council highways department.

DAVID D. STEED
D.H. Steed & Co,
The Badleys,
Great Waldingfield

Help for troops

GREAT Waldingfield woman Maureen Hammond is looking for items to fill the many cardboard boxes in her house so she can help servicemen and women in The Gulf.

Maureen said:"I want to do my bit for the armed forces.

"The Ministry of Defence has sent me a list of things that will be ideal including toothpaste, foot powder and soap but I have also prepared a list of luxuries like sweets, biscuits, book, air mail pads and envelopes."

Anyone who wants to contribute to the parcels can drop items off at Great Waldingfield Primary School or Great Waldingfield Post Office.

Further details on the lists are available by phoning Maureen on Sudbury 77796.

CONCERT — This Saturday sees the very welcome return of Mixed Reviews, a talented young amateur company. Originally the young people used to sing together at university, the operas of Gilbert and Sullivan being a favourite. Now, even though they work in different parts of the country, they still manage to meet together and perform shows for charity.

So far they have raised at least £2,500 for different charities. Last year they performed Ruddigore at Gt Waldingfield and this was thoroughly enjoyed by all present; so much so, that they have been persuaded to return to perform a concert version of Iolanthe, in Gt Waldingfield School Hall at 7.30 pm. The proceeds will go to the church roof repair fund. Tickets are limited, but can be obtained from the school, church or post office.

CLASS 2
1991

HORTICULTURAL SHOW — The seventh spring horticultural show was held in the village hall on Saturday, April 13. Judging by the magnificent sights and smells in the hall, it looked as though the date was just right; in fact there were more entries this year than ever before. According to the judges, the exhibits were again of an extremely high standard.

Flower section winners were — daffodils, single: 1 Chris Francis, 2 George Albion, 3 Christine Tompsett; double: 1 Tom Nice, 2 Maureen Shinn, 3 D. Thompson; narcissi: 1 L. A. Haxell, 2 Maureen Shinn, 3 M. E. Armour; jonquils: 1 F. C. Shinn, 2 Maureen Shinn, 3 Chris Francis; tulips, single: 1 George Albion, 2 F. C. Shinn, 3 Edna Allen; double: 1 E. V. Eliot, 2 L. A. Haxell; miniature daffodils: 1 Mary Jackson, 2 F. J. Radley, 3 George Albion; pansies: 1 F. Radley, 2 M. E. Armour, 3 A. A. Valdy; polyanthus: 1 D. Hamilton, 2 D. Armour, 3 M. E. Armour; other primula: 1 M. E. Armour, 2 D. Hamilton, 3 Edna Allen; flowering shrub or tree: 1 F. Radley, 2 E. V. Eliot, 3 Mary Jackson; spring flower selection: 1 Chris Francis, 2 M. R. Shinn, 3 Jean Misselbrook; pot plant, flowering: 1 D. Hamilton, 2 Anne Francis, 3 C. Adams; non-flowering: 1 Mary Jackson, 2 Chris Francis, 3 D. Hamilton; other spring flower: 1 George Albion, 2 Chris Francis, 3 A. Albion.

Flower arranging — spring flowers in basket: 1 Anne Francis, 2 Mary Adams, 3 Jean Misselbrook; silver wedding arrangement: 1 Anne Francis, 2 Jean Misselbrook, 3 Maureen Mitchell; miniature: 1 Anne Francis, 2 Jean Misselbrook.

Novice flower arranging — spring flowers in a basket: 1 Pat Leathers, 2

Ready for work ... Acton and Waldingfield cubs down by the riverside
Contributed picture

Mr D Floyd recently donated a cup to Great Waldingfield School. The cup is to mark over 20 years of service, by Mr Floyd, to the school as a manager and a governor, and is to be awarded each term for achievement. The first recipient is Michael Welsh, here seen receiving the cup from Mr Floyd, at the end of last term.

GOVERNOR'S CUP

Customers say thankyou as 'lovely couple' shut up shop

ELSIE and Bill Green thought they would shut up shop quietly on Monday when they closed Heathway Stores in Coronation Rise, Great Waldingfield, for the last time after 21 years. But their grateful customers had other ideas.

Nina Butcher, who lives nearby, had got together with friends Nita Walker and Mary Nice and between them canvassed all the Greens' customers in the village. They collected enough money to buy a suitable surprise gift and express their appreciation to "a lovely couple".

Bill (71) was quietly tidying up the shop on Tuesday morning when Nina suddenly arrived with a crowd of customers who had gathered to wish them well.

The couple were presented with a library clock for their living room, a basket of flowers, a floral arrangement and two large cards signed by

Customers crowd round retiring shopkeepers Bill and Elsie Green.

everyone who had contributed.

"They were absolutely overwhelmed and for once, stuck for words. We were very pleased because they really deserved it," said Nina. "We wanted to express our thanks because they have been ever so good and have bent over backwards to be

helpful. They are what village shops are all about."

Elsie (75), who was a little tearful at the presentation, said the surprise had been a bit of a shock but "it was lovely to know so many people thought of us."

She has not been well over the past couple of

years and as her husband could not carry on without her they decided the time had come to shut up shop and retire.

"We felt we had had enough but have thoroughly enjoyed it. We have plenty of good friends round us and couldn't wish for better people," she said.

Gt. Waldingfield

Women's Institute: The first signs of snow were in the air on Feb. 6, the evening of the W.I. meeting, but despite the very cold night, there was a good attendance in the Village Hall. A report was given on resolutions raised at the Triennial General meeting held at Whiting Street on Jan. 23 and attended by Mrs. D. Thorpe, M. Jackson and F. Bates. Thirteen resolutions were listed and all present voted their choices, in order of what they merited most urgent. The annual pantomine at Newton Green provided lots of fun and was enjoyed by those who went to see it. Refreshments and raffles were also available. New member Mrs. Eileen Winscoll was welcomed and greetings for birthdays went to Mrs. Sheila Lester, Gillian Nuttall and Grace Parish. This year's delegate for Gt. Waldingfield at the Federal general meeting in Birmingham, will be secretary, Mrs. Ann Holloway. Guest speaker, Mr. Ken Brooks, gave a most interesting talk about his work on the Bench at the County Court as a Justice of the Peace. Mrs. Frances Bates thanked him for his talk. Next meeting at village Hall on March 6 (7.30 pm).

FAREWELL GIFT FOR RETIRING PRESIDENT

TOM Wells (right) receives his farewell gift from festival vice-chairman Robert Hewett.

SUDBURY Festival organisers gathered at Uplands Middle School on Saturday for a special surprise presentation to Tom Wells, retiring after ten years as president

The former Clare Primary School head, who has been involved with the Clare and Sudbury festivals for over 40 years, officially steps down in June.

He received a landscape print by local artist Michael Carlo from vice-chairman Robert Hewett, who said Mr Wells would be sorely missed by everyone.

Mr Wells (80) moved to

Surrey in 1981 following the death of his wife Joy but has maintained close links with the festival which has grown into a major annual celebration of music, speech and dance involving hundreds of people.

On Saturday he presented the open piano class cup in memory of his wife and promised to keep returning to the festival as long as his health permits.

In Surrey Mr Wells serves on the committee of the Goldalming Music Festival and continues to give occasional singing lessons at Charterhouse School, where his son is head of music.

WI build on history of bricks

PETER Minter of the Bulmer Brick Company enthralled Great Waldingfield Women's Institute with the story of bricks and brickmaking covering 3,000 years, showing slides of churches and chimneys, fireplaces and stately homes — all the while telling the history of his own brick company.

Top award for guides

THE highest honour for guides, the Baden Powell award, was presented to two 14-year-old Great Waldingfield girls last week.

Jo Challacombe, whose sister Becky received the award two years ago, and Jennie Lloyd were presented with the Baden Powell badges and certficates by Shirley Ansell, South West Suffolk divisional commissioner, for four years of hard work and dedication to the movement.

Their work for the Baden-Powell award included learning sign language and lip reading for their Friends to the Deaf and studying the Common Market for their Eurpoean award.

Fellow guides joined them in their celebrations at Great Waldingfield village hall where Mrs Ansell praised the girls for their efforts.

Jo Challacombe (left) and Jennie Lloyd receive their Baden-Powell awards from South West Suffolk divisional commissioner Shirley Ansell.

"It is quite rare for the guiding movement to give this award but these two girls really deserve it," she said.

"It is always nice to see guides been rewarded for their hard work and Jo and Jennie are a shining example to all guides."

Gifts for Romania wanted

SUDBURY Town Hall will be open next Thursday and Friday to anyone who wants to donate something to the local charity Christian Cargo.

Norman Ridge from Great Waldingfield set up the charity to help Romanian orphans who live in poverty.

Clothing, toys and jigsaw puzzles are needed and anyone who wants to give anything can leave items at the town hall between 10am and 4pm on March 14 and 15.

Unsuitable clothing will be sold and the proceeds used to buy drugs and medicine in time for the next delivery by Christian Cargo to Romania on April 7.

Gulf parcels generosity

MY husband and I would like to say a very big thank you to everyone who contributed to the parcels that we have been sending to the Gulf over the last few weeks.

I'm happy to let you know that 61 parcels have been sent so far, which without your readers' generosity would not have been possible.

A special thank you also to United Carriers for their collections.

MAUREEN & PAUL HAMMOND

Kenyon Drive,
Great Waldingfield

NORA CRACKNELL — The funeral took place on Thursday, March 21, of Nora Cracknell of Great Waldingfield, who died at the age of 85. The Rev Lawrence Pizzey officiated at the service in Great Waldingfield Church and at the burial at St Mary's Church, Little Thornham, which she had attended as a child.

One of the youngest of a large family, on the death of her mother Miss Cracknell embarked on a happy and fulfilling life as a social worker and particularly running a children's home in Grantham, Lincolnshire. A lover of young people, she brought happiness, security and hope to many needy children.

She retired to Great Waldingfield, where she lived for 25 years and found happiness and contentment in her home, garden and participation in church and local activities. After a short stay in hospital in Bury St Edmunds over Christmas, she was cared for by members of her family at Great Henny, where she died.

Hearty thanks

THANK YOU from the British Heart Foundation to all the people of Sudbury, Lavenham and Long Melford who contributed to our flag day and street collection on Saturday, April 13. The total for the day was a magnificent £782.42.

PETER HOLLOWAY,
Hon. Sec., Sudbury & District BHF,
8 Holbrook Close,
Great Waldingfield.

Help with family trees

ANYONE compiling a family tree can now consult five volumes which have been supplied to the town's library by Sudbury Freemen's Trust.

The books contain local parish registers of baptisms, marriages and burials from 1564 to, in some cases, 1837 and they are only for reference.

Library manager Anne Lockley says the public have already shown an interest and the books could be most useful for researching family histories. Parishes covered include All Saints, St. Gregory's and St. Peter's in Sudbury, Great Cornard, Little Cornard, Acton, Great Waldingfield and Little Waldingfield.

Any information that cannot be found in the volumes can be obtained from the Record Office in Bury St. Edmunds (0284-763141, ext. 2522).

Thank-you

NOW that Mathew's appeal has been closed, I would like to take this opportunity to thank everybody who helped to raise money for his wheelchair. Without the Free Press coverage of his story, this would not have been possible.

PAULA TURKENTINE,
39 Badleys Close,
Great Waldingfield.

BABERGH DISTRICT COUNCIL

Setting of Personal Community Charge

NOTICE IS HEREBY GIVEN that at a meeting held on the 19th February 1991, the Babergh District Council, in accordance with Sections 32 and 33 of the Local Government Act 1988, set for the year beginning on 1st April 1991 and ending on 31st March 1992 the amounts shown below as the personal community charge for the undermentioned areas:—

For the Parishes of	Amount of Community Charge £	For the Parishes of	Amount of Community Charge £
Acton	372.24	Kersey	368.85
Aldham	367.26	Kettlebaston	374.04
Alpheton	368.55	Lavenham	376.09
Arwarton	365.00	Lawshall	367.28
Assington	369.79	Layham	371.41
Belstead	366.98	Leavenheath	372.79
Bentley	368.91	Lindsay	368.74
Bildeston	373.01	Long Melford	374.93
Boxford	372.65	Milden	365.00
Boxted	365.00	Monks Eleigh	371.96
Brantham	376.25	Nayland	376.32
Brent Eleigh	374.47	Nedging	366.00
Brettenham	371.92	Newton	370.08
Bures St Mary	376.91	Polstead	370.39
Burstall	369.49	Preston St Mary	366.91
Capel St Mary	372.54	Raydon	372.51
Chattisham/Hintlesham	369.57	Semer	366.92
Chelmondiston	373.30	Shelley	365.00
Chelsworth	365.00	Shimpling	367.76
Chilton	369.21	Shotley	369.64
Cockfield	368.92	Somerton	368.17
Copdock/Washbrook	372.50	Sproughton	376.85
Cornard Great	378.50	Stanstead	370.83
Cornard Little	367.59	Stoke By Nayland	372.65
East Bergholt	374.10	Stratford St Mary	370.42
Edwardstone	371.85	Stutton	369.50
Elmsett	369.10	Sudbury	380.73
Freston	365.00	Tattingstone	368.11
Glemsford	372.42	Thorpe Morieux	370.74
Groton	370.24	Waldingfield Great	379.27
Hadleigh	382.91	Waldingfield Little	368.61
Harkstead	372.42	Wattisham	369.82
Hartest	371.07	Wenham Magna	365.00
Higham	365.00	Wenham Parva	365.00
Hitcham	367.45	Whatfield	368.04
Holbrook	368.87	Wherstead	369.14
Holton St Mary	369.04	Woolverstone	370.18

R. G. SALMON
Secretary

Council Offices
Hadleigh, Ipswich
Suffolk, IP7 6SJ
February 1991

New number

SUDBURY police station's telephone number has changed to Sudbury 881000.

Council bids to beat the bogus bookers

GREAT Waldingfield parish council has warned that all bookings for the village hall must be backed by a letting agreement and a deposit following a bogus application by schoolchildren.

The hall was booked by letter for an event on November 24 but the address turned out to be false.

Further enquiries revealed that schoolchildren had made the reservation and sold tickets for a dance but schools were alerted that it could not take place.

Three days before the event another letter with no address was received containing a £5 booking fee and as the council do not expect this to be claimed it is being donated to Children in Need.

The council says the incident wasted a lot of time on the part of schools, the police and the hall's letting secretary and hopes it will not happen again. Dance and disco bookings also need the names and addresses of two people aged over 25.

GREAT WALDINGFIELD

PARISH COUNCIL — The parish council held their meeting in the village hall, when discussions on the future use of the land off Ten Trees Road were postponed as information was not available from the bowls club.

The council are aiming to officially list the footpath from Rectory Road to Upsher Green and the necessary forms are being completed. The footpath along Hole Farm Road from the Church towards Little Waldingfield has been officially listed as Footpath 14.

The parish council chairman and the clerk had met on site with Mr D. Steel on Friday, January 18 to discuss the condition of Folly Road. The problems of drainage and collapse of the road edge were noted and a report was approved and forwarded to the highways department for comment.

Planning applications for a garage at the Old Rectory and an extension at Compass House were recommended for approval. Changes of plans for houses at Bantocks Field were discussed but the council reported that the design of detached four-bedroomed houses was not what was wanted in the village. A small low-cost home would be more acceptable.

A donation of £75 was made to the Suffolk Age Concern unity centre in Sudbury. The scheme for transferring the trusteeship of the village hall charity was nearing completion but there were a few points still to be cleared.

A complaint was received about cars parking on the grass in Coronation Rise and this would be followed up with the district council. Two street lamps had been damaged in vehicle accidents and the council had followed up the cost of repair with the parties concerned.

An exhibition on planning consultation in the village hall on Friday, February 22 will be open to the public from about 10am to 7pm. Various road signs and fences were reported as broken and missing and these would be repaired.

The next council meeting will be on Tuesday, February 26, at 7.45, in the village hall.

Kuwait is a prison camp

AS I write the bombers are going in to "liberate" Kuwait.

President Bush has finally lost patience, having done as little as possible to find a peaceful solution.

John Major rightly described Kuwait as a prison camp. By the time liberation is over it will be a graveyard. Like the rest of the Middle East! May God forgive us! It's a Holy War!
BILL SKINNER
Garrison Cottage
Gt Waldingfield

Generator theft

THIEVES stole a generator worth £500 from a garage in High Street, Great Waldingfield, on Saturday night. It belongs to Barry Heavens, of Chelsworth.

PARISH MEETING: The annual parish meeting was held on Tuesday, April 23, in the village hall. Mr David Flloyd, chairman of the parish council, welcomed those present. He introduced Mr Neil Greg, planning consultant, who talked about the proposed Babergh plan for the area.

As the local plan for the area had to be updated to include more industry and housing, it was decided to look at the Chilton airfield area, the proposed plans of new roads, industry, housing and community woodland had been on view previously but various questions were asked about roads, type of trees, provision of low cost housing, pedestrian and cycling pathways, and the problem of heavy traffic.

The chairman's report covered the problems of trying to provide local needs housing and the goods vehicle licensing system. There is now a speed limit in the village and an improved junction at Valley Road. The process of taking over the village hall is nearly complete.

New items of play equipment with safety surfacing had been erected on the playing field. Vandalism was still a problem, costing the parishioners about £2 a head per year.

A footpath walk around the Waldingfields had been completed with most of the work undertaken by Mr Hammond, with finance for publishing coming from the county council.

There were now eight places on the parish council and in fact only eight nominations had been received, so those people would be returned with no election. Mr Floyd thanked the parish councillors for their hard work and support during the previous year.

Mr Selwyn Prior, county councillor, addressed the meeting. He was hopeful that the Suffolk County Council would not be fragmented but stay as it is.

Mr Colin Spence spoke on behalf of the district councillors. Over 95 per cent of the people in Babergh district had paid their poll tax during the previous year – those not paying would be pursued. It was hoped the revised bills for this year will be out in early summer.

Good wishes were given to Mrs Viven Pryke who was not seeking re-election to the district council this year.

Chief Inspector Durrant addressed the meeting and spoke about the problems of policing the area. He urged people to be aware of people visiting homes on any pretext and later returning to burgle the house. Properties and vehicles should be locked and secured. The public could cut down the present incidents of vandalism and thieving if they were vigilant and reported anything unusual to the police.

The treasurer presented the accounts and these were adopted. She pointed out that without a community council or village hall committee to raise funds, the parish council would have to spend more so the precept for 1991 would have to be higher.

Reports were presented by the WI, school governors, Braithwaite Trust, brownies, rangers, guides, playgroup, bowls, horticultural committee and the parish magazine committee.

WI — The beautiful display of decorated goose eggs, transformed into pretty and ingenious ornaments, brought gasps of admiration from her audience, when Mrs Summerhill brought out one by one the amazing fruits of her skill and hobby, when she was guest speaker at the WI meeting on April 3. Mostly mounted on small gold or silver stands, they were cleverly cut, painted and decorated with sequins, braid or flowers, and inside could be seen miniature figures, some of which were bridal pairs. Several layers of paint are used to make the shells strong for this purpose, and the variety she creates, made this a very interesting subject. An ostrich egg with scenery both inside and out, towered over them all and completed this lovely collection.

Future outings and events were on the agenda, including trips to Mr Minters brick works at Bulmer Tye, a visit to a vineyard, a cruise on the River Derham, a jumble sale in May, a bowls fun day, plans for the carnival and several other promising future plans for the coming year.

There is always room for new members in the local WI, and Gt Waldingfield is no exception. Women of all ages are there, and three visitors, at a low entrance fee, can provide a "make your mind up" trial period. To find out more information, phone Sec A. H. Holloway, Sudbury 79227.

Next month's speaker will be Mrs Iona Pettit talking of The British Heart Foundation, May 1 at 7.30 pm, village hall. So many interesting subjects and creative hobbies can be enjoyed with others, at the WI meetings.

PARISH COUNCIL

The Parish Council held their first meeting following the Local Government elections on Tuesday 14 May 1991 at the Village Hall.

The election of officers was held and the Council now stands as follows:

Chairman	–	Mr David Floyd
Vice Chairman	–	Mrs Jean Misselbrook
Councillors	–	Mr Bill Skinner, Mr Alan White, Mrs Vickie Haynes, Mrs Frances Bates, Mrs Sheila Marchant and Mrs Christina Richardson.

The Council now run two equal sub-committees to deal with both the Village Hall and the Pavilion and Playfield Equipment.

RAMBLING ROUND THE WALDINGFIELDS

SUDBURY Ramblers have got together with Suffolk County Council to organise an inaugural four-mile walk round the Waldingfields on Sunday, May 19.

The walk will launch a footpath guide leaflet, published by Great and Little Waldingfield parish councils with the help of the Countryside Access Project.

The leaflet was compiled and illustrated by parish councillor and retired teacher Leslie Hammond, who has lived in Little Waldingfield for the past 27 years.

Leaflets are available from the Sudbury tourist office, Great Waldingfield post office or parish clerk Lyn Chamberlin.

The ramble starts from Little Waldingfield church at 10am.

The drivers are local haulier Christian Bridge, helped by co-driver Roger Layzell, and Norman Ridge, a founder of the Sudbury-based charity group Christian Cargo, who is making his fifth journey

Mayor of Sudbury Ray Smith hands over a packet of pens to lorry driver Christian Bridge before he sets off for Romania.

Mayor sees off more supplies for Romania

GT WI WALDINGFIELD

Giffords Hall, a small-holding near Hartest, that contains on its 33 acres a vineyard, sheep, cultivated flowers, organic vegetables and its own small winery, all owned and managed by the Kemp family and surrounded by lovely country views, was the venue for Gt. Waldingfield's "Birthday Outing" on June 4th.

A tour and information was given by a son of the family, taking in the vineyard, where the young vines start their grape-producing life, which are later, with a lot of work and experience, transformed into their tasty, clear white wine. A video showed the various stages behind the scenes, and the machinery, modern-type vats, plus corking and labelling machines were shown, all housed in the Winery, with a free tasting to conclude.

The giant-sized, multi-coloured sweet peas cultivated in a nearby "plastic" greenhouse, brought gasps of amazement from the members - these are cut and sold. Well set-out rose beds formed a large rose garden area overlooked by a beautiful landscape and the house.

A varied and enjoyable buffet with as much as one could eat, washed down with piping hot coffee, in their cosy tea room, ended a very "happy birthday" celebration of the WI.

FARM MACHINERY PRESERVATION SOCIETY

VINTAGE RALLY

SATURDAY, JUNE 29 12-5.30
SUNDAY, JUNE 30 10-5.30

GT. WALDINGFIELD SUDBURY, SUFFOLK

STEAM ENGINES, COMMERCIAL VEHICLES
CARS, TRACTORS, MOTORCYCLES,
STATIONARY ENGINES, DISPLAYS,
TRACTOR POWER TESTING, CRAFT TENT,
PLUS STALLS AND GRAND RING EVENTS
SPECIAL ATTRACTION: TERRIER RACING

ADMISSION: ADULTS £1.50 CHILDREN £1

All steamed up for the farm machinery and traction show

A loving polish for a tractor classic – the Fordson Major

STEAM engines of all shapes and sizes thrilled visitors to Great Waldingfield at the weekend when the Farm Machinery Preservation Society held its annual show.

Restored tractors, engines and cars numbering over 200 were the main attractions at the show which was enjoyed by almost 4,000 people over the two days.

Chairman of the FMPS, Ron Mansfield said the number of people at the rally, which was held on land owned by David and Colin Steed, was a record.

"It was a marvellous weekend and the weather was just brilliant. The show has been going for eight years and this year was by far the biggest," he said.

"The whole weekend went with a swing." Other attractions included stalls and a car boot sale.

Long Melford-based organisation Project 7 will receive approximately £2,000 raised from the day, for distribution to local charities.

GREAT WALDINGFIELD LIBERAL PARTY

We wish to let former members know that unless we receive any objections from them it is our intention to transfer the £82.90 in the Great Waldingfield Liberal Party account at the Midland Bank, Sudbury to the South Suffolk Liberal Democrat Election Fund account. We will then close the account at the Midland.

Shirley Rose.

NEW BUS ROUTE

Eastern Counties Bus Service have included a new bus route which operates in conjunction with the Suffolk College at Ipswich. It means that a bus operates on Mondays through Fridays leaving Great Waldingfield at 7.55 am and arriving at the Old Cattle Market at 8.47 am and leaves again at 5.15 pm arriving back at Waldingfield at 6.03 pm.

FIRST WOOD:-After a successful couple of years since the rink first opened, Waldingfield Bowling Club has raised enough money to make major renovations including a new carpet for the rink that was official re-opened by England international Roy Cutts. He is seen rolling the first wood watched by, l to r, Lilian Haxell, ladies captain, John Sparkes, men's captain, Colin Mitchell, chairman and Doug Armour, vice-captain.

IF ACCESS is needed in North Street for delivery vehicles, it is also needed for orange-badge holders.

If they cannot park in any one street, that street is effectively closed to them. In fact many, like me, with limited walking, have to park within very few yards of the shop they are visiting. Could parking be allowed for orange-badge holders anywhere in the street, with fewer restrictions of any kind than for other cars?

S RANSON,
Lavender Cottage,
Great Waldingfield.

An Evening Out with Great Waldingfield WI

A visit to Mr Peter Minter's Brick Company at Bulmer is a combination of interest and information linking past with present.

Contrary to expectations, the scene is not of hundreds of bricks being churned out by machinery. Amid trees and natural greenery there are numerous sheds and workshops built by the owner's father and grandfather for what was and still remains a busy and useful industry.

Among the thousands of bricks, hand-made in specially constructed wooden and local clay moulds, are ordinary house bricks and an endless range of bricks and tiles of all shapes and sizes. An enormous col-

lection of different moulds, some a hundred or more years old, with their destined addresses written on the sides for reference, are stacked and stored for restoration of many of our old houses, churches and other historic buildings. Replicas of broken and worn bricks and chimney stacks, for example, can be supplied, blending present-day craftsmanship with that of the past and keeping alive the beauty of these treasured structures.

The kiln, built during the last war, replaced the old one whose fires were open and visible from the air. Hundreds or bricks are stacked manually there every week to be slowly fired. Walking

round the inside of this kiln, with its glowing coal fires, added to the feeling of "going back in time".

Mr Minter, a man who obviously loves his work, was our guide. His forefathers' skills, now in his hands are being passed to his sons.

After an initial demonstration, the group's secretary made a tile-shaped brick with a lovely flower-shape moulding which when it has been fired will be presented to her as a memento of our visit.

GT WALDINGFIELD

Giffords Hall, a small-holding near Hartest, that contains on its 33 acres a vineyard, sheep, cultivated flowers, organic vegetables and its own small winery, all owned and managed by the Kemp family and surrounded by lovely country views, was the venue for Gt. Waldingfield's "Birthday Outing" on June 4th.

A tour and information was given by a son of the family, taking in the vineyard, where the young vines start their grape-producing life, which are later, with a lot of work and experience, transformed into their tasty, clear white wine. A video showed the various stages behind the scenes, and the machinery, modern-type vats, plus corking and labelling machines were shown, all housed in the Winery, with a free tasting to conclude.

The giant-sized, multi-coloured sweet peas cultivated in a nearby "plastic" greenhouse, brought gasps of amazement from the members - these are cut and sold. Well set-out rose beds formed a large rose garden area overlooked by a beautiful landscape and the house.

A varied and enjoyable buffet with as much as one could eat, washed down with piping hot coffee, in their cosy tea room, ended a very "happy birthday" celebration of the WI.

GREAT WALDINGFIELD SCHOOL

Obviously our most important item of news this month is to welcome Mrs Shinn back into school, and what a term to come back to.

While the autumn and spring terms are just busy in school, the summer term seems almost frantic. Since the last edition of this magazine we have held a Jump Rope for Heart afternoon, a collection of toys for the children of Romania, a Beetle Drive organised by the Friends of the School, an Open Morning and our Parents Evenings. All classes worked for the Science Fair held in Sudbury Town Hall. This included the studying of plant growth by classes 1, 2 and 3. Class 4 carried out a detailed study of the school pond.

'Beware burglars' warning

POLICE are warning residents in Great Waldingfield to be on their guard following a series of break-ins and attempted break-ins in the village.

Numerous incidents have been reported in Bantocks Road, Brandeston Close, Holbrook Close and the Heath Estate areas.

Intruders who broke into a house in Bantocks Road in the early hours of Monday morning stole a stereo system, portable television and a selection of compact discs worth a total of £1,000.

Anyone who has seen anything suspicious should contact Sudbury police on 881000.

ACTON & WALDINGFIELD

TRIP: A trip to Great Yarmouth early in July gave members of Acton and Gt Waldingfield Friendship Club a delightful day out. All appreciated the crosss-country route, the comfort of the coach and the cheerfulness and courtesy of Andy, the driver. New members welcome. Meetings held fortnightly in Acton village hall, transport available. Contact Sudbury 311108 or 78837.

Airfield burglars

THIS WEEK the police need your help to catch the people responsible for break-ins at industrial premises on Chilton Airfield near Sudbury.

Over the night of Monday, June 24, burglars forced their way into Brian Anderson Haulage and Chilton Grain.

A small amount of cash was stolen but a considerable amount of damage was caused to office equipment and furniture.

Do you know who is responsible?

If you know anything about this or any other crime — ring Crimestoppers on Freephone 0808 555111. You don't have to give your name.

July 4 tribute to US servicemen

SUDBURY'S deputy mayor, Syvia Cann, laid a wreath at the memorial to the American 486th Bombardment Group — stationed at Great Waldingfield during the second World war — near St. Gregory's Church, Sudbury, on American Independence Day, July 4.

Prayers were said by the Rev Hugh Wake on behalf of the Royal British Legion and by the Rev Derrick Stiff, Rector of St. Gregory's, Sudbury. Another wreath was laid earlier by an American air force representative. The ceremony, which takes place every year on Independence Day, was well attended by councillors, Royal British Legion members, honorary members of the 486th Bombardment Group and townspeople.

New look for filling station

VILLAGERS at Great Wadlingfield can expect to see a totally new look to their only petrol and service station, soon. Situated at the heart of the village where it serves a wider area, Great Wadlingfield Garage supplies Murco fuels, with stocks of competitively priced used cars on its forecourt. Looking after MoT's on a while you wait basis is Neil Jolly. He is pictured left, on the left, with colleagues, Patricia Buckler and Roy Dodd.

Sponsor a swimmer

£200 home raid

THIEVES who forced a patio door to break into a house in Great Waldingfield in the early hours of Saturday morning escaped with £200.

GREAT WALDINGFIELD LIBERAL PARTY

We wish to let former members know that unless we receive any objections from them it is our intention to transfer the £82.90 in the Great Waldingfield Liberal Party account at the Midland Bank, Sudbury to the South Suffolk Liberal Democrat Election Fund account. We will then close the account at the Midland.

Shirley Rose.

GREAT WALDINGFIELD

Mrs M. Shinn, Hollies Cottage.
Gt Waldingfield. Tel 76747

CHURCH CONCERT: On Saturday, July 20, one of the occasional village concerts was held at the church. It was entitled Memories of Childhood and presented a "distillation of reminiscences of times long ago – and not so long ago", and was presented by villagers and friends.

The excellent programme included a Joyce Grenfell reading by Christine Tompsett, the original choir of St Lawrence's, the St Lawrence handbell ringers, the school choir, conducted by Sarah Douglas, Chris Northall on guitar, country music from Fred Wheeler, Greg Wright and John Mills, an item by Norma Chambers, Emma Rayner and Jane Ryan and a version of Cinderella by the Hengists. There was of course lots of audience participation, particularly singing nursery rhymes. All in all it was another successful concert thanks to Patrick Friend, the producer.

BARBECUE: After being postponed because of bad weather, the church barbecue was held at Churchgate House, by kind permission of Mr and Mrs Lawrence-Jones, directly after the concert on Saturday, July 20. It proved to be a very enjoyable evening, when apart from plenty of food and drink on offer, there were sideshows, stalls selling a variety of goods, including the new church souvenirs and children's races. Although not intending to be a fundraising event, over £100 was made.

JOHN HOPKINS SERVICE: A special service was held in St Lawrence's Church on Sunday, July 21, to commemorate the work of John Hopkins, rector of Great Waldingfield from August 1561 to October 1570 and also rector of Chilton for most of that time.

Hopkins, in his time, had helped to produce a "hymn-book" for the ordinary people. He had taken the psalms and written them for folk to enjoy singing; they were produced in Sternhold and Hopkins' Psalter. The tunes were in a simple meter for easy memorising.

The service was introduced by Mr Tom Wells, choirmaster of St Lawrence's from 1963 to 1976. He gave a thumbnail sketch of the life and works of John Hopkins.

The service was led by the Rev Lawrence Pizzey and the singing was led by an augmented choir of St Lawrence's, conducted by Mr Patrick Friend. The service partly followed the pattern of Mattins from the 16th century, the psalm-hymns being Hopkins's own translations.

HORTICULTURAL COMMITTEE: At a recent meeting of Gt Waldingfield horticultural show committee final arrangements were made for the eighth autumn show on Saturday, September 21, in the village school hall. It is later in the month than usual so that it can be held in conjunction with the three villages fete and carnival on the playing field.

The schedule follows a similar format to other years and includes sections for vegetables, flowers, flower arranging, handicraft, domestic and children. The schedules will be available from committee members and main points in the village including the church, the post office, the White Horse, the bowls club and the school. There is no charge for the schedules and the classes are open to residents and non-residents. The committee are hoping for record entries this year.

VCP SCHOOL: The end of term has been a busy time for pupils and staff. The whole school spent a day at Holland Haven, in glorious sunshine on July 4. The following week class two visited Bulmer brickworks. They were shown round by Mr Minter and found it extremely interesting. Still elbow deep in clay, Mrs Philpot, a potter, helped them to produce pots on a wheel the following day.

On July 17, Mrs Tompsett and the Friends of the School organised a fashion show by Seconds Out. This proved to be a relaxing evening in a hectic end of term and £175 was made for school funds.

The traditional sports were held on Friday, July 19 after being moved back just one day because of rain. The pupils (and later on the parents and toddlers) were able to show their prowess at running, skipping and other traditional events. The popular "potted sports" were held on Tuesday, July 23. Here all children, whatever their athletic ability, are able to join in an afternoon of activity, with the help of about 40 parents, governors and friends.

Children from the school entered the Cramphorn's Garden Centre painting competition and on July 24 presentations were made to Joanna Hart and Michael Walsh, who were first and second in the five to eight years section, and to Victorian Howe, who won third prize in the nine to 12 years section. The school was pleased to receive a voucher for £50.

During the end-of-term assembly the school said goodbye to Mrs Sarah Douglas, who is leaving to teach at Stoke-by-Nayland Middle School. The chairman of governors, the Rev Lawrence Pizzey presented her with a barbecue and accessories from the children and later she received a patio plant, a watch and a teapot from the staff and governors.

At the same assembly the governors' cup for achievement was presented to Louisa Shirley, by Mr David Floyd, chairman of the parish council and donor of the cup.

Village raiders

POLICE are investigating three burglaries and four attempted burglaries on Sunday night at Great Waldingfield.

Video, hi-fi and compact disc equipment worth at least £1,000 was taken from a house in Bantocks Road, while another house in the same street and one in Brandeston Close were also entered.

Elsewhere in the village the raiders' attempts to gain access to four other houses were unsuccessful.

"The thieves must have made some noise and someone probably heard them but no reports of anything suspicious were received," said a Sudbury police spokesman.

"I would urge anyone who hear suspicious to contact police imme 999, and not wait until the mornin

Muriel Eldridge. . . her first book at the age of 90.

Muriel writes book to set the world to rights

A 90-year-old Great Waldingfield woman, disillusioned with the way the world is going, has written a book describing her version of Utopia.

Muriel Eldridge, of Heath Estate, has spent 20 years on and off setting down her 500-page story, The Event, which tells the tale of a castaway who returns to England after 25 years and finds everything changed.

She is in the process of having the book published privately and it is due out next month.

A dedicated conservationist, Mrs Eldridge thinks the world is "going all wrong" and said her thoughts had nagged her until she set them down in the form of a book.

She described The Event as a fictional tale based on fact and New Age ideas.

"We are living in the age of grab and everything has to be made into money. I honestly believe we may get to the point of Armageddon," she said. "I had the urge to complete the book before I died and a clairvoyant has told me it is seven years before its time."

A retired teacher, Mrs Eldridge taught all over the country and spent eight years in South Africa.

She is also a self-taught artist and has exhibited at Sudbury, Braintree, Bury and other towns in Suffolk.

1990

Better bus service for villages

FROM September 1 local villages will benefit from an improved bus service which will take passengers into Ipswich.

Long Melford, Acton, Assington, Nayland, Stoke-by-Nayland, Leavenheath, Glemsford and Great Waldingfield are among villages which will benefit from the new services.

Leaflets detailing new services and changes in timetables are available from libraries, tourist information offices and some local shops.

Do views change anything?

AT THE Sudbury town hall meeting on September 30 about the loss of the casualty unit, Sir Colin Walker, Regional Health Authority chairman, laid great emphasis on their desire to listen to the views of Sudbury citizens, the customers of the Health Authority.

Over 300 people came to express their views, including Sudbury authorities and medical practitioners. They almost unanimously expressed the need for a casualty service in the new hospital rather than in Bury St Edmunds.

Sir Colin then suggested the meeting was not representative of the people of Sudbury and he wanted to know what were the views of those who did not attend!

A resolution was then put to approve of a referendum of all electors in Sudbury on the issues, and this was passed almost unanimously. Whereupon Sir Colin stated that he did not agree with a referendum!

It must be fairly clear that, in spite of his charm and minor concessions, the authorities, and especially the managers of the West Suffolk Health Authority, have no intention of changing their minds.

After all, if they were not wearing the straight-jacket of government restrictions, would they have insisted on closing the casualty service in the first place?

J. W. SKINNER,
(Waldingfield and District
Labour Party)
Garrison Cottage,
Great Waldingfield.

THE coffee morning held at "Junipers", Upsher Green on July 19 in aid of the St Nicholas Hospice, raised £1,286. Our sincere thanks to those people who contributed or attended the event and to our band of helpers who worked so hard, it is very much appreciated.

MILLY & DON SHATFORD,
"Junipers,"
Upsher Green,
Gt Waldingfield.

COFFEE MORNING

A Coffee morning in aid of the St Nicholas Hospice will be held at 'Junipers', Upsher Green, Great Waldingfield on Wednesday July 18th at 10.20 am. Raffle, Tom-Bola, Bric-a-Brac, Cakes, Dress Material and plant stalls will be there. Admission 10p Children Free Ample off-road parking available.

No trendy street furniture for Sudbury, please

BETTY Doughterty's letter (October 3) about Hadleigh hit all the nails (or bollards) on the head, and the planners' picture would be laughable were it not a threat. Those High Street houses and those pavings juxtaposed?

Sudbury is under the same threat. There are two separate questions: 1. Would pedestrianisation pure and simple improve Market Hill? Yes.

2. Would it have to alter the look of Market Hill? No.

Old towns have matured unselfconsciously. The best old towns are those where money was not abundant enough for destroying and rebuilding (Lavenham was poor for centuries); money can do much damage.

Artistic, "antique look" slabs/ bricks are wrong in streets next to genuine old architecture. Together with bollards, tubs, funny gutters, sweeping curves of pavement, they are pretentious, artificial, "naff" and oh so boring. They say: "look at me; I am smart", when attention should be drawn not to them but to the buildings. They will also go out of fashion, precisely because they are now a fasionable "image".

Wouldn't sleeping-policemen and a couple of no-nonsense straight-sided bottlenecks slow the cars, or a pay and display or toll deter them? For the rest, leave things as they are, dear Babergh, so that the Market Hill will look natural, workaday and uncluttered, just as it does early every day.

SUSAN RANSON,
Lavender Cottage,
Great Waldingfield.

HORTICULTURAL SHOW: The eighth autumn horticultural show was held on Saturday, September 1. This year it was held in the village school hall as part of the three villages carnival held on the nearby playing field.

There was a good number of exhibitors with a high number of entries in spite of the difficult growing season; the fuchsia class was particularly spectacular.

Prizewinners were:—

Vegetables and fruit – White potatoes: 1 D. Armour, 2 J. W. Skinner, 3 Tom Nice; coloured: 1 M. Jackson, 2 Tom Nice, 3 D. Amour; onion, under 10oz: 1 B. L. Cousins, 2 M. Jackson, 3 Tom Nice; over 10oz: 1 B. L. Cousins, 2 Tom Nice, 3 D. Amour; shallots: 1 W. Flockhart, 2 D. Armour, 3 Tom Nice; beetroot: 1 Tom Nice, 2 D. Amour; tomatoes; 1 A. Whittaker, 2 D. Thompson, 3 W. Francis; courgettes: 1 J. W. Skinner; carrots: 1 B. Radley, 2 E. Haxell, 3 B. L. Cousins; marrow: 1 B. L. Cousins, 2 J. W. Skinner, 3 J. Hughes; runner beans: 1 B. Radley, 2 M. Jackson, 3 J. Hughes; any other veg: 1 W. Flockhart, 2 L. Bloomfield, 3 J. Hughes; eating apples: 1 A. Whittaker, 2 T. Bloomfield, 3 E. J. Berry; cooking apples: 1 A. Whittaker, 2 J. W. Skinner, 3 C. Kyte; pears: 1 R. Dawe; other fruit: 1 W. Francis, 2 L. Bloomfield, 3 W. Flockhart and Mrs V. Francis.

Flowers – HT rose: 1 G. Eliot, 2 Lilian Haxell, 3 R. Dawe; floribunda roses: 1 M. Jackson, 2 E. V. Eliot; marigolds: 1 D. Hamilton, 2 M. E. Armour, 3 E. V. Eliot; dahlias: 1 W. Flockhart, 2 D. Hamilton, 3 J. Hughes; chrysanthemums: 1 E. J. Berry; spray chrysanthemums: 1 E. J. Berry, 2 M. R. Shinn; mixed flowers: 1 R. E. Dawe, 2 J. Misselbrook, 3 Mrs V. Francis; asters: 1 R. E. Dawe, 2 Anne Francis, 3 J. Phillip; other flower: 1 M. R. Shinn, 2 D. Hamilton, 3 W. Flockhart.

Fuchsias – pot size 6in: 1 Mrs S. Collins, 2 D. Hamilton; 8in: 1 D. Armour, 2 D. Hamilton, 3 M. R. Shinn; hanging basket: 1 D. Hamilton, 2 F. Batley, 3 H. Batley.

Flower arranging – autumn foliage: 1 J. Misselbrook, 2 M. Mitchell; special occasion: 1 M. Mitchell, 2 J. Phillips, 3 J. Misselbrook; dressing table arrangement: 1 J. Misselbrook, 2 Anne Francis.

Novice flower arranging – autumn foliage: 1 Sally Brinton, 2 Pat Leathers, 3 Lilian Haxell; special occasion: 1 R. E. Dawe, 2 Pat Leathers, 3 J. Phillips; dressing table arrangement: 1 Lilian Haxell, 2 Sally Brinton, 3 Pat Leathers.

Handicraft – pencil sketch: 1 Cherry Skinner, 2 John Hughes, 3 J. Phillips; puppet: 1 Victoria Flute, 2 L. Bloomfield; hand knitted garmet for adult: 1 Mrs S. Collins, 2 M. Jackson, 3 Anne Winstanley; hand knitted garment for child: 1 Paula Barry; birthday card: 1 Victoria Flute; handcrafted article: 1 Anne Francis, 2 Paula Barry, 3 Mrs S. Collins; hand sewn garment: 1 Paula Barry; article of needlecraft: 1 A. W. Scott, 2 Paula Barry, 3 J. Phillips; photograph a church: 1 Neil Cheese, 2 C. Bradstock, 3 Lilian Hazell; calligraphy: 1 C. P. Smith, 2 Sally Baldwin, 3 D. W. Thompson.

Domestic – fruit cake: 1 Lilian Haxell, 2 M. Jackson, 3 Mrs V. Francis; gingerbread man: 1 M. Jackson, 2 Lilian Haxell; chocolate eclairs: 1 M. Jackson; jam: 1 J. W. Skinner, 2 C. V. Kyte, 3 M. Jackson; marmalade: 1 P. E. Westley, 2 C. V. Kyte, 3 Sally Brinton; chutney: 1 Anne Winstanley, 2 Lilian Haxell; decorated cake: 1 Lilian Haxell; brown rolls: 1 Lilian Haxell, 2 Brian Skinner, 3 D. W. Thompson; white loaf: 1 D. W. Thompson, 2 Lilian Haxell; sweeet wine: 1 J. Hughes, 2 P. Alexander; dry white wine: 1 P. Alexander; sweet red wine: 1 P. Alexander, 2 J. Hughes; dry red wine: 1 P. Alexander, 2 J. Hughes.

Children, pre-school age – painting, My mum: 1 Nathan Bloomfield, 2 Laurence Mitchell, 3 Kelly Paul; Lego model: 1 Adam Butcher, 2 Verity Butcher, 3 Nathan Bloomfield. 5-8 years, birthday mobile: 1 Gemma Page, 2 Amy Mitchell, 3 Catherine Page; jam tarts: 1 Stephanie Hart, 2 Amy Mitchell, 3 Catherine Page; flowers in an unusual container: 1 Amy Mitchell, 2 Gemma Page, 3 Samuel Haynes. 9-12 years, butterfly mobile: 1 Joanna Hart, 2 Emma Barber, 3 Lucky Barber;

jam tarts: 1 Emma Barber, 2 Joanne Hughes; flowers in an unusual container: 1 Emma Barber, 2 Joanne Haynes, 3 Lucy Barber.

PARISH COUNCIL: The parish council held their monthly meeting on Tuesday, September 24, at the village hall.

The first item on the agenda was the problem of heavy goods vehicles using the roads through Waldingfield and Acton. A request yet again for a weight restriction on Valley Road had been made to the highways department but the reply had been that such matters would be included in a county-wide appraisal due to take place early next year. A request for yellow lines on the Heath Estate junction was being considered in conjunction with the local police.

The council have considered the possibility of entering into the USAAF reunion in 1992 when American airmen will be returning to this country during a wide ranging reunion event. It was suggested that a joint venture between the parishes of Great Waldingfield, Chilton and Acton should be undertaken, possibly in the form of an exhibition and open day. Further details of how this could be planned will be available for the October meeting.

A planning application was considered for the retention of porch covers at Jasmine Cottage which is a listed building. The council considered the porches, although not on the existing rebuilding plan, were not out of keeping with the property and recommended approval for their retention. The council also considered the provision of a brick built garage at No 6 Chilton Cottage, which is in the parish of Chilton, but does have bearing on the visual aspect of Waldingfield. It was felt that a brick garage was more in keeping with the cottage than the existing asbestos one.

It was reported that two new seats have been provided in the playing field and the old ones would be refurbished for use elsewhere in the village. The schoolchildren would be asked to help design a play area on the large heap near the seats, using a supply of telegraph poles which are in the council's possesssion. A small prize would be given to the best design.

It was reported that the village hall was in the process of getting a facelift. Thanks were due to Mr Ron Cowe for the interior painting and Mr Pooley is currently painting the exterior. Mr Eric Elliott put in a request for another postbox for Bantocks Road.

Babergh Council are holding an open day on Saturday, October 12, and any members of the public are welcome to visit the offices to see how local government operates.

An appeal from the 1992 Olympics Appeal local branch was considered and a grant of £25 given.

Approval was also given to clean the pond at the school which was overgrown with reedmace. The work would be carried out by the Suffolk Wildlife Trust.

The next meeting of the parish council is on Tuesday, October 22, at the village hall at 7.45 pm and all members of the public are welcome to attend.

The following awards were presented by Mr Geoff Chatters, headteacher of the village school:—

Braithwaite Cup for vegetables and fruit to be shared by Mr Tom Nice and Mr B. L. Cousins. Horticultural Committee salver for flowers to be shared by Mr R. Dawe and Mrs Hamilton. Bowls Club Cup for fuchsias to Mrs D. Hamilton. Rural Community Council Cup for flower arranging to Jean Misselbrook. St Lawrence Cup for novice flower arranging to be shared by Sally Brinton and Pat Leathers; Parish Council Cup for handicraft to Paula Barry; Cagienard Cup for domestic to Lilian Haxell; Misselbrook Cups for children to Nathan Bloomfield and Emma Barber and the Shinn Cup for children to Gemma Page. The WI Cup for the best rose in the show was presented to Anne Winstanley. The Magazine Cup for the best exhibit in the show to Lilian Haxell for her decorated cake; the village hall cup for most entries to Mary Jackson; and the Great Waldingfield challenge cup to the Great Waldingfield resident with most entires in section one to Mr Tom Nice.

After the prizegiving Mr Ron Dawe auctioned the donated entries and the chairman, Mr Chris Francis thanked everybody for working together to produce another very highly successful village show.

Firemen free two drivers

FIREMEN spent over an hour cutting two drivers from their vehicles after a crash on the Lavenham to Great Waldingfield road on Friday.

The accident happened shortly after 9am on the B1070 near the turn-off to Little Waldingfield when a lorry carrying concrete was in collision with a transit van.

Firemen about to clean up look at the van from which Michael Otto was freed with both legs broken.

Mean and miserable

HAVING taken part regularly in evening classes for the last 20 years, like two or three million other people in Britain, I was shocked to discover that the government proposes to abandon its support for adult education, except that for 'vocational' use.

Retired people particularly need the opportunity they may have missed earlier in life to take part in cultural and recreational activities. Many of them cannot afford to pay three to ten times as much for evening courses, as the Workers Educational Association points out.

There can be no excuse for this mean and miserable policy which will seriously reduce the quality of life for many people.

Please support the united opposition to this measure, and take advantage of the wide variety of courses offered this autumn by the adult education services.

J. W. SKINNER,
Political Education Officer,
South Suffolk Labour Party.
Garrison Cottage,
Great Waldingfield.

CRIMESTOPPERS NEEDS YOU!

POLICE are investigating house burglaries in the villages of Bures, Groton and Great Waldingfield.

A house in Sudbury Road, Bures, was broken into between September 2 and 7. Property stolen included an oak chest, Pembroke table, Victorian desk, bureau, jewellery and seven pewter mugs engraved with the name D. E. Tolhurst. About two weeks earlier two men claiming to be CID officers went to the house seeking directions to a nearby farm.

A cottage on the Groton to Daisy Green road was entered on Monday September 9 during the morning.

The burglars removed property from the house but made off leaving the property piled up outside the house.

Three burglaries and four attempted burglaries took place over Sunday night, September 8, in Great Waldingfield. Houses in Bantocks Road, Heath Estate, Brandeston Close and Holbrook Close were attacked.

At one house in Bantocks Road a Technics hi-fi, portable television and compact discs were stolen.

Tidy up, command

BABERGH planners are expected to give the green light to legal action forcing the owners of two untidy gardens in the district to tidy them up.

One site, at 157 Bures Road in Great Cornard, has been unoccupied since 1989 and the front garden, open to the street, is filled with builder's rubbish and old vehicles.

The other, Homeleigh in Tentrees Road, Great Waldingfield is strewn with builder's waste, old car parts, tyres and household items, some of which are dumped in a skip.

The owner of the house in Cornard does not live in the region and has proved difficult to trace. Homeleigh's owner has refused to clear the site despite requests from the council.

Joanne's marathon swim for church

Congratulations for Joanne Haynes as she salutes the completion of her 200-length sponsored swim.

GREAT Waldingfield girl Joanne Haynes took just three hours and 50 minutes to complete a marathon 5,000 metre charity swim on Saturday.

The ten-year-old's amazing swim – 200 lengths of Sudbury's Kingfisher pool – raised over £200 for St John's Methodist Church building fund.

Looking remarkably fresh after her gruelling three-miles, Joanne, of Green-acres, said the swim was 40 lengths more than she'd ever done before.

"I pulled a muscle in my right arm," she said. "But I carried on anyway. I love swimming and the church wanted some money raised so I decided to do it."

Staff at the Kingfisher opened up early so Joanne, a keen member of Sudbury Swimming Club, could start her swim at 6am.

Joanne's mum Vicky said she was very proud of her daughter's efforts.

"I'm absolutely delighted – especially considering she suffers from asthma."

A LIFETIME'S fascination with other people's houses has brought commercial success to one Sudbury interior designer.

Georgie Grattan-Bellew, who runs Upstairs in North Street, has just been admitted to the Interior Decorators and Designers' Association.

The group consists of some 250 professionals throughout the country and is designed who can guarantee certain standards of excellence and expertise.

So far, only four Suffolk design companies have been admitted — Tessuto in Long Melford, Judith Wiesner of Rendlesham, Dorothy Boyer Interiors of Laxfield and now Upstairs of Sudbury.

Accolades

It is the latest in a series of accolades for Georgie, who founded her business 15 years ago above a delicatessen in Friars Street.

Since then she has worked on houses in East Anglia and London, sometimes working with architects and other designers, sometimes alone.

Professional discretion forbids her from name-dropping, but she does admit to helping redecorate Delia Smith's Suffolk home, creating a set of Royal racing cushions for presentation to the Queen Mother and designing the interior of a suite of offices at St Catherine's Dock in London.

were absolutely fascinating.

However it was not until she came to decorate a newly-built extension at her own home in Great Waldingfield that her hobby became a career.

SEPTEMBER 1991

We really do WANT the casualty unit

Dear Sir,

AT THE SUDBURY Town Hall meeting on September 30 about the loss of the casualty unit, Sir Colin Walker, Regional Health Authority chairman, laid great emphasis on their desire to listen to the views of Sudbury citizens, the customers of the Health Authority.

Over 300 people came to express those views, including Sudbury authorities and medical practitioners. They almost unanimously expressed the need for a casualty service in the new hospital rather than in Bury St. Edmunds.

Sir Colin then suggested that the meeting was not representative of the people of Sudbury, and that he wanted to know what were the views of those who did not attend.

A resolution was then put to approve a referendum of all electors in Sudbury on the issue, and this was passed almost unanimously. Whereupon Sir Colin stated that he did not agree with a referendum!

It must be fairly clear that, in spite of his charm and minor concessions, the authorities, and especially the managers of the West Suffolk Health Authority, have no intention of changing their minds.

After all, if they were not wearing the straight-jacket of government restrictions, would they have insisted on closing the casualty service in the first place?

J. W. SKINNER,
Waldingfield and District
Labour Party,
Garrison Cottage,
Gt. Waldingfield.

Interior designer Georgie Grattan-Bellew with part of her range some of which are exclusive to her business called Upstairs, at North Street Sudbury.

BARGAIN OF THE WEEK

Amazing value 4/5 bedrooms, 2/3 reception rooms, solid oak kitchen, gas central heating, double garage, utility room, en-suite shower room, quiet location. Reduced by £25,000 to only

£89,995
Phone now to view

UPSHER GREEN
Delightful listed period semi-detached thatched cottage in need of improvement in lovely rural setting. Entrance hall, timbered reception rooms, kitchen/breakfast room, entrance lobby, bathroom, 2 attractive bedrooms. Shingle driveway £80,000

In Bantocks Road, **Great Waldingfield** is an executive–style detached residence, quietly positioned overlooking farmland to the front on the edge of a popular sought after residential development.

The property is being offered at £89,500 with gas fired central heating and the **spacious** accommodation comprises: hallway, cloakroom, lounge, dining room, kitchen, utility room, bedroom with ensuite shower room, three further bedrooms and bathroom.

There is a small open plan garden to front, a double garage and a fully fenced rear garden.

Great Waldingfield: £89,500.

PRICES 1991

Boy who touched all your hearts

BY NICK CROWN

LOCAL people have been saddened by the sudden death of brave six-year-old Mathew Turkentine who touched the hearts of townsfolk with his courageous battle against the crippling effects of a rare disease.

The disabled youngster – one of Sudbury Town Football Club's most fervent young fans – died at West Suffolk Hospital on Friday after suffering a massive brain haemorrhage at his Great Waldingfield home.

Mathew in his wheelchair wearing Sudbury Town colours.

TURKENTINE on the 18th October 1991 suddenly but peacefully in hospital. Matty aged 6 years of Gt Waldingfield. Treasured son of Paula and Geoff and grandson of Chris. Nephew of Andy. Private funeral service at Stanstead church on Friday 25th October followed by cremation at the West Suffolk crematorium at 3.45pm. Family flowers only but donations if desired to the Jennifer Trust S.M.A. Co-Op Funeral Service.

It would be hard, nowadays, to sustain the argument that the manufacture and sale of armaments sustains peace. How many people can now see any sense in the slaughter of the flower of Europe's youth in the trenches of the First World War? How many nuclear weapons are necessary to stop the destruction of Dubrovnik?

How many people would be wearing a poppy, red or white, if there were no international arms trade?

J. W. SKINNER,
Garrison Cottage,
Great Waldingfield.

PARISH COUNCIL: The parish council held their monthly meeting on Tuesday, October 22, at the village hall. Three members of public were present.

The chairman welcomed the new beat policeman, PC Gibbens, who lives locally in Acton. PC Gibbens hopes to be able to assist the villagers with problems such as vandalism, theft and the traffic congestion experienced through the village.

Under the main items of the meeting, the chairman reported on a meeting with a resident in Clayhall Lane who has problems with a footpath crossing his property. He has agreed to remove the blockage placed across the footpath and the county footpath officer is looking into the possibility of sorting out the anomalies associated with the footpath and possibly diverting the path to the edge of the properties it crosses. The parish council will be kept informed of the progress.

It was agreed to replace the brass plaque on the USAAF memorial at the entrance to the airfield at Chilton. The memorial was erected by Great Waldingfield Community Council and is in need of repair as well as alteration.

A letter of thanks was to be sent to the county council highways department for the work they had carried out at Morris Farm, Folly Road, which involved considerable kerbing and strengthening of the road. It is hoped the heavy traffic which uses the road will treat the new works kindly.

The next meeting of the parish council will discuss the precept requirements for the 1992/93 financial year and it was agreed that both the playing field committee and the village hall committee meet to discuss the requirements before the full financial matters are discussed in November.

The roll of honour has now been replaced in the church following restoration work which was financed by the parish council. The scroll had suffered from the damp conditions and had been cleaned by an expert from the county archivists department in Ipswich. It has now been rehung in such a way as to let an airflow around the framework.

Various reports of problems with street lights, rubbish dumping and vermin were noted and would be taken up with the appropriate authorities.

The next meeting of the council is on Tuesday, November 26, at 7.45 at the village hall.

Village mourns loss of artist Cuthbert

A FAMILIAR sight to Little Waldingfield villagers will be missing with the death of local artist Cuthbert Bell.

Cuthbert, 68, was often seen out and about in the village with his sketch pad and easel.

He was well respected by villagers who will remember him for his kindness, charm and friendly nature.

"He was one of the few people that you would term a true gentleman," said a family friend.

A water-colourist, he was particularly renowned for his beautiful Turneresque skies, and his work was exhibited in London and all over Europe.

He died suddenly in the West Suffolk Hospital last week. His funeral was held at the West Suffolk Crematorium on Monday.

He leaves a widow, Raine.

BABERGH DISTRICT COUNCIL
REFUSE COLLECTION
CHANGES TO COLLECTION DAYS

Due to a change of tip site considerable alterations will be made to the collection rounds from Monday 4 November 1991.

Notices will be distributed to those properties having a change of collection day. The notices will be left with the wheeled bin during collections the previous week.

All residents are advised that collection times will vary until the new rounds have settled down and bins should be available from 7.00 a.m.

Further information can be obtained from the Cleansing Section, on Hadleigh (0473) 825882.

J. S. SLATER
Chief Environmental Services Officer
Council Offices,
Hadleigh.

Moscow welcomes the Suffolk WI

THREE representatives from the Suffolk West Federation of Women's Institutes are preparing for an historic trip to Moscow to meet their Russian counterparts.

The visit is the first ever exchange between the National Federation Women's Institutes and the Soviet Women's Committee.

Last year, three members of the Russian organisation spent nine days in Suffolk and next week, three local women will make the return visit.

June D'Cruze of Glemsford WI,

Kate Riddlestone of Rattlesden WI and Ann Holloway of Great Waldingfield WI fly out to Moscow for a week in which they hope to meet as many Russian women as possible.

"International understanding is much too important to leave to the politicians!" says Mrs. Holloway.

"We really just want to meet with as many ordinary women as possible, talk about their lives and further cooperation between our two organisations."

Now members of the trio are organising their luggage which will include

gifts of everyday items such as cotton wool, coloured tights, soap and gloves, none of which are readily available in Russian shops.

British Airways have helped them in their task by giving an extra baggage allowance free of charge.

They are also busy polishing up their Russian vocabulary, although they will be accompanied by an interpreter throughout their visit.

"We really are excited about the trip — it's such an historic time over there and conditions are changing all the time," said Mrs. Holloway.

Taste of the country

ORIGINALLY opened to sell the farm's own home produced beef, Oak Tree Farm shop, Lavenham Road, Great Waldingfield, near Sudbury, now stocks a good selection of other produce with that local taste too. Offering all that is best in country fare, the shop also specialises in free range farm turkeys, with orders currently being taken to reserve birds for the Christmas feast. Just a mile and a half from the village, Oak Tree Farm is open from Wednesdays to Sundays inclusive, 10am until 5.30pm, when Peter and Claire Wilson are delighted to see customers old and new.

PICTURED above, Claire Wilson of the Oak Tree Farm shop, busily stocking up with all the extras that make Christmas such a memorable feast.

There's lots of East Anglian goodies on sale, including honey, jams and preserves, plus delicious mustards to add that extra special tang to meat

and cheese dishes.

Also available in time for the festive season, is farm made Christmas pudding ice cream, a novel way of enjoying a traditional taste in a lighter, more refreshing way.

Dried flowers and other decorative items are also to be found in the shop.

Tapes stolen

THIEVES stole blank cassette tapes from a Nissan car in Badleys Close, Great Waldingfield on Thursday.

Raid on garage

THIEVES who broke into a workshop at Great Waldingfield Garage, Lavenham Road, Great Waldingfield on Monday night stole eight spark plugs worth £20 and caused £20 damage to a window.

PARISH COUNCIL: The parish council met on Tuesday, November 26, in the village hall.

It was decided that after the Christmas break the council would look into the condition and legality of the footpaths in the village with regard to a full rationalisation of the footpath map.

The plans to recognise the USAAF reunion in 1992 are to be held in abeyance until news of when the area would be visited by Americans. This would ensure that anything arranged would have the greatest impact.

The new houses in Bantocks Road were in the final stages of completion and should be occupied by the beginning of December. In line with other roads in the area, the close has been named after another local hall — Lynn's Hall Close.

An application for the re-roofing of a bathroom extension at Garrison Cottage was given approval, as was a rear conservatory at 1 Greenacre.

The council then set to considering the precept requirements for the forthcoming year. Following the high level of precept last year due to commitments which have yet to be met, the council elected to open a contingency account to maintain a level of savings for future access. With this account financed from the amounts still held by the parish council, the precept for next year was set at £7,500, an amount of approximately £7 per community charge payer.

A grant of £75 was made to the Citizens Advice Bureau. The village hall was to be supplied with a new set of crockery. It was felt that with the possible introduction of stringent health and hygiene regulations the kitchen at the hall should be gradually upgraded and a consistent set of crockery would be a start in the right direction.

Eastern Electricity would be approached at the highest possible level to explain the serious delay in reinstating lights in Badleys Close area which have been out of order for months. It is understood that underground wires are at fault but recently a hole has been dug and left unguarded and poses serious problems for anyone using the area at night. The electricity company have been phoned weekly on this matter but can give no answer as to when it will be rectified.

The chairman ended the meeting by wishing everyone a Merry Christmas. The council meet again in January.

November 14, 1991

Bed push

STAFF from Somerfield Foods, Sudbury, are taking part in a sponsored bed push through the town to Melford, Acton, Waldingfield and back to Sudbury on Sunday to raise money for Children in Need.

Applause Costume Hire of Friars Street are lending fancy dress and Walnuttree Hospital is providing the bed. The push starts from Somerfield at 10am.

Friday, November 22.
Illustrated talk on London Gardens, *Great Waldingfield Village Hall*, 8pm, in aid of Horticultural show committee.

THANK you to all the readers who responded to my letter just before Christmas and gave their unwanted gifts to the British Heart Foundation, Sudbury and district branch.

We were delighted with the response and all gifts will be used as tombola and raffle prizes to raise money towards BHF research.

We appreciate, very much, the kindness of both Carpet Connections and John Hilary Travel who allowed our boxes to be displayed. Several people were also prompted to give donations of money and wished to remain anonymous.
PETER HOLLOWAY,
Secretary, Sudbury BHF branch,
8 Holbrook Close,
Great Waldingfield.

Couple float a winning idea for gardeners

A SUDBURY couple have won £50 in a competition to find Britain's most original gardening tips.

Frank and Olga Cadge, of Waldingfield Road, won the prize in a year-long competition run by BBC Gardeners' World magazine and sponsored by Guinness Original.

Mr Cadge, a retired motor engineer, gave a suggestion on how to prevent a garden pond freezing over in winter.

The tip, featured in February's edition of the magazine, is to float a car or lorry inner tube on the surface of the pond.

An upturned dustbin lid placed on top of the inner tube will also serve as a bird bath if filled with water.

If Mr and Mr Cadge are judged the overall winners in March, they will win a two week holiday in Thailand.

January 24, 1992

Villagers battle on to get public house re-opened

HOPES are still high that pints might yet be pulled again at a closed village pub which brewers have claimed cannot be revived as a viable licensed premises.

Residents at Little Waldingfield have been battling to get their only local, the Swann, re-opened since it was closed by Greene King nine months ago.

Alan and Richard Halsey, tenants of the Bull, Troston, confirmed they hoped to have the necessary finance in place soon to complete a £120,000 purchase of the Swann.

In the meantime the brewers have re-submitted a planning application to Babergh District Council to allow the pub to become a private home.

Babergh threw out a similar bid several months ago when it said Greene King had not tried sufficiently hard to market the premises as a pub, which was an important element of the village's social well-being.

In their new bid, the brewer's agents say the asking price, which began at £140,000, has been steadily reduced. Although some offers have been made, they have not been followed through, proving commercial use of the property is unviable.

It is also claimed that campaigners fighting to see the pub re-opened have based their case on emotive rather than objective issues.

Despite this assertion, Babergh's planning officers are recommending that Greene King should carry out a more intensive marketing exercise of the premises.

Cyclist dies in training

Neil Miller

A CYCLIST who was battling to regain a place in the British Olympics team collapsed and died on a training run.

Neil Miller, a member of Cycle Club Sudbury, was climbing a hill in Bournemouth – he was staying there with his parents for Christmas – when he collapsed.

Neil (31), who was living in Sandy, Bedfordshire, still had a home in Great Waldingfield. He had been working to regain peak fitness after breaking his leg and pelvis in a training crash.

CC Sudbury's Harold Raymond said: "It is sad news for all involved in cycling. He had just started to come back again after the crash ... it's almost impossible to take in."

January 16, 1992

Crash rescue hero gets Italian bravery award

MOTORIST Andrew Spain, who helped save the life of a police officer trapped in a road crash, received an Italian bravery award on Thursday.

The presentation was made by Sudbury police chief, Superintendent Alan Hartup, at the town's police station.

Mr Spain (29), a sales manager, of Upsher Green, Great Waldingfield, came across a crash on the M11 at Woodford Bridge in November 1988.

With two other motorists and a police officer, he rescued PC Alan Minnis from beneath a blazing Ford Sierra.

PC Minnis, of the Metropolitan Police traffic division, attended the ceremony with his wife Sonya.

The Giancarlo Tofi diplomas commemorate the courage of an Italian killed helping a road crash victim. Mr Spain is one of only six recipients in this country.

Mr Spain, whose bravery has already been recognised by

Metropolitan Police constable Alan Minnis and his wife Sonya with his rescuer Andrew Spain and Supt Alan Hartup (left).

the Royal Society for the Prevention of Accidents, said he was surprised to receive the award and hoped anyone in the same situation would react in the same way.

The Village

Changes & Improvements

Village Hall opened —and Waldingfield's dream is fulfilled

SATURDAY saw the fulfilment by Great Waldingfield villagers of a 40-year-old dream—the opening of their own village hall.

It was during the first World War that plans were first made for a village hall and since that time the post of treasurer has been held by Mr. George Hazell.

The hall, which will provide a centre for all village activities, is on the main Sudbury-Stowmarket road and has been built largely by voluntary labour.

Sir Henry Corry, who lives in the neighbouring village of Edwardstone, performed the opening ceremony on Saturday. He congratulated the villagers on completing their enterprise despite the many difficulties.

Fresh efforts

The hall was crowded for the opening ceremony, which was presided over by Mr. A. W. Heard, chairman of the Hall Committee. He traced the history of the effort from its beginning during the first world war. Interest lapsed and the money was used for a memorial to the fallen. Fresh efforts were made during the last war and around £700 was raised.

Again interest faded, but in 1953 a well attended village meeting decided to press on with the project.

He thanked all who had helped, especially those who had worked on the building of the hall, and the ladies, who had not only helped to raise money, but had helped with the painting and decoration of the hall.

More work

Mr. Heard said that expenditure on the building to date was £1,686 14s. 7d. There was still a balance in hand, but more work remained to be done. It was hoped to further improve the forecourt and to erect a cycle shelter.

After the opening there was a bazaar and various sideshows and stalls.

A free social was held in the Village Hall on Saturday evening. Mr. F. Abbott and other members of the committee organised games and dancing, and refreshments were served by the ladies' committee. Winner of a competition was Miss S. Ashford.

A WARTIME fancy dress event for children in Great Waldingfield provides this week's glimpse into days gone by. It was lent by Beryl Ruse of Newton Road, Sudbury, who is pictured with other children at the 1943 event held at Wade's Farm.

Left to right: Beryl Ruse, David Ayres, Derek Carter, Robin Carter, Rhoda Ball, Roy Moss, Joan Pogson, Jean Rowland, Joan Spraggons, Connie Roper, June Capon, Betty Poulson.

TESCO'S plan for a major edge-of-town store for Sudbury should go ahead.

THE town centre development will take place eventually. Tesco must be of good design not like our "carbuncle" friend Great Mills. Hopefully the monthly Sainsbury and Tesco shoppers will return to Sudbury.

Mrs F. Bates,
Rectory Rd, Gt Waldingfield

LARGER powerful groups such as Tesco should not be encouraged. They are prepared to break the law to further their own ends. The effect on Sudbury as a retail area would be devastating.

J. Schofield,
Post Office, Gt Waldingfield.

BABERGH councillors have approved an overall poll tax level of £260.29 after 11th hour moves to keep the charge at the current level of £234.88 failed to win support.

The 8.7 per cent increase approved by members of the council's policy and resources committee on Thursday was £3 more than originally expected due to a last-minute increase in Suffolk County Council's recommended charge.

Thursday, February 6, 1992

Tesco hold fire

TESCO bosses say they will decide within the next month whether to appeal against Babergh Council's controversial decision to reject their edge-of-town supermarket scheme for Sudbury.

Townspeople – who have called on Babergh to reconsider their refusal of the Woodhall scheme – are still waiting to hear if the supermarket giant will challenge the authority.

Meanwhile, Suffolk Preservation Society have added their opposition to the multi-million Kimberley Securities town centre shopping redevelopment plan which they have branded a disaster.

The society claims the whole approach to the scheme is wrong and say planners have failed to consider how best to enhance and conserve the town centre before embarking on a major new development.

PARISH COUNCIL: The parish council, meeting on Tuesday, January 28, were told of confirmation of a visit by members of the USAAF reunion tour to Sudbury on Tuesday, May 19. Final details for the day would be known by the middle of February.

Following discussions on costs, it was agreed to put the majority of the street lights in the village on to photo-electric cell operation. This would mean a more efficient lighting system operating from dusk until dawn. The only area not to be converted is on Greenacre, where the lamp standards are in need of replacement in the near future and such work would not be economical. These lights would be considered for replacement during the next financial year. Eastern Electricity would also be asked to study two dark areas – in Coronation Rise and Folly Road, near the pond.

The highways department have advised that once again they are without funds to repair footpaths in Heath Estate but might find sufficient funds to do the worst areas of Folly Road. A letter requesting urgent reconsideration is being sent, with copies to the district councillors and county councillors.

PC Gibbons reported a fall in the number of crimes in the village. The residents of Folly Road have started a Neighbourhood Watch scheme and the council agreed to buy two signs for the area.

The parish council considered the planning application for the erection of 37 houses on Bantocks Road. While the number has been increased, the council felt that the provision of over 20 two-bedroomed houses justfied this and agreed to the development, provided that the layout and size of houses was not altered in subsequent plan changes.

An application for extensions at Red House Farm, Lavenham Road was recommended for approval.

An application for a house in the garden of 1 Coronation Rise was approved out of meeting and Babergh Council have added a provision that it should be a bungalow.

The local scout group had put forward a tentative suggestion for a single-storey building on Ten Trees Road site and the council considered that as long as it was sited on the same side as the bowls club, they could welcome the idea. Further information would be needed on the development.

The letting fees for the village hall were reviewed for the first time in two years and would take effect from April 1.

Mrs Misselbrook reported that the school was being fitted with an alarm system to counteract the vandalism problems.

The parish council agreed to enter a team for the quiz night being organised by Friends of the School on Saturday, March 7.

The next parish council meeting is on Tuesday, February 25 at 7.45 pm.

£500 for Matthew

A CHARITY Valentine's dance at Great Waldingfield has raised £504 to help brain-damaged Sudbury youngster Matthew Lockett. The money will boost the 12-year-old's Helping Hands Fund for revolutionary physiotherapy treatment.

NEIGHBOURHOOD WATCH: A large number of residents from Folly Road, Chapel Close and Chestnut Close met in the school on Monday, January 20. Concern has been expressed about the increasing number of break-ins and the problems of vandalism and nuisance to property. The meeting was convened by Mr Brinton and he introduced the police crime prevention officer who spoke about the positive values of setting up a Neighbourhood Watch scheme. All present were in favour of such a scheme, including the local beat policeman. It was agreed that the area covered be Folly Road, Chapel Close and Chestnut Close. The scheme will be co-ordinated and run by Mr Brinton assisted by Mr Presneil.

Proposed development at Chilton Airfield, Chilton, Sudbury, Suffolk

I give notice that Countrywood Leisure is applying to the Babergh District Council for planning permission to convert existing Grain Store into 20 lane 10 Pin Bowling Centre and alterations to existing vehicular access and car park together with installation of Bio-Disc Treatment Plant.

Members of the public may inspect copies of the application, the plans and other documents submitted with it at 5 King Street, Sudbury, Suffolk, during all reasonable hours until 20.03.1992.

Anyone who wishes to make representations about this application should write to the Council at Corks Lane, Hadleigh, Ipswich, Suffolk.

ROGER BALMER
On behalf of Countryside Leisure
Date: 28.02.1992

501IC04/10

BOWLS CLUB NEWS

The Christmas party was held on 7 December – once again a successful evening, with the very popular quiz game getting the proceedings off to a good start.

Another competition consisting of wall posters containing a list of anagrams, which formed the names of birds caused much brainwork: nobody got all the answers.

The refreshments once again provided and served by the ladies, were very much enjoyed, and the evening was rounded off by the presentation of trophies played for during the past month or so.

The John Raymond Cup, a triples competition was won by G & D Daw and G Rowland.

The Chairmans Cup, for novices pairs was won by J & S Sparkes.
The Norma Bacon Cup, a singles event was won by D Armour with G Rowland as runner-up.
The Ladies Pairs was presented to Ruth Lock and Mary Jackson.

Finally the Fours League Salver, a league game played over the last three months, was won by J & S Sparkes and D & M Armour.

NEIGHBOURHOOD WATCH

A large number of residents from Folly Road, Chapel Close and Chestnut Close met in the school on Monday 20 January. Concern had been expressed about the increasing number of break-ins and the problems of vandalism and nuisance to property.

The meeting was convened by Mr B H Brinton and he introduced the Police Crime Prevention Officer who spoke about the positive values of setting up a Neighbourhood Watch Scheme. All those present were in favour of such a scheme, including the local beat policeman who was present.

It was agreed that the area covered be Folly Road, Chapel Close and Chestnut Close. The Scheme will be co-ordinated and run by Mr B H Brinton, assisted by Mr A Presneil.

Derek Moore & Sandra Wood

THE wedding took place at Holy Trinity Church, Long Melford, of Sandra Jane Wood, of 26 Bantocks Road, Great Waldingfield, and Derek Michael Moore, of 2 Westropps, Long Melford.

Tattoo-mad Andrew East from Great Waldingfield, Sudbury.

WHEN Andrew East was 14 he had his first tattoo.

Just one, he told his mother, this will be the first and last.

Now, twelve years later, he could be the most tattooed man in East Anglia.

By the time he was 17, and in fact it's illegal before the age of 18, he had 30 tattoos. Then he stopped until a couple of years ago when he resumed.

Andrew, of Great Waldingfield, says: "I went with a friend to Colchester and had more done. In August 1990, I had seven hours work done in one go. Dave Ross, the tattooist, worked round those I had done earlier by a local man.

"If you are really determined you forget about the pain because in the end you find it is worth it.

"The longest and most painful session was one of eight hours when he went round my ribs and stomach."

Martin Richards & Donna King

THE wedding took place at Bildeston Parish Church of Donna Marie King and Martin John Richards.
   The bride is the daughter of David and Bella King, of 21 Badleys Close, Great Waldingfield, and the bridegroom is the son of Lionel and Rosemary Richards, of 77 Wattisham Road, Bildeston.

GT WALDINGFIELD

QUIZ NIGHT: The Friends of the Village School organised a quiz night in the vilage hall on Saturday. The event was planned and co-ordinated by teacher Miss Christine Bradstock working with the Friends.

It proved to be a very popular event with 29 teams of four people taking part — the maximum that could be seated in the hall. Quiz master was Mr Richard Stainer and scorers were Mr Gerry Higginson and Miss Bradstock. A ploughman's supper was enjoyed in the interval and there was a licensed bar.

The chairman of the school governors, the Rev Lawrence Pizzey, presented the prizes. First prize and a cup to be competed for annually went to the governors, second were the parish council team and joint third were two teams made up of Friends.

Pensioners' butter

PENSIONERS in Great Waldingfield can collect free EEC surplus butter from the village hall today between 9am - 5pm. It is being distributed by the parish council.

Machines pay out

POLICE are investigating two burglaries in which cash was taken from game machines on Sunday.

Thieves who broke into Great Waldingfield Bowls Club smashed a window and forced game machines causing £75 damage. They escaped with an estimated £200 in cash.

Game machines were also forced at the club house at Newton Green Golf Club when thieves broke in. The amount taken is not known.

SETTING OF
PERSONAL COMMUNITY CHARGE

Notice is hereby given that at a meeting held on February 19, 1992, the Babergh District Council, in accordance with Sections 32 and 33 of the Local Government Act 1988, set for the year beginning on April 1, 1992, and ending on March 31, 1993, the amounts shown below as the personal community charge for the undermentioned areas:—

For the Parishes of	Amount of Community Charge £	For the Parishes of	Amount of Community Charge £
Acton	260.29	Kersey	250.68
Aldham	248.67	Kettlebaston	248.88
Alpheton	250.14	Lavenham	258.43
Arwarton	246.44	Lawshall	251.50
Assington	251.32	Layham	252.88
Belstead	250.63	Leavenheath	253.52
Bentley	249.62	Lindsey	255.00
Bildeston	255.97	Long Melford	258.15
Boxford	252.63	Milden	246.44
Boxted	246.44	Monks Eleigh	254.33
Brantham	256.93	Nayland	255.64
Brent Eleigh	255.58	Nedging	248.88
Brettenham	251.68	Newton	252.17
Bures St. Mary	257.18	Polstead	253.44
Burstall	250.36	Preston St. Mary	248.48
Capel St. Mary	254.20	Raydon	256.22
Chattisham	250.78	Semer	250.01
Chelmondiston	255.49	Shelley	246.44
Chelsworth	248.42	Shimpling	247.88
Chilton	250.81	Shotley	251.81
Cockfield	250.62	Somerton	246.44
Copdock	252.44	Sproughton	259.27
Cornard Great	263.77	Stanstead	249.59
Cornard Little	248.71	Stoke By Nayland	255.14
East Bergholt	254.74	Stratford St Mary	252.37
Edwardstone	254.10	Stutton	252.63
Elmsett	251.79	Sudbury	264.25
Freston	248.44	Tattingstone	250.83
Glemsford	254.79	Thorpe Morieux	249.57
Groton	249.22	Waldingfield Great	253.11
Hadleigh	267.02	Waldingfield Little	251.61
Harkstead	255.11	Washbrook	252.44
Hartest	253.23	Wattisham	252.77
Higham	246.44	Wenham Magna	246.44
Hintlesham	250.78	Wenham Parva	246.44
Hitcham	249.35	Whatfield	249.52
Holbrook	252.61	Wherstead	251.04
Holton St Mary	251.92	Woolverstone	256.37

R. G. SALMON
Secretary

Council Offices
Hadleigh, Ipswich
Suffolk, IP7 6SJ
5 March 1992

ACTON AND GREAT WALDINGFIELD FRIENDSHIP CLUB

Members, tea ladies and guests met to enjoy a traditional Christmas dinner at Acton Village Hall. Mr Blazey, Chairman, gave a welcome and presented gifts in appreciation to Mrs Ball for fund-raising, Mrs Grant for year-long greetings cards, and Mrs Cozens in her capacity as secretary.

Entertainment included a humorous Suffolk song and folk dances from Eastern Europe performed by the Friendship Dancers, in colourful costumes.

GREAT WALDINGFIELD SCHOOL

SHOES needed

We have an outlet for your old shoes – not the ones with splits, holes or collapsed heel backs but any style of shoes including high heels, sandals, leather-style fashion boots, working boots etc, etc – men's, women's and children's in reasonable condition – heavy wear to soles or heels does not matter. (No slippers, wellingtons, flip flops, canvas or plastic shoes.)

We will receive 25p a pair for the shoes – they are exported to West Africa where local labour is used to repair the shoes, which are then sold on market stalls. The organisers are not a charity, but hope to make a profit whilst helping the local people.

PARISH COUNCIL

The Parish Council met on Tuesday 28 January at 7.45 pm. The Council were told of confirmation of a visit by members of the USAAF Reunion Tour to Sudbury on Tuesday 19 May. Final details for the day would be known by the middle of February.

Following discussions on costs, it was agreed to put the majority of the street lights in the village onto photo-electric cell operation. This would mean a more efficient lighting system operating from dusk until dawn. The only area not to be converted were those on Greenacre, where the lamp standards are in need of replacement in the near future and such work would not be economical. These lights would be considered for replacement during the next financial year.

Eastern Electricity would also be asked to study two dark areas, namely in Coronation Rise and Folly Road, near the pond.

The Highways Department have advised that once again they are without funds to repair footpaths in Heath Estate but might find sufficient funds to do the worst areas of Folly Road. A letter requesting urgent reconsideration is being sent, with copies being sent to the District Councillors and County Councillor.

PC Gibbens reported a fall in the number of crimes in the village. The residents of Folly Road have started a Neighbourhood Watch Scheme and the Council agreed to purchase two signs for the area.

The Parish Council considered the planning application for the erection of 37 houses on Bantocks Road. Whilst the numbers are increased the Council felt that the provision of

over twenty two-bedroomed housed justified this and agreed to the development, provided that the layout and size of houses was not altered in subsequent plan changes.

An application for extensions at Red House Farm, Lavenham Road was recommended for approval.

An application for a property to be erected in the garden of 1 Coronation Rise was approved out of meeting and Babergh District Council have added a proviso that the property should be of a single-storey style.

The local Scout Group had put forward a tentative suggestion for a single-storey building on the Ten Trees Road site and the Council considered that as long as it was sited on the same side as the Bowls Club, they would welcome the idea. Further information would be needed on the development.

BOWLS CLUB

On 21 March the club organised another Beetle Drive, ten tables were needed, and at half time a fish supper was brought in, the proceedings being resumed after refreshments. A half-time prize was awarded to P Whitby, the winner at the finish being V Beer. The booby prize was won by P Chamberlin.

1992

Babergh has set aside £770,000 for housing association grants which will help build 15 homes at Great Waldingfield, of which five will receive Department of Environment funding, as well as six at Stoke-by-Nayland and six at Cockfield.

APRIL 1992

£350 bike taken

A THIEF who entered the back garden of a house in Bantocks Road, Great Waldingfield, on Thursday night, stole a £350 mountain bike from a greenhouse. The orange and red Yankee Yukon machine belongs to Gavin Fincham.

A GREAT Waldingfield couple living in fear of the builders' bulldozer say developers are making their life unbearable.

Farmworker James Mayhew and his fiancee Heidi Carsboult are among tenants of four condemned prefabricated houses in Bantocks Way who face homelessness when the buildings are eventually demolished to make way for a housing estate.

But as earthworks and rubble continue to pile up around their home, the couple claim they are being "harassed" by Essex-based Chelmsford Developers who they believe are trying to push them out.

"Last week I came home and and my driveway had disappeared – they've pulled up the concrete and dumped it on my lawn," said Heidi.

"It seems they're trying to harass us into moving out because we won't go into temporary accommodation. I ended up in tears last night. I just can't cope with it," she explained.

Heidi and James say the work by the builders is making their life intolerable.

"You worry if you'll have a house to come home to at night and the piles of rubble are building up all over the place.

"Now we've been told to clear out of our shed because they want to knock that down," said James.

This week Babergh Council said all four sets of tenants were regarded as being "in urgent need of rehousing" and had been offered temporary hostel accommodation.

FRIENDS OF GREAT WALDINGFIELD SCHOOL

PRESENT

A QUIZ NIGHT

on

SATURDAY MARCH 7th *1992*

at

GREAT WALDINGFIELD VILLAGE HALL

Enter a team of 4(18 years+) from your club, family, neighbourhood, workplace or wherever.

£6 per team to include ploughmans.

BAR   **RAFFLE**

Entry forms available from Christine Bradstock at the School Telephone 74055. To be returned by Wednesday 4th March.

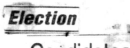

Candidates

APRIL 9TH 1992

● Tim Yeo   ● Kathy Pollard   ● Stephen Hesford   ● Tom Aisbitt

CONSERVATIVE   LIBERAL DEMO   LABOUR   NATURAL LAW

Thanks on behalf of the children

CHRISTIAN CARGO were delighted with the magnificent amount collected by Brian Cook through the Sudbury Fun Run on Good Friday.

He was in fact the highest fundraiser in the run and has handed to us £590 – which will go towards the children's centre planned for a village called Dragoslavele in Romania.

The centre is to provide outdoor facilities, training, some rehabilitation, all manner of "normal" experiences for deprived children from the orphanages and individual families.

Thank you Mr Cook – you may never know what changes your efforts will make to little lives but "thank you" on their behalf.

ELEANOR RIDGE,
7 Braithwaite Drive,
Great Waldingfield.

CRIMESTOPPERS NEEDS YOU!

CAN you help solve a burglary at a club in Great Waldingfield or do you know who is responsible for a burglary at a school in Glemsford?

Burglars got into the primary school in Lion Road, Glemsford, some time over the May Day bank holiday weekend (Friday, May 1 to Tuesday, May 5).

A Nimbus computer, a Panasonic video recorder, three headphone sets and two Coomber radio cassette players were among items stolen.

Great Waldingfield Bowls and Social Club in Tentree Road was broken into at around midnight on Thursday, April 29.

Having broken a window to get in, the burglars managed to take an electronic games machine containing about £200 cash.

If you know anything about these or any other crime, phone Crimestoppers now on 0800 555 111.

Your call is strictly confidential. You do not have to give your name and address. You could qualify for a Community Action Trust cash reward.

£200 stolen

MORE than £200 was stolen from a game machine at Great Waldingfield's Bowls and Social Club last week.

Flag week success

A TOTAL of £3,368.92 was raised during the recent flag week in aid of Sudbury branch of the Royal National Lifeboat Institution.

Collection details were: Flag Day £563.13; Sudbury house-to-house £537.75; factories £99.91; villages £2,168.13.

Flag Week organiser Mrs S. H. Whitney said the committee wished to thank all those who had helped.

Individual village totals were: Assington £57.59; Newton Green £92.73; Nayland £197.61; Leavenheath £253.17; Borley £23.74; Foxearth £27.99; Liston £20.56; Little Waldingfield £104.03; Long Melford £311.91; Acton £157.02; Great Waldingfield £125.12; Bures £112.97; Little Cornard £38.34; Henny St. £7.76; Lamarsh £61.70; Alphamstone £92.53; Middleton £63.24; Bulmer £27.47; Great Cornard £108.29; Pentlow £39.78; Glemsford £145.35; Cavendish £61.78; Stanstead £37.45.

APRIL 25ᵗʰ 1992

BEAUTIFUL flowers were on display in Great Waldingfield on Saturday when villagers and visitors gathered for the eighth annual spring flower show.

Held in the village hall, the show attracted a steady stream of visitors throughout the day who admired bunches of flowers and flower arrangements.

Villager Anne Francis (pictured) won first prize in the flower arranging class and secretary of the Great Waldingfield Horticultural Committee, John Hughes said the day had been very enjoyable.

"Those who were exhibiting bunches of flowers had to grow them themselves but flower arrangers could buy their flowers from shops. The flowers were of a very high standard and everyone enjoyed themselves," he said.

HORTICULTURAL SHOW: The eighth spring horticultural show was held in the village hall on Saturday, April 25.

The organisers were worried that there would be very few entries because of the mild winter and the early flowering of spring flowers. However, they need not have worried because onced again it was a very pretty and successful show.

The only section poorly supported was the flower arranging.

The judges were Mr C. Hurr, flowers; Mrs Riddlestone, flower arranging and Mrs P. Higginson, children.

APRIL 30ᵗʰ

Blaze in prefab house

TWO fire crews from Sudbury were called to Great Waldingfield last Friday afternoon after fire broke out in a derelict prefab house in Bantocks Road.

The blaze, which was reported at 4.09 pm, severely damaged two rooms of the wartime building, which has been empty for some time, and is scheduled for demolition to make way for new housing.

Firemen were able to bring the blaze under control within 20 minutes.

Bike stolen

THIEVES stole a Yankee Yukon mountain bike worth £350 from a greenhouse in Bantocks Road, Great Waldingfield, over the weekend.

THIS IS the only way in which we can say thank-you to all the customers of the Ipswich Co-operative Society who donated their dividend to share no 118474. We are delighted to say that £618 has been raised through their generosity.

These Co-op customers can be sure that the money you have donated to us will be wisely used by the British Heart Foundation to fund their ever-increasing research programme into the causes, prevention, diagnosis and treatment of all aspects of heart disease.

We do hope that people will go on supporting the work of the BHF by donating their dividend throughout 1993 to share no 118474 when they shop at the Co-op In-store in Sudbury or at Long Melford Co-op.

PETER HOLLOWAY,
Secretary,
Sudbury district branch BHF.
8 Holbrook Close,
Great Waldingfield.

Barry Spooner, 11, and Alistair Argent, 11 of Great Waldingfield try out a vintage tractor at the rally.

Memories of the war

A REPLICA of the artwork on B17 bomber Goin' Jessie, based at the old airfield outside Sudbury during the war, was just one exhibit at Great Waldingfield village hall when former American airmen returned this week. Pictured, from left to right, are replica artist Roger Lane and Goin' Jessie crew members James W Nugent and Gene Hamilton. Full story on page three.

A "lift" in a jeep at the Waldingfield exhibition for former White Horse landlady Vera Butcher with American visitor Peter Ruplenas at the wheel.

SURVIVORS of one of the greatest air battles in history returned to base in Suffolk, 50 years on, as veterans of the US Eighth Army Air Force revisited the haunts of their youth.

The reunion involved more than 100 former members of the 486th Bombardment Group (H), formerly based at Great Waldingfield near Sudbury, and their wives and friends.

OLD memories were rekindled and new friendships were forged as the Yanks returned to Sudbury and surrounding villages this week – 50 years on from their days as young airmen during World War Two.

Members of the 486th Bomb Group who were stationed at the airfield which lies in Acton, Great Waldingfield and Chilton returned to Suffolk and a warm welcome by Sudbury Mayor Sylvia Cann and her husband Brian on Monday.

Their busy day came on Tuesday when, after a service in St Gregory's Church, they laid wreaths on the American memorial near the church to remember comrades who died during the war. They also attended a lunch at the town hall.

Waiting for them at Great Waldingfield Village Hall were members of the three parish councils, villagers and an exhibition about the airfield and the 486th Bomb Group.

An old video of World War Two aircraft was showing in Great Waldingfield village hall as locals and Americans exchanged stories and walked round the exhibition.

Local historian David Johnson set up an exhibition on local history including ghost stories and tales from the past.

Vera Butcher who ran the White Horse pub in Great Waldingfield said she remembered the American airmen very well.

"I remember them arriving." she said. "It was very early morning – not even light. They used to come in the pub and were generally very pleasant."

US veteran is killed

ONE of the American airforce veterans who returned to Suffolk for the 50th anniversary Return to England celebrations has been knocked down and killed by a London cab.

Robert Pearsall was one of a group of 100 former members of the 486th Bombardment Group (H) who revisited their old haunts in Sudbury and Great Waldingfield, where they were stationed during the war.

The accident occurred the following day as Mr. Pearsall was enjoying the sights of central London accompanied by his son, Jeff.

Previously an air traffic controller in the RAF, PC John Gibbens is married with three children and gives sea angling among his interests. He is responsible for Acton, Great Waldingfield and Little Waldingfield.

Harvest time... pupils at Great Waldingfield school, with some of their crops. They are (from left) Louise Nayes, Jay Meekings, Lewis Rockwood, Jake Charles, Mia Hoy and Connor Sparkes

Picture by Victoria Spofforth 7vs0709016

GREAT WALDINGFIELD

Mrs M. Shinn, The Hollies Cottage, Chilton. Tel 76747

PARISH COUNCIL: The annual parish council meeting was held on Tuesday, May 26, at the village hall.

Mr David Floyd was elected chairman and Mrs Jean Misselbrook was elected vice-chairman. All other representatives to organisations were elected as the previous year.

The USAAF reunion exhibition and tea on Tuesday, May 19 and was a resounding success.

The only problem arising on the day was making room for the veterans when they arrived at the hall – the exhibition and the WI tea proved very popular with the locals and the hall was filled to capacity for most of the afternoon.

It was noted that an exhibition to cover the amendments to the Babergh Plan was due to take place on June 1 and a parish council meeting will be held to discuss the implications on July 7.

A planning application for the use of No 20 Coronation Rise for a dental distribution business was recommended for approval.

A planning application for the erection of a detached dwelling on land at the rear of the Red House, Lavenham Road was recommended for refusal on the grounds of poor highway access and unnecessary infilling.

In the treasurer's report it was noted the council have purchased a small photocopier and this was available for small numbers of copies at reasonable charges.

The playing field committee are making arrangements to fit two refurbished seats on the field and place new surfacing at the foot of the slide.

Mr Elliot of Holbrook Close is experiencing problems with children on the field and this will be taken up by the council.

The entertainments licence for the village hall has been renewed but with a proviso that the tiles in the toilets are repaired. The council will obtain quotes for the replacement and repair.

Fishing theft

FISHING rods and equipment worth £300 and four CB radios worth £130 were stolen from a barn at The Heath, Great Waldingfield, on Friday.

AUGUST 14 '92

Housing project

THE LAST four houses in the second phase of a Babergh Council social housing development built by Chelmsford Developments at Bantocks Road, Great Waldingfield, will be handed to the Orbit Housing Association on Monday, seven weeks ahead of schedule. The project has been jointly funded by the association and the council.

Police probe Waldingfield straw blaze

POLICE are treating as suspicious a blaze which destroyed two tonnes of bailed straw at Brandeston Hall, Great Waldingfield, at the weekend.

The fire started in the early hours of Sunday morning and firecrews from Long Melford and Sudbury tackled the fire.

Anyone who saw anything suspicious just after 1am on Sunday should contact Sudbury police on 0787 881000.

Golden day for first firewoman in town

SUDBURY'S first firewoman Lilian Haxell celebrates a golden day with husband Edward on Saturday.

The couple, of Lavenham Road, Great Waldingfield, will be joined by family, including daughter Trisha and grandchildren Rachel and John, and friends at the Bull Hotel in Long Melford for a party to mark their golden wedding.

"I served in Sudbury as a firewoman during the war and it's my claim to fame being the town's first firewoman," said 70-year-old Lilian, who was born in Great Waldingfield.

Her husband Edward (73) was born in Little Waldingfield and spent most of his working life on farms, continuing farm work during World War Two. He then founded A and H Motors in Great Waldingfield.

Edward and Lilian Haxell... married 50 years.

For 25 years they both enjoyed old time and sequence dancing and now play bowls at the Great Waldingfield club.

"We are looking forward to our get-together at The Bull and no doubt a lot of memories will be rekindled," said Lilian.

Arson probe after dutch barn blaze

A BLAZE which ripped through a dutch barn destroying 1,200 round straw bales is believed to have been started deliberately.

Fire crews from Sudbury and Long Melford tackled the blazing building in Folly Road, Great Waldingfield, after a passer-by alerted gamekeeper Denny Ellender.

The barn, owned by Oliver Farms,

of White Hall Farm, Great Waldingfield, was completely destroyed by the fire which crews managed to stop spreading to adjoining buildings.

A Sudbury brigade spokesman said the barn was well alight when crews arrived shortly after 8.30pm on Friday. After it was brought under control the straw was allowed

to burn itself out. Firemen stayed at the scene throughout the night and most of the following day.

The fire is still being investigated but on Tuesday Mrs Liz Oliver said the cause was being put down to arson.

"We believe it was started deliberately, possibly by children," she said.

PAROCHIAL CHURCH COUNCIL

We had agreed to make new hassocks for the Church once the roof and heating had been completed. We agreed to make a start on this project. The Rector will obtain lengths of canvas and parishioners are invited to work a hassock in cross stitch, either to their own submitted design or one made for them. All the hassocks must have the same colour red as a background. Hopefully a number of people will make hassocks or sponsor the cost of one.

CRIMESTOPPERS NEEDS YOU!

FISHING tackle worth a total of over £400 was stolen from a garage and a van in two incidents in the Sudbury area last month.

In Great Waldingfield during the day of Friday, August 14, a garage on the Heath Estate was entered and a number of fishing rods in a bag and other tackle was stolen.

HORTICULTURAL SHOW: The ninth autumn horticultural show was held on Saturday, September 12, in the village school.

This was another successful show with 314 entries from 72 exhibitors with all sections being well supported.

Escort theft

A BLUE Ford Escort was stolen from its owner's driveway in Folly Road, Great Waldingfield, last Monday. The car is a GL model, registration number VGV 617X.

GREAT WALDINGFIELD

Mrs M. Shinn, The Hollies Cottage, Chilton. Tel 76747

PARISH COUNCIL: The parish council met at the village hall on Tuesday, October 27, for their monthly meeting.

The problems which appear to have arisen over the numbering of Lynns Hall Close were explained in a letter from Babergh District Council. It would appear that houses fronting on to Bantocks Road needed to be included in the existing numbering and therefore slight alterations were made to accommodate these new properties.

The parish council were having considerable difficulties in getting street lighting repairs carried out since Eastern Electricity had moved their lighting department to Ipswich. It was apparent that the computers were set up to take instructions only on column serial numbers and not location details, but these numbers have yet to be printed on the actual lights by the Electricity Board. As a result it is taking a considerable amount of "persuasion" to get the work carried out.

The bowls club have requested an application for a new noticeboard at the entrance to the Ten Trees Road site and the parish council will follow this up for advertising consent.

The scout group have also approached the council for permission for a building on the remaining land on the Ten Trees Road site. The council have requested outline details of the building and the actual siting plan for consideration and discussion with the owners, the county council.

Appeals for grant aid were received and it was agreed to give £100 to Citizens Advice Bureau, £100 to the St John's Methodist hall expansion and a commitment of a donation of £150 to the development of a Sudbury Volunteer Centre.

The insurance for the council through Municipal Mutual Insurance Company is still valid until the renewal date next June.

Mr Skinner gave a report on the area meeting.

The council have agreed to take over the responsibility of the Remembrance Day wreath as from next year, the WI having supplied it in the village for a number of years.

Reward offered after burglary

A FAMILY is offering a reward of £5,000 for information which could catch the gang who stole antiques and jewellery worth thousands of pounds from their country home.

The unidentified house, between Great Waldingfield and Lavenham, was stripped of items worth a total of £11,000 in the first of two major burglaries in the area in nine days.

Among the items taken was an oil painting by Dutch artist Johannes Ykens, depicting an old man holding a skull and accompanied by young women dressed in pink.

The picture, painted in 1651 and entitled *The Brevity of Life*, measures 40 by 30 inches with its frame and 28 by 33 inches unframed.

Jewellery

Also taken were a mahogany Georgian firescreen bearing a tapestry picture of a parrot and a mahogany Sheraton easy-chair upholstered in blue tapestry.

A Chippendale table measuring three feet by two, three prints of stage coaches and a circular chestnut pendulum clock were also stolen, along with ornaments and personal jewellery.

The raiders struck on October 6, but it took more than a week for the value of the haul to be calculated.

Anyone who recognises any of the stolen items or has information about the theft can contact Sudbury police on (0787) 881000.

The police are also investigating a £2,000 burglary at a house in Bantocks Road, Great Waldingfield, on October 14 or 15.

Among the items stolen were three wrist watches — a round-faced Omega with a gold bracelet, a square Longines with a gold strap and a Timex in a gold and silver case.

Two engagement rings, a diamond solitaire and a blue opal set in diamonds, a 22-carat Chinese gold bracelet, a gold charm bracelet and a gold necklace and earrings were also taken.

I WOULD like to thank the young couple who looked after me and put me in a taxi after I fell on some uneven pavement near Borehamgatre Precinct in Sudbury just before 11 am last Thursday.

Also, thank you to the taxi

Thank you

driver who was so helpful.

Mrs M RAINE,
33 Badleys Close,
Great Waldingfield.

MRS V D HAXELL

It is with sadness that we record the death of Mrs Vi Haxell, aged 92 years, of Hillside, Great Cornard, formerly of Bridge Bungalow, Little Waldingfield.

Vi first came to Great Waldingfield as Miss Coward – Headmistress of the Village School, which was then next to the Church, residing in the School House. She soon became involved with the affairs of the village – she was clerk to the Parish Council, secretary to the Braithwaite Trust, Church Warden at St Lawrence's and was president and secretary of the WI.

She married local farmer George Haxell in 1944 and on their retirement they moved to Bridge Bungalow, Little Waldingfield, but she still kept her connections with Great Waldingfield.

At 80 years old she moved to Hillside Home, where she spent twelve pleasant years, until she fell and broke her leg, which led to her death in hospital.

MILDEN United's football-team of 1952-3 are the subject of this week's Memory Lane picture, loaned by J R Sparkes of Great Waldingfield.

Pictured are, left to right, back row: Bertie Richardson, Charlie Bowers, Don Carter, John Sparkes (capt), Bill King, Bill Byford, Billie Everett and Arthur Griggs (secretary); Front row: Ron Griggs, Les Sparkes, Claud Alliston, Freddie Game and Gerald (Jake) Goodchild.

FRIENDS OF GREAT WALDINGFIELD SCHOOL PRESENT

A QUIZ NIGHT

on

SATURDAY 17 OCTOBER 1992

in **GREAT WALDINGFIELD VILLAGE HALL**

at **7.30 P.M.**

Enter a team of 4 (18+) from you family, club, workplace, neighbourhood or wherever.

£6.00 per team to include a Ploughmans

BAR   **RAFFLE**

Entry forms available from the School, phone 74055.
To be returned as soon as possible.

ENTRY WILL BE LIMITED TO THE FIRST 30 TEAMS THAT APPLY!

GT WALDINGFIELD PLAYGROUP

An under-10's disco was held on 18 September to celebrate our 21st birthday. A cake made and donated by Mrs Wilson (Supervisor) was cut and enjoyed by everyone. £56 was raised as profit.

HORTICULTURAL SHOW

The Ninth Autumn Horticultural Show was held on Saturday 12 September in the Village School.

This was another successful show with 314 entries from 72 exhibitors with all sections being well supported.

PARISH COUNCIL

Distribution Road – the council seriously objected to the stoppage of the Sudbury/Waldingfield Road to all traffic and suggested a physical width restriction to allow local car and cycle use but remove access to bigger vehicles. A similar suggestion was put forward for Valley Road, which faces a similar closure order. The Council also objected to the closure of Acton Lane to Sudbury as this was essential for direct access to the Middle School and its closure could result in increased traffic coming into Gt Waldingfield.

BOWLS CLUB

On Tuesday 6 October the Club Captain organised an outing to a leisure complex in North Norfolk.

A coach took eight teams of four players each to play a similar number from the Norfolk club, and every Great Waldingfield player experienced two hours of playing under quite different conditions.

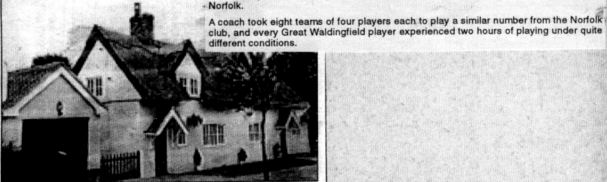

GREAT WALDINGFIELD: Large 3 bedroomed Grade II listed cottage in pristine order. Re-thatched in 1991, fully renovated with all original features, ground floor shower room, 2 reception rooms with beams and original fireplaces, luxury oak fitted kitchen, detached lodge in grounds, full gas fired c.h., viewing essential .... **£125,000 o.n.o.**

PARISH COUNCIL

The Charity Commission have agreed to change the existing charity status of the Village Hall to a scheme whereby the land and the hall are entrusted under one scheme with the Parish Council as Trustees. This would alleviate the need for a ground rent and retain the land for the Parish.

The Council have agreed to take over the responsibility of the Remembrance Day wreath as from next year, the WI having supplied it in the Village for a number of years.

THE PAROCHIAL CHURCH COUNCIL

The PCC will, as usual, be inviting all senior citizens in Great Waldingfield to partake of tea in the Village Hall – on Sunday 6 December. Christmas music, carols etc to follow. Invitations will be dropping through your doors shortly. Replies please (to ensure sensible catering) by the beginning of December.

Flower Festival and Harvest. We are grateful to Anne Francis and the large band of volunteers who produced such a splendid result – £680 was raised.

Any Other Business. It was suggested and agreed that we reserve a spot directly near the church for cars of disabled people. Cones will be obtained. These will be marked and the sidesmen of the day will place them outside.

Suzanne reported that we have a new Third World child called Bolina.

MIXED REVUES IN CONCERT

An audience of seventy-five people filled the School Hall for the third visit of this talented group. The format was different this time. The first half was a shortened version of the Mikado. The story was narrated, and the music performed by the group. The up-to-date list of people who wouldn't be missed, written and performed by the Lord High Executioner, was much enjoyed, as was the high standard of the singing. During the interval everyone was able to enjoy a ploughmans supper and chat to friends and members of the cast. The second half of the concert consisted of a variety of songs from musicals, old and new. Solo's, duets, quartets, and the whole company singing together provided much variety. Songs ranged from *'Forty Second Street', 'In the Mood', 'She's My Girl'* to the love duet from *'Phantom of the Opera'*. The unaccompanied four-part singing was a particular delight. The ladies of the company also performed a dance which was well choreographed – dressed in black tights, dinner jackets and top hats they looked most professional. The Rector thanked everyone at the end of a most enjoyable evening. A raffle was held in aid of the charity *'Save The Children'* which is where all the money Mixed Revues have been paid the last few months has been sent. The total raised was £71.

Thank You. The cast of Mixed Revues would like to take this opportunity to thank all the people who made their recent visit so enjoyable. Maureen Shinn, who never seems to mind giving up time to open the School for us, so that we may rehearse during the day. The Churchwardens who moved chairs from the Gospel Hall to the School on Saturday morning, and then back again early Sunday morning. Thanks also to the Gospel Hall for lending the full sized chairs – what a difference this made to the audience who usually crouch on infant sized chairs. The ladies and gentlemen under the guidance of Judith Kiddy who prepared all the ploughmans suppers, and even remembered cold drinks for the cast, as well as tea and coffee. We always enjoy our visit to Great Waldingfield. The warmth of our welcome is very special.

Lesley sheds 4½ stones

AFTER - "Did I really wear skirts this size? the new slim-line Lesley.

IT'S away with the voluminous size 20 skirt and on with an average size 14 for a Great Waldingfield woman who shed four-and-a-half stone to become Slimmer Clubs UK East Anglian finalist.

After only six months of careful calorie-counting, Lesley Plumb (33) of Heathway, Great Waldingfield, slimmed down from a chunky 14½ stone to her ideal weight, a steady ten stone.

Lesley's efforts were rewarded on Monday when area manager Sarah Bingham presented her with a collection of body-firming and toning products at the weekly class.

Admitting she had always been overweight, Lesley said she began her slimming regime after realising her bathroom scales were moving steadily up.

"I couldn't kid myself any longer and realised something had to be done," she explained.

"I'd gained weight before, during and after having my two daughters and never lost it. I was eating man-sized portions and snacking on biscuits."

by PAT BRAY

She started attending Slimmer Clubs UK classes at Long Melford Old School and followed their healthy diet, always counting her calories.

"I had to weigh everything but found it really easy and the weight just came off," she said.

"Now I'm eating normally, but my diet is much healthier and my weight's steady. I feel great, but all my clothes are too big!"

Husband Graham, who is delighted with the new Lesley, was supportive throughout and even managed to lose four stone himself on the same diet.

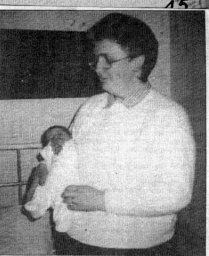

BEFORE – Lesley Plumb, pictured with her young niece a year ago, when she weighed 14½ stone.

Her adviser Lynn Halifax, who also holds a class at Glemsford's United Reformed Church Hall on Tuesdays, said Lesley had been "absolutely brilliant."

"She stuck to her diet 100 per cent," she said.

"Lesley lost steadily every week and only took six months to reach her goal."

ACTON AND GREAT WALDINGFIELD FRIENDSHIP CLUB

The last meeting of 1992 was a double celebration for the Club, combining the 25th anniversary of its founding with the Christmas lunch. Mr Blazey, Chairman, welcomed the tea-lady guests and thanked all helpers. Gifts were presented to Ms Fraser and Doel, long-standing Committee members, to Mrs Cutt for sending greetings cards, and to Mrs Ball for fund raising. A superb lunch was enjoyed. After party games the decorated cake was cut and distributed, portions being sent to those who could not attend. Mr Lee thanked the Chairman for all his hard work during the year.

GREAT WALDINGFIELD SCHOOL

We would like to thank you for your continued support of our school and its activities. We were able to send a cheque for £52.00 to the Children's Hospice and one for £194.96 to the Children's Society before Christmas.

We quickly collected 5,000 Christmas cards for the Babergh appeal and any surplus will be put to good use.

Babergh have initiated a new scheme in conjunction with the Aluminium Can Recycling Association. We would be very pleased to receive your aluminium cans in School.

QUIZ NIGHT

Thank you to everyone who supported the Friends of Great Waldingfield School Quiz Night on Saturday 17 October.

SHOES ... SHOES ... SHOES

BRING US YOUR OLD SHOES! We have found an unexpected way to make money for our school fund. Shearwater Export Ltd will pay 25p per pair for shoes in a reasonable condition. They export the shoes to West Africa where local labour is used to repair the shoes which are then sold on market stalls. We have sent two loads to date and have received £38 and £21, very useful additions to school fund.

POLICE are mystified over the cause of a tragic crash on Friday evening which left a teenager dead.

Richard Britton (19), of Great Waldingfield, was killed in the accident on the A1092 near Clare.

He was a passenger in a VW Camper van, which left the road about a quarter of a mile on the Clare side of Cavendish at about 8pm.

The van driver, Richard's former schoolfriend Patrick Ince, of Long Melford, was discharged from the West Suffolk Hospital, Bury St Edmunds, on Tuesday after receiving treatment for a broken collar bone.

Richard, who had an elder brother and sister, Douglas and Lisa, lived with his parents, Marion and David, in Bowling Green.

HEATHFIELD, Blanche died very peaceably at 58 Bantocks Road on 12 November 1992. The much beloved wife of Edward Heathfield who would like to thank all the friends and neighbours for their support during her illness, the many gifts, flowers and cards were a great source of comfort to my dear wife. God bless you all.

Rubbish blaze

SUDBURY firemen dealt with a small rubbish fire at the White Horse, Great Waldingfield, on Thursday afternoon.

Council tax bill average £426 in Babergh

HOUSEHOLDS in the Babergh district are likely to pay an average council tax on their properties of £426 from April 1.

The figure is expected to be approved today (Thursday) by Babergh Council's policy and resources committee and is based on properties in valuation band C (£52,000 - £68,000).

This compares to an average community charge of £257.45 levied on each adult in Babergh during the current 1992-93 financial year.

The committee is being asked to approve the use of £823,000 from the authority's working balances to bring its total expenditure for 1993-94 to £657,000 below the government's standard spending allowance target for the council.

If approved average council tax charges for each property band will be as follows:

- Band A (up to £40,000): £319.
- Band B (£40,000 - £52,000): £373.
- Band C (£52,000 - £68,000): £426.
- Band D (£68,000 - £88,000): £479.
- Band E (£88,000 - £120,000): £585.
- Band F (£120,000 - £160,000): £692.
- Band G (£160,000 - £320,000): £798.
- Band H (over £320,000): £958.

In his report to the committee, council treasurer John Covsh, who is due to retire this month, says the figures are based on the assumption that Suffolk County Council budgets to spend at its 1993-94 SSA set by the Government.

He adds that taking the £657,000 figure from Babergh's balances would still leave an estimated £1,107,410 in its general fund and £3.9 million in its general services reserves at March 1994.

Wages are too low

HAVING read that Job Centre staff are to visit 250 local employers to help find vacancies in Suffolk blackspots, I hope the employers, whoever they be, will pay a decent wage.

I have been to the Job Centre in Sudbury with my husband and most of them are paying around £3.50 an hour which is about £140 a week.

Then you would have to look at stoppages which would bring you down to about £115 a week.

Most married men I know say they are better off staying at home as they are better off on the dole.

To keep up with the cost of living you need to earn £4 to £5 an hour and no way are employers prepared to pay that kind of money. If there are, could you let me know? By the way, my husband used to be a lorry driver. Any offers out there?

L WELSH
11 Coronation Rise,
Great Waldingfield.

Tributes to airmen lost in action

SUDBURY paid its annual Independence Day tribute on Sunday to the US airmen lost on wartime bombing operations from a local airfield.

Mayor of Sudbury Elizabeth Wiles, accompanied by town councillors, laid a wreath at the town's 486th Bomb Group memorial outside St Gregory's Church.

Graeme Garden, himself a former Mayor, laid a second wreath on behalf of the Friends of the 486th BG, of which he is president.

His wife Joan also paid her own floral tribute to the 400 US Army Air Force aircrew who lost their lives flying from nearby Great Waldingfield.

Mrs Wiles then placed a wreath on the memorial to the town's own war dead, which stands nearby.

Man injured in dustcart crash

A MAN was treated in West Suffolk Hospital for facial injuries after his car was in collision with a dustcart near the White Horse Club, Great Waldingfield.

Darren Parkinson, of Bradleys Close, Sudbury, was discharged after treatment. Dustcart driver David James, of Mountbatten Court, Great Cornard, was not hurt.

PARISH COUNCIL: The parish council held their first meeting of the year on Tuesday, January 28, at the village hall. The first item on the agenda was the forthcoming Babergh Plan inquiry which starts in February.

The parish council have resolved various matters but will be making representation regarding the closure of local roads and the proposed new link road on Tuesday, March 23, at Sudbury Town Hall. Mr Peter Blackwell from Sudbury had submitted alternative plans and these would be considered before the next parish council meeting.

The local scout group submitted suggested site plans for the erection of a single-storey building on the land opposite the bowls club in Ten Trees Road. The council could see no objection to the development but said local opinion would have to be sought when an official application was made. They agreed to assist with the fees for the application should it be submitted.

Royal Mail have agreed to erect a post box in Bantocks Road.

Planning appeals have been made for the erection of a house behind Red House, Lavenham Road, for which the parish council had recommended refusal, and the use of a room for office accommodation at 20 Coronation Rise for which the parish council had recommended approval. The council decided they would not change their decisions on either appeal.

Planning permission was recommended for an extension at Ye Olde Cottage, The Heath.

PC Gibbons, in a short report on the crime statistics, said burglaries are causing concern as are thefts from cars.

The village hall is at present preparing for a considerable facelift in the kitchen area. With the recent inspections from virtually every health and safety officer, a programme of improvements has been undertaken costing approximately £5,000.

The hall is to be fitted with a fire alarm system and back-up electrical services. The heaters in the extension have been refurbished and replaced and a new hot water heater in the men's toilets and new soakaways to the store room are planned.

The largest job however will involve replac-

...ng the kitchen units which are being replaced in line with the health and hygiene recommendations and replacing the two cookers with one more robust commercial grade cooker.

The finance for this work is available from a contingency fund and it is hoped that the work will begin during the half-term holiday starting on February 15. When this is complete, the village hall will present a very acceptable face to the world and will offer good value for the letting fees charged.

The WI have kindly offered to supply a new sign for the hall as part of their 75th birthday celebrations.

The council have arranged a meeting with the Charity Commissioners in London to resolve the outstanding problems of the charity status of the hall.

The parish council have agreed to make the pavilion available on Saturday, July 10, for the Acton and Waldingfield carnival.

The next meeting of the parish council is on Tuesday, February 23, at 7.30 pm.

Suffolk Show quiz winners

WINNERS of the National Farmers Union countryside quiz at the Suffolk Show included Emma Stifane of Coronation Rise, Great Waldingfield, Lauren Warden of Cornard Road, Sudbury, and D Honeybone of Naughton Road, Whatfield.

Not so merry

THIEVES have stolen a "Robin Hood" bicycle valued at £40 from Bantocks Road, Great Waldingfield.

Since the last edition of this Magazine, we have been saddened by the sudden deaths of Richard Britton (19), Lucinda Turner (71) and John Steed (49). We extend our sympathy to the families of all three in their bereavement.

Industry objection

A FORMER airfield site north-east of Sudbury earmarked for industry in alterations to the Babergh Local Plan should remain a greenfield site, say Acton villagers.

Instead factories should be located at Acton Place in the opposite direction towards the Melford bypass, Acton Parish Council clerk Christine Johnson told inquiry inspector Michael Shaw on Thursday.

The compromise was suggested as the parish registered its opposition to plans to zone land north of Waldingfield Road, Chilton, and east of Acton Lane for general and prestigious employment use.

But John Holt for Babergh Council, said the parish council's suggestion posed potential problems in terms of traffic access onto the bypass. The area also did not meet the needs for presti-

THIEVES entered Great Waldingfield Primary School in Folly Road last Wednesday afternoon, stealing two handbags containing various items.

Sudbury Police community affairs officer Dave Gilson said: "We would like to hear of anybody acting suspiciously and ask all schools to be on the look-out."

RATCLIFFE: Peacefully on March 23, 1993, after a long illness bravely borne, Laurence George, aged 69 years, formerly local butcher at Baxters Butchers. Beloved husband of Doris, also a dearly loved father, grandfather and father-in-law. Funeral service at Great Waldingfield Parish Church on Tuesday, March 30, at 2pm, followed by burial. Family flowers only, donations if desired to St Nicholas Hospice, c/o Co-operative Funeral Service, Cornard Road, Sudbury.

Thursday, March 18, 1993

Death crash cause is still a mystery

MYSTERY still surrounds the cause of a crash in which a 19-year-old teenage passenger died from his injuries after a van hit a garden wall and bounced across a road, an inquest was told on Thursday.

Passenger Richard Britton, of Great Waldingfield, died of internal bleeding at the scene of the crash near Clare despite efforts by a passing motorist and his wife to resuscitate him using heart massage.

West Suffolk Coroner Bill Walrond recorded a verdict of "accidental death."

VW van driver, Patrick Ince, told Mr Walrond he could remember nothing about the December 11 crash on the A1092 at Clare.

Mr Ince, of St Catherine's Road, Long Melford, who was found lying on a grass verge yards from the scene, said he could remember coming up just before a bend but the next thing he knew he was waking up in hospital.

He added he could not remember whether he or Mr Britton were wearing seatbelts.

Dr Henry Fell, of Gedding, said he was driving along the road when he saw something "going across the road from left to right." When he stopped his car to investigate he found Mr Britton halfway out of the passenger doorway of ther van.

He was jammed in the doorway and both Dr Fell and his wife tried to resusitate Mr Britton.

In a statement read to the inquest pathologist Dr Hussaine Al-Rufaie, said death was caused by internal bleeding.

PARISH COUNCIL: The parish council meeting was preceded this month by a meeting of the voluntary committee of the village hall to officially resolve to wind up the charity covering the hall and to hand over the assets to a new charity which will be managed by the parish council as trustees.

This decision was taken to ensure both the future of the hall and the land on which it stands. This has been let to the village hall in the past by the parish council. The resolution will be advertised and officially noted at the annual parish meeting in April.

The Babergh plan inquiry opened on Tuesday, February 23, and the parish council will be represented on March 23 to discuss the proposed road schemes. By a majority vote the council agreed to offer support to Mr Blackwell from Sudbury in his attempt to have the relief road merged with the far end of Valley Road to avoid the need for two roads running parallel with each other. This, however, would be dependent on the local councils being successful in keeping the Waldingfield-Sudbury road open to local traffic.

Plans are in hand to erect extra lights in Folly Road, Coronation Rise and Kenyon Drive, but final costs are still awaited from Eastern Electricity.

The WI have offered to provide a sign for the entrance to the village hall and final details are being obtained as to cost. The refurbishment of the hall is well in hand and the parish council were pleased with the progress so far.

The council were pleased to note that for a trial period of 12 months, Babergh Council will alllow a parish council representative to attend planning site meetings.

A request had been received from Mrs May of Walnuttree Cottage to raise funds for new play equipment. The council are to check with the district auditor on the legal implications of accepting gifts and their future maintenance.

The council were disturbed to note that three horse riders have been using Mill Field path and in doing so forced a pedestrian into the field. This problem must be addressed and action is being taken to find out the identity of the people involved.

The next meeting is on Tuesday, March 23 at the village hall.

RED NOSE DAY: Red Nose Day was celebrated in school with the children organising various events. These included baking and selling cakes, setting up a bring and buy stall and participating in various games. Children paid to wear optional dress and to have their faces painted. They raised £56 for Comic Relief.

A PASSING doctor who arrived at the scene of a road crash may have helped to save the life of a badly injured motorcyclist.

The doctor applied a tourniquet to slow the blood loss from 20-year-old Graham Ludford's leg after the Essex rider was in collision with a car outside the White Horse pub at Great Waldingfield at around 5pm last Wednesday.

Mr Ludford, of Rayne, was taken to the West Suffolk Hospital at Bury St Edmunds with multiple injuries following the crash. His condition is described as "comfortable."

Car driver Peter Verhaest, of Minsmere Way, Great Cornard, was uninjured.

The doctor, who arrived at the scene of the crash by chance, was helped by White Horse landlady Linda Warner who helped to make Mr Ludford comfortable until an ambulance arrived.

Appeal after £5,000 raid

POLICE have appealed for witnesses after a £5,000 raid on a house in Great Waldingfield on Monday.

Thieves smashed their way through a patio door to get into the house in Folly Road between 9 am and 11 am.

Their haul included an Olympus zoom lens camera, a JVC video, a briefcase and £1,000 in cash.

They also took jewellery including a silver charm bracelet and a 22 carat gold man's watch with white face, Roman numerals, a sapphire on the face and a black strap.

APRIL 1993

MUSICAL blockbuster Joseph and the Amazing Technicolour Dreamcoat had audiences at Great Waldingfield Primary School joining in the tunes and tapping their feet this week.

Masterminded by musical director Faith Marsden, the colourful production staged on Monday and Wednesday involved all 75 pupils, with Peter Gostling (pictured front) in the leading role.

His many-coloured, patchwork coat was borrowed for the occasion but all the other costumes were made by parents or in school. Parent and artist Steve Povall created the huge Pharaoh's head.

Headteacher Geoffrey Chatters said the school had not done a nativity play at Christmas but liked to stage something special every year.

"Everyone enjoyed taking part and we had a good crowd of parents in to see the production," he added.

THESE children from Great Waldingfield were among youngsters from all over the district who have been taking part in funtime sessions laid on by Babergh Council during the holidays to encourage their interest in sport.

Sessions for youngsters aged eight to 12 are usually fully booked, with games on offer including volleyball, skittle ball, unihoc and snowball.

"We aim to provide kids with an introduction to sport and entertain them as well," said Babergh's sports activities officer Kris Lamb.

GT WALDINGFIELD £65,000 Freehold Non-estate location

SPRING HORTICULTURAL SHOW: The 9th annual Spring Show was held in the village hall on Saturday, April 24.

The committee were rather concerned about the early spring and wondered if there would be any flowers left to exhibit!

As it turned out, it was once again a successful, pretty show with entries in nearly every class. The children's classes were particularly well supported.

The judges were Mr C Hurr, flowers and plants; Mrs L Henwood, flower arranging, and Mrs P Higginson, children's classes.

Winners (first, second and third): single daffodils, Olivia Miller; Chris Francis; Anne Francis; double daffodils, Mrs M Armour; Ruth Lock; Mrs A Albion; narcissi, Maureen Shinn, Mary Jackson, Mrs A Albion; jonquils, Jean Misselbrook, G. Albion, Chris Francis; single tulips, Chris Francis, Fred Shinn, Edna allen; double tulips, Mr T. Nice; miniature jonquils, Jean Misselbrook, Ruth Lock, Derek Jackson; pansies, Mrs M. Armour, Jean Misselbrook, Edna Allen; polyanthus, Mrs M Armour, Derek Jackson, Mary Jackson; other primulas, Maureen Shinn, Derek Jackson, John Hughes; flowering shrub, Mrs M Armour, Ruth Lock, Mr T Nice; spring flowers, Jean Misselbrook, Maureen Shinn, Anne Francis; flowering pot plant, Mrs V Acton; picture of a dragon, Emily Taylor, Oliver Haynes, Verity Butcher; flower mobile, Verity Butcher, Oliver Haynes; model building, Oliver Haynes, Verity Butcher.

5-6 years: dragon picture, Ben Taylor, Kay Leathers, Jemma Taylor; flower mobile, Laura Haynes, Kay Leathers, Robyn Kaye; model building, Bryony Marsden, Robyn Kaye, Adam Butcher.

9-12 years: dragon picture, Olivia Miller, Peter Gostling, Gemma Page; flower mobile, Joanne Haynes, Samuel Haynes, Gemma Page; model building, Lucy Barber, Janne Haynes, Benjamin Taylor.

The section winners' prizes were presented by Mr Bill Skinner to Margaret Armour, Dianne Quilter, Sally Brinton, Oliver Haynes, Kay Leathers and Joanne Haynes.

Highest number of points: Jean Misselbrook.

The chairman, Chris Francis, thanked everyone for their hard work and support.

He urged people to look out for the schedules for the tenth anniversary show, to be held in the marquee on the playing field on July 10.

This should be a grand show, with hopefully many people entering. Schedules will be available soon.

Richard is running for playfield

GREAT Waldingfield runner Richard May is taking part in the London Marathon on Sunday to raise money for adventure playground equipment for the village playing field.

Richard (36), a computer systems analyst, of The Street, who has been accepted for the marathon after applying for four years, keeps in training by running in various organised events all over the area.

He has left sponsor forms in the White Horse pub, the local shop and the school and hopes villagers will support him.

His wife Kathryn said the family had moved a year ago to Waldingfield from London where there were adventure playgrounds galore and Richard wanted to help fund new equipment for the village.

"We're expecting him to finish," she said. "It's the first time in recent years that money has been raised for play equipment."

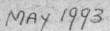

MAY 1993

Pauline Higginson, left, and Maureen Shinn, take a look at some of the old photograpghs on display at the "Village Life Past and Present" exhibition at Great Waldingfield Parish Church.

Village life past and present

FASCINATING photographs, documents and artefacts reflecting village life past and present in Great Waldingfield were the subject of a special bank holiday weekend exhibition to boost funds for roof repairs to the village church.

Staged at St Lawrence's Church, the event included exhibits provided by residents, the village school and church and archive material from the county records office.

Visitors were able to delve through the parish records as well as browsing around displays evoking memories of the U.S Army Air Force's 486th Bombardment Group based at the old airfield.

These included a fragment of the engine of Bomb Group aircraft lost in a crash in the area.

Proceeds from the exhibition will go towards the fund which has a target of £30,000 to pay for essential repairs to the church roof.

Lost sign

DOES anyone know the rightful home of a red Babergh Council sign saying "Residents parking only"?

This colourful sign was attached to the bus shelter in Great Waldingfield a couple of weeks ago. We hope someone will claim it.

FRANCES BATES
Ramla
Rectory Road
Great Waldingfield

**Great Waldingfield Women's Institute
founded in June 1918**

**Invite you to join them in celebrating
their 75th Anniversary**

Come for Tea and Biscuits

**Wednesday 2 June 1993
Great Waldingfield Village Hall
from 2.30-4.30pm**

No charge! We just want to meet you

Thursday, May 27, 1993

Promising firm crashes

A SUCCESSFUL Sudbury company who began the year with plans to expand their dental supplies operation has crashed with the loss of 12 jobs.

Firmadent European has ceased trading and laid off all its staff after a bankrupty order was made against company founder Martin Lindsay.

The firm was started by Mr Lindsay and his wife Hazel in 1991 at their Great Waldingfield home and in January this year relocated to a factory unit in Sudbury's Alexandra Road.

Specialising in supplying the dental materials market, the couple were looking for a £60,000 cash injection to aid further growth and expand the sales side of their operation.

However, this was not forthcoming from private investors and the firm were unable to protect their niche in the market against major companies like Bayer.

The firm dealt with manufacturers in Europe and the US and had enjoyed a £410,000 turnover since being launched.

WI birthday invitation to village

AN ENTIRE village is being invited to tea and biscuits on Wednesday to help Great Waldingfield WI celebrate their 75th anniversary.

The celebrations are being staged at the village hall from 2.30-4pm and an exhibition of WI memorabilia, scrapbooks and articles belonging to members will be on show.

A special booklet highlighting Great Waldingfield WI's previous celebrations and contrasting them alongside national and local events of the time has been compiled by branch president Ann Holloway and treasurer Edna Allen and will also be available to view.

● The celebrations continue with a 1918 old time music hall birthday party in the village hall for past and present members and guests from neighbouring WI groups.

Gardening gifts for retirement

A TREE lopper and a cold frame were among gifts presented to keen gardener Geoff Chatters when he retired as head teacher of a village primary school.

Mr Chatters, who is leaving Great Waldingfield Primary School after 16 years, was showered with gifts and tokens of affection at the school's end-of-term summer concert.

"I'm very sad to be leaving, but at least I will have the time to get on with all the things that haven't been done in the last 16 years," he said.

Retiring Great Waldingfield head teacher Geoff Chatters with pupils in the school's garden.

We welcome Mrs Jill Penrose as our new headteacher from September and look forward to having her here working in the village, and in our school.

CONGRATULATIONS

Our congratulations go to Louise Eady of Heath Estate who has just been awarded an LLB (Honours) degree from the University of Teeside. Louise gained a second class honours division 1. Louise was a pupil at Gt Waldingfield School, All Saints Middle and later became head girl at the Upper School. Well done Louise!

● A THIEF who entered the premises of Motor City auto traders in Great Waldingfield scratched one car causing £500 damage and stole four wheel trims worth £50.

SELF-employed farmworker Peter Mayhew drove an uninsured car shortly after buying it, Sudbury magistrates were told told on Tuesday.

Mayhew (39), of Greenleaves Bungalow, Folly Road, Great Waldingfield, was fined £250, ordered to pay £30 court costs and had his licence endorsed with seven penalty points.

Music exam successes

MUSICIANS have received the results of examinations they took while studying with Great Waldingfield teacher Dorothy Rattray Allan.

The following grades were obtained in the Incorporated Society of Musicians, which is the oldest established music associaton in the UK.

Piano: Helen Claye 1 (merit), Nicholas Lowe 2, Laura Brown 4, Frances Petty 4 (merit), Laura Border 5, Isobel Lindsell 6, Penny Stratham 8 (merit): Theory: Isobel Lindsell 5.

UPSHER GREEN   **£170,000**

A most attractive and interesting period house, surrounded by delightful gardens of 0.82 acres in a peaceful hamlet. Reception hall, cloakroom, drawing room, kitchen/breakfast room, dining room, utility room, sitting room/bedroom, 2 bedrooms, 2 dressing areas, bathroom, garage, outbuildings and garden.

WHEN John Misselbrook took the job of borough accountant in Sudbury 28 years ago the town was very different.

For example, the development on land on the outskirts of town, now the Springlands estate, was still being discussed, the police station was in a building near the old outdoor pool and Boreham-gate Precinct didn't even exist.

Colleagues and members of the town council said goodbye on Tuesday and presented him with a painting of old railway engines by Sudbury artist Terry Oben.

From leaving school in Hampshire John trained as an engineering draughtsman and then spent three years in the RAF.

After that he joined a private firm of accountants and then went into local government in Petersfield, Hampshire.

He became Sudbury's borough accountant in 1965 and then borough treasurer. After the local government reforms in 1974, he became town council treasurer.

"I have seen Sudbury change so much over 28 years. There has been so much development, some good and some bad but Sudbury has still remained a nice town," said John who lives in Great Waldingfield with his wife Jean.

John (66), who officially retired in July, added he is looking forward to spending more time on his major hobby – model railways.

"I am also interested in wartime aviation and I have my garden railway to keep me occupied."

Retired town treasurer John Misselbrook with his garden railway

Basil Martin (left) from Great Waldingfield discusses his 1955 Nuffield tractor with Eddie Weeks of Leavenheath

New head at Waldingfield

CHILDREN and staff at Great Waldingfield Primary School are getting to know their new headteacher who started at the beginning of term.

It is Jill Penrose's first job as a head teacher although she has been teaching in Suffolk schools for many years.

She said has received a warm welcome and is very enthusiastic about the school which caters for children from both Great and Little Waldingfield.

The red and yellow-coloured bike with a Danger Mouse motif and white wheels stolen from Great Waldingfield this week.

Baker beats his own record

MASTER Baker John Haynes from Great Waldingfield chopped 26 seconds from his own world record of baking bread in a Suffolk field on Saturday.

His mission was to bake 13 one pound loaves, from harvesting the grain to putting the baked loaves on a table to be judged edible, as quickly as possible.

BBC TV cameras came to film the event at Buxton Farm, Alpheton, along with new Record Breakers presenter and former Olympic athlete Kris Akabusi.

Car stolen — with insurance

A BEIGE Peugeot 309 hatchback, registration number C563 HYD, has been stolen from the Heath, Great Waldingfield.

The car, which contained a number of documents from the Combined Insurance Company of America, disappeared last Thursday.

AFTER nine years of selling stamps and a lot more besides, John and Vanessa Schofield have decided to call it a day as proprietors of Great Waldingfield Post Office Stores.

They are going to move to Hartest and take stock of their lives before making another career choice.

John (58) and Vanessa (56) have not only sold postal items at the store, they have sold locally produced hams, cheese and sausages and locally grown fruit.

Tributes to you both, and those nine years, could fill the whole of this issue of the Parish Magazine but, suffice to say from all the villagers, *"Thank You John and Vanessa"* – for all those years, you have been at the heart of the village and we shall all miss you both.

John and Vanessa Schofield outside Great Waldingfield Post Office Stores.

the community life and the regular contact with the locals of Great Waldingfield.

"We have very stong feelings for this trade – this sort of business becomes your life. You can't really do it otherwise," he said.

The Schofields have a grown-up son and daughter, both living in London.

The new proprietors of the Post Office Stores will be Stuart and Christine Hogg.

PARISH COUNCIL MEETING

The Parish Council held their meeting on Tuesday 28 September at the Village Hall. The first item raised was the matter of the nuisance from The Piggeries. It was reported that a statutory notice had been issued on 13 September to carry out remedial work by 31 December. The situation would be monitored as numerous complaints were still being received.

Friends of Great Waldingfield School present

A QUIZ NIGHT

7.30 pm on Saturday 6 November *1993*

Head teacher Jill Penrose with Kathryn Cole, Stacey Parker and Andrew Ruffell at Great Waldingfield Primary School.

Jill Penrose, head teacher at Great Waldingfield Primary School said the study of history was of crucial importance.

She welcomed Sir Ron's promise to slim down the national curriculum at the primary level, but said his plans for the subject at secondary level were a mistake.

History was not simply the study of facts, but a life skill which enabled pupils to question motives and understand the world in which they lived, she said.

By allowing pupils to drop the subject at 14, schools were in danger of stunting that intellectual growth.

"Even at primary level, history is an opportunity to challenge the printed word, looking at bias, cultural differences and points of view.

"It is crucial that people think and are critical in a positive sense and if you don't go on refining the skill, you have a childlike rather than an adult appreciation," she said.

Mrs Penrose believes a basic grasp of history is a "guardian against fascism and political extremes" and that it should be a compulsory subject right through to A level.

"If you have no historical understanding, then you have no context in which to operate, no set of values about what other people are trying to do," she said.

Sing it with feeling: Great Waldingfield Primary School pupils enjoying their nativity play, which has a cast of 68.

Village school to get an Easter holidays facelift

A VILLAGE school which won an architectural award back in 1971 is to undergo major refurbishment to bring it in line with National Curriculum demands.

The work, at Great Waldingfield primary school, is expected to cost between £15,000 and £20,000, and will be carried out during the Easter holidays.

It includes roofing over an outside courtyard, re-sanding the hall floor, knocking down partitions within classrooms, carpeting, new doors and levelling the floors of two "quiet" rooms to maximise their potential use.

"It's going to make an enormous difference," said headteacher Jill Penrose yesterday. "It's going to make life so much easier for children and teachers.

"Since we're a small village school with small classes, having more self-contained areas within the building will be particularly beneficial."

Mrs Penrose added that although the school had won an award from the Royal Institute of British Architects in 1971, changes were now necessary to meet the demands of the National Curriculum.

GT WALDINGFIELD

Mrs M Shinn, The Hollies Cottage, Chilton. Tel 376747

PARISH CHURCH: A series of addresses were given by the rector, the Rev Lawrence Pizzey, every Wednesday in Lent. These were followed by the evening service of compline.

On Maundy Thursday the children of the Friday Club met in church for a workshop based on Easter activities. These included making an Easter garden, puppets, cards, chicks, cake icing, painting pictures and banners, place mats and badges. Many of these things were used to decorate the church on Easter Sunday.

On Good Friday the three-hour service, based on the seven last words of Jesus from the cross, was led by the rector, the Rev Lawrence Pizzey, and Maureen Shinn, lay reader. In the evening a choir of men's voices from the surrounding villages and our own choir sang compline to plainsong.

Easter Sunday was celebrated by well attended services. The family service was led by the newly formed worship group who just sing informally, but who desperately need more musicians to accompany Mark Gant and his guitar.

The next praise evening service will be on Sunday, April 24 at 6.30 pm. This is an informal service with music and songs led by Karl Hunnibell and friends, based on the shorter version of ASB evening prayer with slots for music from Karl. The first service was very well receivd and anyone is very welcome to attend.

SCHOOL PLAY: The end of term was marked by the whole primary school taking part in a version of Wind in the Willows.

All the staff were involved with the production but the main direction was by Mrs Faith Marsden (music) and Mrs Kate Hart, main characters.

The younger children performed dances. Parents provided the costumes and the scenery was made and painted by Mr Povall and Mr and Mrs Noad and the children, with a large backdrop being loaned by Mr Neil Cheese.

The evening performance included refreshments in the interval when the Governors' cup for achievement was presented by Mr D Floyd, chairman of parish council, to Cathy Page, year three. The school's 100 club draw was made at the same time.

All the children of the school, with teachers, parents and friends, attended an Easter service in St Lawrence's Church, on Thursday, March 18, to mark the end of term. The story from Palm Sunday through to Easter was told in word and song by the children and a talk was given by the Rev Lawrence Pizzey.

A PRIMARY school at Great Waldingfield, which won a design award when it was built in 1970 but turned out to be an architectural nightmare, was made education-friendly — at a cost of £24,000. Originally hailed as an open-plan showpiece, the school had suffered a catalogue of disasters, including rain seeping beneath the hall floor off a flat roof, alcove partitions which proved impractical for teaching, and a pottery kiln which released fumes into the school.

WE would like to thank Sudbury people for their kind support of the Oxfam market stall on September 3.

The amount raised for Rwanda was £107. Many thanks indeed.

BRIAN SKINNER,
(Membership secretary,
Sudbury Campaigning Group),
Garrison Cottage,
Garrison Lane,
Great Waldingfield.

Beware the wrong signs

THREE WEEKS ago I was walking home after getting off the bus when a car pulled up and the driver asked me the way to Sudbury, as he had got lost.

He told me he had followed the signs at the crossroads from which I had just crossed over.

When I looked over I saw the sign was pointed the wrong way and pointed him the right way. When I got home my father-in-law said they had been like that all week.

The same day in the afternoon my husband was out walking with the dogs when a car pulled up and asked the direction to Long Melford.

He told my husband he had followed the sign at the crossroad and ended up at Bildeston.

I rang the police to let them know the sign post was round the wrong way they said they would do something to get it put right.

That was four weeks ago. Now for a warning to all drivers who come through Great Waldingfield.

When you come to the crossroads make sure you are going the right way!

MRS L WELSH,
11 Coronation Rise,
Great Waldingfield.

Mike comes a cropper

JULY 1994

A WILD promise made by Mike Stewart at his local, The White Horse at Great Waldingfield, led to a rude awakening on Saturday evening.

In casual conversation, he said that he would have his long hair cut off if Chelsea beat Luton in the cup semifinal.

But the remark was heard by both the landlord, Ian Fleming, and his barmaid, Samantha Gibbons — and when Chelsea did beat Luton it was decided that Mike would have to keep his promise.

Samantha, who trained as a hairdresser, had the clippers ready when he arrived and soon gave Mike a crewcut to remember!

The landlord was so impressed with Mike's pluck in keeping his promise, that he also made a promise; if Chelsea go on to win the cup, he will have ALL his hair cut off, provided customers sponsor the event for a local charity.

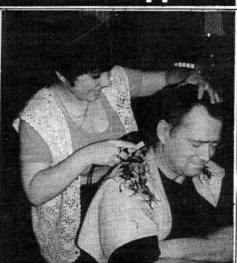

● Cut final: Mike Stewart pays the ultimate penalty as barmaid Samantha Gibbons lops off his locks.

STEWART, Harry. Formerly of Great Waldingfield, passed peacefully away on July 15, 1994, at Walnuttree Hospital. Funeral at Colchester Crematorium on Monday, July 25, at 12 noon. Family flowers or donations for Hazell Court may be sent to W A Deacon Funeral Services, Lavenham.

Bike stolen

A BLACK ten-speed mountain bike was stolen from a garden in Badleys Close, Great Waldingfield, over the weekend.

A BICYCLE valued at £210 was stolen on Sunday from the garden of a house at Great Waldingfield. The pink Raleigh Manta went missing from Laurel Cottage between 12.30pm and 9.30pm.

A PURPLE Raleigh mountain bike, worth £180, was stolen from a garden in Alexander Drive, Great Waldingfield, last week.

UPSHER GREEN, GREAT WALDINGFIELD £80,000

A two bedroom
period semi-detached
thatched cottage, with
rural location, garage
and far reaching
views.

The Theobalds

MY GREAT, great grandmother emigrated to Queensland, Australia, in 1875. I am researching my family tree.

Emma (possibly Harriet Emma) Theobald grew up in Great Waldingfield with her brothers and sister – Robert, Ann, Charles, Joshua and George – in the 1830s and 1840s.

Her parents were James Theobald and Clarissa (Clara). When Emma married John Medley in London in 1858 they went to live in Chelmsford.

I would like to contact anyone who may be related to this family or with someone who may know of them in the area around Great Waldingfield, Edwardstone, Sudbury and Groton.

Your help would be greatly appreciated if you would publish these details in your newspaper in the hope that a contact might be made with my Suffolk relatives.

MRS BEVERLEY WALL,
7 Hobart Avenue,
Campbelltown,
NSW 2560,
Australia.

MEMORIES of war were rekindled when American air force veterans returned to the area to mark the 50th anniversary of their first arrival in 1944.

The veterans were members of the US Army Air Force 486th Bombardment Group, who were based at Sudbury airfield between Great Waldingfield and Acton in 1944 and 1945, and flew almost 200 missions from the airfield.

They arrived on Wednesday and were met by Sudbury mayor Mike Gould at the Mill Hotel where they stayed.

On Thursday they attended a memorial service at Sudbury's St Gregory's Church where the Rev Derrick Stiff welcomed them.

The lessons were read by the Rev Laurence Pizzey, rector of Great Waldingfield.

After a service in St Lawrence's Church, Great Waldingfield, a memorial plaque was unveiled and afterwards villagers held a reception for the visitors who later toured the old airfield.

Sitting in an authentic Second World War jeep at the reception for the Americans at Great Waldingfield are Jean Misselbrook, vice-chairman of Great Waldingfield Parish Council, bomb group association commander Bob Cross, Charlie MacGill, past association commander, and 486th association newsletter editor Bob Bee.

Paul Owen & Jacqueline Byham

THE wedding took place at Sudbury Register Office of Jacqueline Maria Byham, daughter of Mr and Mrs J Day, of Great Cornard and Paul Daniel Owen, son of Mr J Owen, and Mrs J Stannard, of Great Waldingfield.

FORMER Great Waldingfield villager May Rigby, who left estate valued at £154,891 when she died on July 21, bequeathed £200 to the repair fund for the village's St Lawrence Church.

May, latterly of Chertsey, Surrey, and formerly of Old Oak Cottage, Great Waldingfield, left £800 effects and half the residue to personal legatees.

The other half will be shared by the Save the Children Fund, Shaftesbury Society, Royal National Institute for the Blind, Arthritis and Rheumatism Coun-

A taste of the past on 'Victorian' day

By Rachel Jenkins
East Anglian Daily Times

A LOCAL rector made sure Victorian values were being upheld when he ran his keen eye over the performances of school children.

Governors' chairman at Great Waldingfield Primary School the Rev Lawrence Pizzey took on the role of school inspector when the establishment put the clock back 100 years.

The Victorian day was the climax of a year's study based on 1891 census records, which the school has undertaken as part of its national curriculum work.

Visits have been paid to investigate the history of neighbouring Little Waldingfield church, plus the Museum of Rural Life at Stowmarket.

The diligent rector tested costumed pupils on their skills at counting, knowledge of the British Isles and its Empire, and also took particular note of handwriting and awareness of the contents of the Bible.

Youngsters at the 76-pupil school, where former county history advisor Jill Penrose is now head, also had their health cared for as they were put through a formal, fitness drill.

Work of regular staff was augmented by four work experience students from Sudbury Upper School, taking on the role of pupil-teachers, who represented a significant proportion of any school's teaching staff in Victorian days.

Catering staff put on a lunch which included vegetable broth, the meal being rounded off with mint humbugs.

A slide show of 19th pictures and a talk on Victorian toys was followed in the afternoon by country and Maypole dancing.

The Council met on Tuesday 28 June at the Village Hall. The first item on the agenda was the introduction of the new Clerk, Mr Mike Cheese and the new councillor Mr Gerry Ball.

The success of the USAAF Reunion was noted and letters of thanks were still coming in from America.

BY ALAN COCKSEDGE

End of design nightmare

JULY 1994

A SCHOOL which won a design award, but turned out to be an architectural nightmare has been made education-friendly at a cost of £24,000.

Hailed as an open-plan showpiece when built in 1970, the premises featured a catalogue of disasters including a flat roof main hall which has had two major floor refits; alcoves in classrooms which proved impractical for teaching; and a pottery kiln which released fumes into the school.

Despite these setbacks, however, governors and staff at Great Waldingfield Primary School have been swift to point out the dedication of teachers and pupils has always ensured high educational standards.

Yesterday, a party was held to mark the revamp of the 64-pupil school, with governors' chairman the Rev Lawrence Pizzey saying the changes had been made to bring the school into line with modern ways of teaching. Of the investment, about £5,000 has come from a

Suffolk County Council insurance claim for treatment to the main hall floor following dampness from water running off the flat roof and into an adjourning open courtyard.

Head teacher Jill Penrose said the courtyard had now been roofed and was providing an important additional resource centre. Previously rain seeped beneath the hall floor, which had already been replaced, about ten years ago.

The kiln, orginally installed on an inside wall, was also now in the courtyard area. It gave off chemicals which meant it could only be fired at weekends when children were not present.

The biggest change, however, was the demolition of alcove petitions in teaching areas, allowing staff to have a better overview of what was happening around them.

▌New beginning: head teacher Jill Penrose overlooking the improved courtyard area at Great Waldingfield Primary School

FREE PRESS, Thursday, October 13, 1994

58

St Flashback: Tony Guercia (front row, fourth from left) and colleagues outside the Waldingfield White Horse after a soft ball game around 1945.

Tony flies back to his favourite corner seat

AS an aircraft belly gunner in the Second World War Tony Guercia was in the hot seat as he flew 25 bombing missions out of the United States Army Air Force base at Sudbury.

Once missions were over he could not wait to get back to his favourite corner seat in the White Horse at Great Waldingfield.

When he was recently back in Suffolk for the 50th anniversary of the 486th Bombardment Group's arrival in England, the ex-serviceman and his wife Rose occupied the same corner seat once again for a photo shot.

During 1944-45 he had posed for an earlier picture outside the pub following a softball game. Reproduced here, it shows the young gunner, then in his early 20, fourth from left in the front row, surrounded by other servicemen and regulars at the pub.

Mr Guercia, who lives in New York with his wife, has been on three re-union trips to Sudbury in recent years, during which

TO WALDINGIELD

● A return visit to Waldingfield White Horse for Tony Guercia and his wife Rose.

Homes plan

TEAMCO Construction have applied to Babergh Council to build three pairs of semi-detached houses and a terrace of three on land at Bantocks Road, Great Waldingfield.

VINTAGE machinery enthusiasts had a chance to put their vehicles into action at the weekend when Monks Eleigh Bygones Collectors Club held their annual road run and working day.

Sixteen old tractors, a vintage car and a two-wheeled garden tractor trundled their way from Edwardstone to Monks Eleigh, finishing at Great Waldingfield on Saturday.

In the evening eight members took part in a night ploughing match, the first one held by the club, using moonlight only as a guide.

"We wanted to do something different," said club chairman and founder Paul Goodchild.

"The oldest tractor dated from 1936 and they ploughed for about an hour.

"It was just for fun and we finished up with a disco in the barn at Northfields Farm," he added.

Sunday was the working day with furrow drawing events and trophies were awarded for drag and mounted ploughing.

Trophies were also presented to Russell Weavers of West Mersea for the best stationary engine and Basil Martin of Great Waldingfield for the best tractor.

"We had a good turnout with plenty of exhibits and quite a few members of the public came to watch," said Mr Goodchild.

SEPTEMBER 1994

Brian Game on his Nuffield Universal Three.

● **YOUNGSTERS** from Great Waldingfield Primary School put themselves in the festive mood with the first public performance of their Christmas show.

Their production was divided into two halves — a Christmas entertainment followed by a traditional nativity play.

The show involved all 68 pupils and proceeds will go towards West Suffolk Hospital's Rainbow Appeal.

, December 22, 1994

Top award for Guide

● *Joanne Haynes after receiving her Baden-Powell Trefoil Award.*

A SUFFOLK girl has been presented with the Baden-Powell Trefoil Award, the highest badge that can be awarded to a Guide.

Joanne Haynes, 14, of Great Waldingfield, had to complete a variety of badges including first aid and international and service badges to earn the award.

A member of the Sudbury Storms swimming club, she completed her service badge by working with the local Avocet Club for handicapped swimmers.

A pupil at Sudbury Upper School, Joanne was until recently a member of the Acton and Waldingfield Guide Company, but has now joined the 1st Chadbrook Rangers.

In addition to gaining her Baden-Powell Trefoil Award, she has also been selected by the county for an international camp and homestay in Sweden next summer — the youngest of 20 girls selected for the trip out of a total of 45 hopefuls.

Joanne was presented with her award by Rose Finch, the recently retired district commissioner for the Chadbrook District, who in turn received a watch in recognition of her efforts over the years.

£30,000 plan for village hall

PLANNING approval has been given for a £30,000 extension to be built on to Great Waldingfield village hall.

Babergh councillors gave the go-ahead for two committee rooms and two storage areas to be provided to replace an old single-storey annexe.

One of the committee rooms will double up as a First Aid area and the store rooms will be used for the kitchen and the village playgroup.

Parish council clerk Mike Cheese, who said part of the cost would be met by grants, heralded the development as important for villagers.

June 8, 1995

TREE WARDEN NEWS

It is now one year since I became Tree Warden for the parish of Great Waldingfield. Just over half the parishes in Babergh District now have a Tree Warden since the scheme began last autumn.

The scheme is a practical response to the large scale loss of trees, woodlands and hedgerows in the landscape since 1945. This has been due mainly to agricultural change, but also drought, storms and development. There is a real need to take positive action now to improve the environment for us and our children.

I am a volunteer with no special powers beyond enthusiasm and some training. I hold copies of Tree Preservation Orders for the parish and other maps. I have done some informal surveys of local hedges and trees. With the help of pupils, I planted some hedge at Great Waldingfield School.

We have some fine hedges but almost no woodland in Great Waldingfield. I can't achieve much on my own so if anyone would like to help with surveys, with suggestions or information, or with actual planting when the time comes, please get in touch. I am at 10 White Hall Close, Great Waldingfield.

David Taylor

The County Council had agreed to provide a kissing gate or stile at a currently inaccessible point on one of the footpaths.

Book week organiser Christine Stainer reads to (left to right) Sam Marsden (eight), Jason Roberts (four), Emily Taylor (six) and Elizabeth Armstrong.

● GREAT Waldingfield teenager Jo Haynes is well on her way to raising enough money to pay for a forthcoming Girl Guide trip to Sweden after a marathon effort on Saturday.

Jo (14), a member of the 1st Chadbrook Rangers, is one of ten girls from the UK to be selected for the international camp and home stay in July and represents Suffolk and Anglia.

Christopher Awdry, son of the Rev W Awdry, author of the much loved Thomas the Tank Engine stories,

Jeffrey Francom, Bantocks Road, Great Waldingfield. Two charges of failing to pay fines of £30 each for breaching parking regulations in Girling Street, Sudbury. Fine £35, costs £60 on each.

FARMING brothers David and Colin Steed took a massive financial gamble to block a new hospital on People's Park, Sudbury. David and Colin Steed went to the High Court to try to prove the 16-acre site is a village green.

Dinner lady dishes up her last orders

● **Pizza pleaser:** Mary Jackson who retires as head cook at Uplands Middle School

BY the time she retires after 28 years in the school meals service, Mary Jackson will have prepared an estimated 250,000 helpings.

But even after she leaves the kitchens of Uplands Middle School, Sudbury, the cooking will continue, thanks to public demand for her home-made jam.

Mrs Jackson, who lives at Great Waldingfield, started in the school meals service in 1967 as a kitchen assistant at Wells Hall primary school in Great Cornard where she remained until 1976 before becoming cook-in-charge at Uplands.

Her working day begins at 8 am. By 10 am the pastries and puddings have been made and the vegetarian meals prepared. From 10 am she usually starts on the pizzas, then it's burgers and sausages and by 11.30 they are ready to put the meals together for lunch at 12.05.

"The food has changed an awful lot," she said. "At Wells Hall the meat came in from the butcher and we had to cut it up ourselves. These days it comes to us frozen.

"Also when I first started there was no choice but now there's a lot more choice for the children."

Apart from jam-making, her retirement will be devoted to her hobbies such as indoor bowls, Women's Institute, gardening and her grandchildren.

In court

October 5

Jackie Ann Parker-Knights (23), Folly Road, Great Waldingfield. Failed to comply with the requirements of a community service order by failing to report for work as instructed.

Convicted, original order to continue with additional 60 hours of community service.

December 22

Marella Kalyan Parker (23), of Folly Road, Great Waldingfield. Drove on the A134 Sudbury bypass, having drunk excess alcohol — 64 microgrammes of alcohol per 100 millitres of breath, when the legal limit is 35 microgrammes. Banned from driving for 12 months, fined £100 with £50 prosecution costs, licence endorsed.

Drugs charge

TWO men charged with possessing and intending to supply an estimated £7,000 of drugs have been remanded in custody.

John Evenden (30), of Nelson Road, Sudbury, and Timothy Young (37), of Bantocks Road, Great Waldingfield, were allegedly caught with cocaine, cannabis and amphetamines on February 1. Young is also charged with possessing an Ecstasy tablet.

The pair appeared before Sudbury magistrates on Tuesday and were remanded in custody for a week.

Overdone

FIREFIGHTERS were called to put out a grill pan fire at a house in Kenyon Drive, Great Waldingfield, on Sunday at 12.30pm.

THANK YOU

I have so many people to thank ....

When I received the news at the beginning of this year that I had further cancer you can imagine how devastated I felt.

However suddenly I was engulfed with love, care and concern from so many. There were the offers of transport, ironing taken away, meals provided, so many cards and messages of love and care and of course the special support of family and close friends.

To me especially the knowledge that so many people were praying for me gave me the strength I needed.

Now after treatment, I'm on the way back! You won't see me in School much but hopefully you'll see me busy with the church work I enjoy, and being able to spend more time talking and listening with people and enjoying my garden and home (after about 33 years of work and dashing in and out!). You might even see me on my bike!

I look forward to making a super scrapbook of all your messages and to still having lots of visitors.

When it comes down to it we must pride ourselves on being a caring, loving community here in Gt Waldingfield.

Maureen Shinn

The Parish Church
St. Lawrence

No Village Scrapbook could be complete without a reference to its Church, around which grew up its little community :-The Village : From birth to death the Church cared for body and soul. It was a foundation of a Welfare State. Food, coals, clothing and a number of charities etc. were handed out to the less fortunate. The sick were visited, and cared for. The Church was their final resting place, both rich and poor. The fine Church of St. Lawrence was re-built in the 15th Century, and without doubt on the site of an older church, of which the present font seems to remind one - Past repairs, and restorations have ensured this noble edifice for this generation, and it is hoped many more to come In 1827 owing to the ravages of time, more restoration was accomplished.

Diamond wedding is at Christmas

ON Christmas Day Mr. and Mrs. Alfred Bowers, of "Cranford," Great Waldingfield, celebrate their diamond wedding. They are the oldest married couple living in the village.

Mr. Bowers is 85 and his wife 84, and they were married at the Parish Church of Great Livermere on December 25th, 1893, by the then rector (Rev. Herbert James). Mr. Bowers has spent all his life in the village. For 47 years he was employed by the late Mr. Stephen Carlton and his son, of Babergh Farm. Mrs. Bowers, who before her marriage was Miss P. Stutters, was born at Stanstead, has lived all her married life at Great Waldingfield.

She was a member of the Women's Land Army during 1914-1918 and an active member of the W.V.S. during the last war. She is a foundation committee member of the Women's Institute, her valued help and keen interest in which has always been a matter of great appreciation to her fellow members.

SIX CHILDREN

Mr. and Mrs. Bowers had a family of six children, three of whom are living, and will spend Christmas Day with their parents. They have one granddaughter who is unable to be with them that day. Gifts and congratulations have been received from a brother of Mrs. Bowers in Australia, and other relatives in Canada.

In 1869 the Rector, the Rev: Bailey and his family rebuilt and redecorated the Chancel, and gave the two beautiful stained windows at a cost of £1100. The people were fortunate in having a rector who was rich and who loved his Church and Parishioners. He was a great traveller, and with his sister visited the Holy Land and the Near East. In the Chancel one sees the Cross of oriental alabaster, which the rector (Rev: Bailey) brought from a ruined temple in Egypt, and granite slabs from Mount Sinai. It might be added here, he also brought two cedar trees from Lebanon, and three cypress trees from the convent of Mt Sinai and planted them in the Rectory Gardens.

In 1887 there were further repairs and replacements which cost £1662 - thanks to the efforts of the Braithwaite family In 1891 the brass lectern was placed in the church in memory of a late Rector (Rev: F. J. Braithwaite) by his wife. It is very gratifying to know these facts were all taken from an old book of Church records compiled by former Rectors during their terms of office

Canons

Retirement

PRESENTATION TO RECTOR AT GT. WALDINGFIELD
Retirement of Canon Alexander

A PRESENTATION to the Rector, Canon T. C. Alexander, who is retiring after over 29 years' service in the parish, was made at Great Waldingfield Church on Sunday after the harvest thanksgiving service. 1955

In the vestry at the close of the service Mr. G. H. Bird, as choirmaster, expressed the sincere regrets of the members of the choir at the rector's departure, and, on behalf of them all, wished him a long and happy retirement.

After the service the congregation gathered outside the church door, where the people's warden, Mr. R. G. Gibbs, accompanied by Col. Darley, rector's warden, made the presentation to the rector. In a brief address he said the occasion was a sad one for the parishioners; it was the last time the rector would officiate in this capacity in Great Waldingfield in this office he had held for over 29 years.

He asked the rector's acceptance of the gift of a cheque to help towards the installation of a figure of St. Lawrence to be erected by the west door of the church.

Illuminated album

He also presented an illuminated album containing the names of over 130 families and individuals who had subscribed to the gift. It was, Mr. Gibbs concluded, "a very small expression of gratitude for all the rector had done for the people, and the parish generally, and a token of good wishes for his health and happiness in retirement."

Expressing his thanks, Canon Alexander said that it had always been his greatest wish that a stone figure of St. Lawrence should be in the possession of the church, and that he was delighted to make his parting gift to the parish and the church.

The rector then proceeded to the lych gate, where he bade farewell to the congregation individually.

THE STATUE of St. Lawrence, which was dedicated by the Bishop on Sunday as a memento of Canon T. C. Alexander's long rectorship of Great Waldingfield. The statue stands in one of the two vacant niches above the west doorway of the church.

Memento of Canon's service
WALDINGFIELD DEDICATION

SUBSCRIBED for by parishioners as a memento of Canon T. C. Alexander's long rectorship of Great Waldingfield, a statue to St. Lawrence has been put up in one of two vacant niches above the west doorway of the church. It was dedicated at an afternoon service of evensong on Sunday by the Bishop of St. Edmundsbury and Ipswich.

Canon Alexander, who has now been in retirement for about a year, came over personally to conduct the service. Parishioners had some time ago expressed a wish to make a presentation to him and it was his suggestion that something material and permanent should be given to his old church instead.

To this the Bishop referred in the address he gave to a numerous congregation at the church. He said it was characteristic of Canon Alexander that he should wish to add further to the parish's indebtedness to him for many unselfish services in the past. It was his old and beloved church that he wished to benefit.

Speaking from a text in the Acts of the Apostles, the Bishop outlined to some extent the history of St. Lawrence, patron saint of the church, who was patron saint also of not a few churches in East Anglia. In the third century A.D., St. Lawrence had been martyred for failing to disclose the whereabouts of church "treasure" to certain evil men who banished Christianity from Rome itself at one time.

When even St. Lawrence's superior in the church had been martyred, St. Lawrence was still allowed to live on for a time, but repeated tortures would—and could—elicit no more from him than the truth; that the "treasure" had been expended by church dignitaries in relieving the sufferings of the poor.

Faithful

Even today there might be such men prepared to be faithful unto death, but Christians were asked little nowadays beyond "faith unto life"; in short, to be more tolerant of the religious views of their fellows and to seek that all should be brothers and good companions under one God.

The Bishop expressed much of his own and of Waldingfield parishioners' gratitude for the ever faithful service of Canon Alexander in the past—and his interest for generations ahead in the church, exemplified by his having desired that the testimonial to him should be an enhancement of the beauty of the ancient fabric. This the statue which, beyond many of its kind, had expression and beauty would certainly do.

The Bishop mentioned that there was now the prospect of a new incumbent of the church to take office before long.

A robed choir was present. Lieutenant - Colonel R. Darley read the lesson, and Psalm 122 and three hymns were sung, including the special hymn dedicated to St. Lawrence.

JOHN HOPKINS
of
GREAT WALDINGFIELD

a

thumb-nail sketch

T.H. Wells.

Bishop institutes new rector at Gt. Waldingfield

PROF. C. F. D. Moule and the Rev. F. S. Skelton, of Clare College, Cambridge, presented the Rev. Francis Kenyon to the living of Great Waldingfield when he was instituted and inducted on Thursday evening.

Induction
Thursday
April 25th 57

There was a large congregation at the church of St. Lawrence for the service. The institution was conducted by the Bishop of St. Edmundsbury and Ipswich (Dr. A. H. Morris) and the induction was performed by the Rural Dean (Canon H. W. S. Cotton, of Lavenham).

The Bishop said it was very pleasing to see the representatives from Cambridge presenting the incumbent on behalf of the patrons. That kind of interest was very gratifying but unfortunately not always observed these days.

Not enough

He said one of the rather unfortunate things of modern church life was that so many parishes had to be united with others. Such a process was, however, inevitable for the livings of single parishes was often not enough to provide a living for a clergyman.

It was important that if they were not merely to have men on the verge of retirement in the rural parishes there should be enough work for them to do.

The Bishop said it was a fact that the village in which the clergyman lived always laid claim to him as "their parson." He thought this was a good thing for it showed the real love of people for their own parson.

The Bishop paid tribute to the long ministry of Canon T. C. Alexander and hoped the parishioners would give the same support to Mr. Kenyon.

Reception

The new incumbent was escorted during the service by the churchwardens, Lt.-Col. R. Darley and Mr. R. Jarvis. The organist was Mr. F. Sykes, Lavenham. Other clergy present were the Rev. G. F. Tricker (Alpheton) and the Rev. A. J. McKinney.

After the service the new rector met parishioners at a reception in the village school.

Mr. Kenyon, who is married with one son, was ordained in 1934. He was formerly vicar of Saltfleetby, Lincs., and before that had given service at St. John's, Buckhurst Hill, Essex, St. Luke's, Bromley Common, Monk Hopton with Upton Crescent and New Bolingbroke, Lincs.

Churchyard

The Consecration of the extension to the Churchyard took place on Sunday Oct: 27th 1957. and the ceremony was performed by the Bishop of Dunwich (The Very Rev: T. Cashmore. The procession, headed by the Churchwardens, Col: Darley & Mr R. Jarvis followed by the Bishop, the Rector, the Rev: F.K. Kenyon & the Choir led the congregation from the church round the new burial ground. The Deed of Consecration was signed & handed to the Rector The procession returned to the church when the Bishop preached an inspiring sermon to a large congregation.

THE CHURCH OF ST LAWRENCE, GREAT WALDINGFIELD

By The Rev Charles Albert Stokes, M.A.

Notes from: Suffolk Institute of Archaeology and Natural History (Est. 1848)
Ancient Arts & Monuments of The County of Suffolk - Vol IX.1897

This Church, in the Archdeanery of Sudbury and Diocese of Ely, is dedicated to
St Lawrence. The tower, nave and aisles were probably rebuilt by John Appleton
at the end of the 14th Century... when the above-named portions of the Church
were re-built, the old chancel was left standing; but the chancel was rebuilt,
as will be described further on, by the Rev W P Baily, Rector, and his family,
in the year 1865-1869.

By the beginning of the present century the Church had fallen into considerable
disrepair: it was partially repaired at a cost of £500, raised by rate, in the
years 1827 - 29. (Rev F Cresswell, Rector). The north Chapel was re-seated,
re-floored and re-roofed in 1875, by John Braithwaite, Esq. of Nottingham, at a
cost of £200.

In the years 1876-77, the Church was thoroughly repaired under the direction of
the Rev Francis Braithwaite, Rector, and a committee, at a cost of £1663,
raised by subscriptions. Mr Hakewill of London was the Architect. The works
done consisted of the following:- the roofs of the Nave, Aisles and Tower were
taken off, and after being made thoroughly sound, were replaced and recovered
with lead. The roofs are of English oak. The Nave, Aisles and Tower were re-
roofed and re-seated. The walls and floors of the Tower were made sound. The
West Arch was reopened, clerestory windows re-glazed, bells re-hung, and one
re-cast. These works were executed before the re-opening of the Church.
A.D.1876. In 1877 the tracery of the Aisle windows was made good and windows
glazed. The South and West doors were repaired and a new North door, an exact
copy of the old one, was hung. South porch was re-roofed and paved and glazed,
and stone work repaired.

These details of the restoration of the Church will serve to show that the
original character of the parts dealt with was preserved. Nothing has been
said so far as to the details of the re-building of the Chancel in 1966 and the
following years. The Architect was Mr Butterfield: the cost, including the
stained glass in the windows was about £1000, undertaken by the Rector, The Rev
W P Baily and his family. The walls were new faced inside and out; new East
and South window frames, new tiles to floor, and oak sittings, new roof. There
were traces left of an Early English east end in a broken 'roll' under the
window. The present East window is of dimensions of another old window found
bricked up in the wall. There was a "Priest's Door" on the South side of the
Chancel. The "Priest's Door" was removed to the School, but the screen is not
in existence now, though it appears to have been used as a vestry screen after
the re-building of the Chancel. The old oak string A.D.1100 was replaced in
the Chancel. The South window before the re-building was a narrow, square-
headed window made up of odds and ends from the old Church. The reredos was
given to the Church by the Misses Emily and Louisa Baily; the marbles, of which
it is formed, having been collected by them from the ruins of temples in Rome
and elsewhere. They were made into mosaics in Rome by Saleri and placed in
their present position under the direction of Mr Butterfield. The Oriental
alabaster forming the cross in the reredos came from a small red granite temple
near the Sphinx, the granite in the slabs over the credence, from Mount Sinai;
the syenite from a fragment of the statue of Rameses II, Thebes. Over the
credence there is the text: "The Lord alone shall be exalted in that day and
the idols He shall utterly abolish".

/Continued over ....

Page 2

The rails in the Chancel sittings and under the Chancel Arch were from the Chancel of St. Micahel's Church, Cornhill, London, a Church of Sir Christopher Wren; they are supposed to have been by Grinling Gibbons. Sir Giles Scott ordered them to be removed as out of character with his improvements in St. Michael's and they were bought by the Rector. The old Altar rails which used to form three sides, are now in the Rectory. The Pulpit was placed in the Church at the time of the Chancel restoration. It is of oak and walnut. There was a corresponding lectern, but that is now in Little Waldingfield Church. The Font is old (with the exception of the cover) but there is no record of its history. The ends of the nave benches are also old, and are worth attention, as also the string-course in the Clerestory with its ornaments. The Vestry was re-built in 1887 at the cost of the Rev F J Braithwaite. Mr Fawcett. Architect. Cost £340. There was a Sacristy but this was pulled down many years ago.

On the South wall (exterior) there is an inscription in black letters: over the West door (exterior) there were carvings relative to the martyrdom of St. Lawrence ..... There appears to be no emblems of the martyr within or without the Church. [NOTE: during the 1950's Canon Alexander gave a statue of St. Lawrence for the niche in outside wall above North door. CSD]

The brass Lectern was given by Mrs Braithwaite in memory of her husband, the Rev F J Brathwaite. Rector. It is an exact copy of one placed in Lt Gidding Church by Nicholas Ferrar. There is an original Lectern, very similar, in Southwell Minster.

Windows

Chancel: 1869 E.window and S.window by Gibbs, London

Church: 1877 W.window - Tracery copied from old window glass - Gibbs.
                   S.Aisle, centre - by Westlake
                   SE.window - old glass re-set
             1886 NW.window - by Lavers & Co
                   N window - by Lavers & Co.

The Organ: is the gift of Mrs Braithwaite.

The five bells as existing previous to 1800 were in that year re-cast into six and re-hung. In 1876 one was re-cast again .... Weight of Tenor, 13 cwt.

The clock was made in 1786 - It may be interesting to note that during the present century a sum of at least £4,500 has been spent .....(on)......the Church ......

The Registers of the Church date from A.D.1339 and are continued to the present day .... The advowson belongs to the Master and Fellows of Clare College, Cambridge and came into their hands in 1727. The Patron before this date was Wm Powle..... The Manor of Waldingfield Hall was granted to Geoffrey Carbonel in the 13th Century. Sir Robert Crane was Lord of the Manor in 1639.

****

GREAT WALDINGFIELD

ST LAWRENCE'S CHURCH — Sunday, December 9, is often known as Bible Sunday. This fact was remembered in the Family Service in church that morning. The newly-formed church Friday groups for children took an active part in the service. The Pathfinders dramatised a short play explaining how the Bible is translated into many versions and languages to suit all ages and nationalities. The youngest children, the Scramblers, dramatised a short poem, while all the children, Pathfinders, Explorers, Climbers and Scramblers, sang three songs. Clare Lindsay and Michael Welsh read the lessons

The magic of Christmas

LITTLE Stacey Parker from Great Waldingfield Primary School captures the magic of many of the region's nativity plays in this picture by Free Press photographer Trevor Forge.

In next week's Free Press we will be featuring school and playgroup festive events from across the region in a four page special called 'The Magic of Christmas.

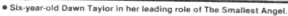

● Six-year-old Dawn Taylor in her leading role of The Smallest Angel.

SENIOR CITIZENS' PARTY — In the afternoon of Sunday, December 9, all the senior citizens of the village were invited to tea in the village hall. Even though the weather was poor about 30 people turned up. They were entertained by St Lawrence's Church members with a festive tea, including trifles, crackers and Christmas cake. All the guests received a small gift. Mr Ted Haxell entertained on his organ and led a sing-song. In the evening the guests were joined by other villagers for a service of carols and readings led by the rector, the Rev Lawrence Pizzey. The evening finished with more refreshments and chat at the end of a very enjoyable get-together.

Sundays in the month.....

1st	8a.m.	Holy Communion
	11.15a.m.	Matins
2nd	11.15a.m.	Family Service ...... Children especially welcome
3rd	9.30a.m.	Holy Communion
4th	11.15a.m.	Holy Communion
5th	VARIABLE, see below	

If you would care for further information, please contact either......

Mr. K. Phillips   Tel: 311258 or

Mr. C. Francis   Tel: 70734

)R AND CONGREGATION

OF

:H OF ST. LAWRENCE,

.T WALDINGFIELD

u to join with them in Worship.

Details of services overleaf.

ord with gladness   Ps.100 v.2

CONCERT — This Saturday at 4pm in St Lawrence's Church, another of the occasional village concerts will be held. These concerts provide local people with a platform to show their various, often hidden, talents. This year the theme is "Name Droppers". Entry is free, but there will be a chance to donate to the roof repair fund on leaving the church.

The programme includes community singing when the audience can show their talents. Also included will be handball ringers, trumpet solos. The choir of Gt Waldingfield Village School, various items of verse and prose, a "dramatic work of art", organ recital and the augmented church choir. There will be light refreshments after the concert.

Everybody is welcome to attend and will receive a warm welcome.

1991

£1,000 bequest

WINIFRED Cagienard, of Bantocks Road, Great Waldingfield, who died in June, left £1,000 to the village's Church of St Lawrence. Her estate is valued at between £70,000 and £100,000.

DEATHS

CAGIENARD - On June 13th. Peacefully at Melford Court Nursing Home. Winifred Eileen, aged 79 years, widow of Alan of Gt. Waldingfield & formally of Ilford, Essex. Service at Gt. Waldingfield Parish Church on Friday 21st June at 1pm followed by cremation at West Suffolk Crematorium, Bury St. Edmunds at 2.15pm. All Winifred's friends are invited to both services. Flowers to Brown Fenn & Parker of Sudbury by 12 noon or donations to British Diabetic Association.

Church bequest

A GREAT Waldingfield woman has left £100 to her local village church and Sunday school. Nora Cracknell, of Heath Estate, Great Waldingfield, who died on March 16 left a net estate of between £70,000 and £100,000.

Village celebrates its hymn writing rector of the past

GREAT Waldingfield parishioners and guests from Chilton held a special service at St Lawrence's Church on Sunday to celebrate the achievements of the village's 16th century Rector, hymn writer John Hopkins.

An ardent reformer, Hopkins began his ministry as Rector at Great Waldingfield in 1561 and of Chilton in 1563.

His Whole Book of Psalms, published in its full form in 1562, was the first universal Anglican hymnbook and enabled Protestants to sing their new-found faith in simple rhymes with catchy tunes.

Sunday's congregation sang several of Hopkins' hymns and the service partly followed the style of 16th century liturgy.

Hopkins's Psalter went into 600 editions over the centuries and the parish is to produce a booklet on him later in the year.

IOLANTHE

MIXED REVUES

Please will you come again? This was the question the cast were constantly asked after the concert performance of 'Iolanthe' in the village school on 16 March.

This was a really 'fun' evening, enjoyed by cast and audience alike. The singing, dancing and acting were of a high standard. From the opening chorus the audience were fully involved and entered with enthusiasm into the world of fairies, wards of court, lords and wicked chancellors. Laughter was never far away, and the songs and music had many feet tapping.

There are no stars in these shows, but I know the cast were very delighted to have Brian Rose accompany them once again on the piano. Several people have said they don't know how Andrew Walter remembered his words in the fast moving, non-stop nightmare song. I understand on good authority, he had a few sleepless nights trying to remember the words!

THE BRAITHWAITE TRUST

There are approximately 40 ten-rod allotments and a 3-acre field on land at Folly Road and Mill Field (opposite the Village Hall). The allotments in Folly Road have a supply of water. Rent for a ten-rod patch is £3.50 and for five-rod £2.00. The Mill Field rent is: ten-rod £2.00 and five-rod £1.00.

We do have some vacant allotments. Any villager interested in renting any allotment please contact Mr F Shinn, Hollies Cottage, Tel: 76747.

THE ANNUAL PAROCHIAL CHURCH MEETING was held in the School on 17 April. Those present re-elected Chris Francis and Ken Phillips as Churchwardens, with thanks for the way in which they have fulfilled their office. Anne Francis and Suzanne Thompson retired from the PCC.

Election of PCC — As members now stand for three years only two places were vacant. Mrs E Ellis and Mr Lawrence-Jones were elected to fill these vacancies. All present sidespeople were re-elected. The Churchwardens may add to the list when appropriate. General discussion then ensued including the giving of help to Kurdish refugees and whether the choir should walk through the church to the vestry.

PAROCHIAL MEETING: The annual parochial meeting of the Church of St Lawrence was held on Wednesday, April 17, in the village hall. The rector, the Rev Lawrence Pizzey, was in the chair.

Mr Ken Phillips gave the churchwardens' report for the past year. Some minor works had been completed on the church building and the rest should hopefully be completed in the near future. This meant they would be able to apply for the promised grant of £28,000 from English Heritage, towards the major roof repairs; other grants amounting to £5,200 had been promised. With £2,000 from the parish council and £10,000 already raised, a further £26,000 was still needed.

Problems had arisen with the proposed heating system planned for the church. However another company had been approached and an efficient heating system should be installed before next winter.

Vandalism had been a problem over the past year with a numbe of windows being broken. There had also been one break-in.

Mr Pizzey expressed his thanks to Mr Phillips and Mr Chris Francis for their dedicated work as churchwardens over the past year. Mr Ken Phillips and Mr Chris Francis were both nominated as churchwardens for the next year and were unanimously voted back to office.

Mr Pizzey reported that the last year had been very productive with the formation of a regular group for children on a Friday evening offering an opportunity for Christian education for all children.

The PCC had met regularly with a fair proportion of the time being spent on the building and all its aspects.

Mr David Rutherford was to be ordained on September 29 to the non-stipendiary ministry. Mrs Cheryl Daines is to continue training as a lay reader and Mrs Maureen Shinn is beginning training.

The treasurer, Mrs Cheryl Daines, gave her report and this was accepted by the meeting.

Reports were given on the deanery synod and children's work. Two vacancies had to be filled on the PCC as Mrs Anne Francis and Mrs Suzanne Thompson had stood down this year. A rota of two people to retire each year had been made and agreed to previously. In their places Mr David Lawrence Jones and Mrs Elizabeth Ellis were elected.

SOCIAL COMMITTEE: The church social committee met recently to discuss the forthcoming fundraising events.

Final arrangements were made for the plant sale to be held at Whitehall, by kind permission of Mr Michael Oliver, on Saturday, May 11 and Sunday, May 12. Last year this proved to be a great attraction and should be equally so this year with many plants being donated as well as other garden items. Most of the work has been done by Mr and Mrs C. Francis and Mr K. Phillips and they will be pleased to receive plants and garden equipment up to the day.

The main item on the agenda was to finalise plans for the main fundraising event for St Lawrence's. This is the annual cream tea weekend. Every year this is held at Brandeston Hall by kind permission of Mr and Mrs O. Kiddy, on the weekend of the late spring bank holiday, May 26/27.

It has grown from afternoon tea many years ago, to two full days supplying food, drink and other attractions. A large marquee seats people not wanting to sit out and enjoy the garden. Already two coaches are booked in for the Sunday afternoon but there is room for all and the committee hope that it will prove to be as popular as ever with people in the area, as well as visitors from all over the country.

Hundreds in church ride

SATURDAY'S fine weather brought cyclists all over the county out in their hundreds to take part in the Suffolk Historic Churches Trust tenth sponsored hike ride.

1991

SPONSORED CYCLE RIDE

The Sponsored Cycle Ride realised a total of £233.50 of which Great Waldingfield Church received half. We would like to thank the riders: Clare Lindsey, Cheryl & Trevor Davies, Mark Kiddy, Ron Coshell and Ross, and anyone else who helped in any way, signing in, sponsors etc.

Mrs. Marjorie Raine-Stoker

The Rector and Parochial Church Council are most grateful for the bequest of £1,765 to the Building Appeal fund from the estate of the late Mrs. Raine-Stoker.

RELATIVE VALUES

One of my favourite pastimes is 'church crawling' and I recently visited a somewhat remote, but beautifully kept little church in the heart of the Suffolk countryside. As I sat in contemplative mood I was joined by the local vicar. During conversation I casually enquired what measure of support he received from the villagers, and he related the following little story which I feel is well worth repetition. Arriving at the church one Sunday morning he found he had a congregation of one, an elderly farm worker who he knew quite well, so he walked along to the pew and said "Good Morning Rueben, you and me are the only people here this morning, what are we going to do about it?" "Vicar", said the old chap, "Oi'm only a 'umble farm warker in charge o' fifty cows, but if only one come in to be milked Oi 'ave tew giv' it the sarvis, an' Oi knows moi roights". "I see", said the Vicar, "I think I get the message". He then proceeded with the service, giving it full treatment, hymns, lessons, responses, creed and the full 20-minute sermon into the bargain. After the service the vicar overtook his congregation walking slowly down the churchyard path, "Well, Rueben", he said, "how did you enjoy the service and my sermon in particular"? "Vicar", said Rueben, "as Oi towd yew 'afore, Oi'm only a 'umble farm warker, ivery day Oi git feed riddy fer fifty cows, but if only one come in, Oi aren't fule enuff tew giv' it the lot".

C W S Hurr

Very observant readers of this magazine will have noticed changes in the personnel section of the St Lawrence's Church notices this month. Firstly, David Rutherford is now entitled, 'The Reverend'. Why? Because he was ordained on 29th September to the office of Deacon. What is a Deacon? During the ordination service, the Bishop explained:

"A Deacon is called to serve the Church of God, and to work with its members in caring for the poor, the needy, the sick, and all who are in trouble. He is to strengthen the faithful, search out the careless and the indifferent, and to preach the word of God in the place to which he is licensed. A Deacon assists the priest under whom he serves, in leading the worship of the people, especially in the administration of the Holy Communion. He may baptize when required to do so. It is his general duty to do such pastoral work as is entrusted to him". So much for David.

Secondly, Ken Phillips, besides being Churchwarden, is now also an Elder. He was commissioned as such – also on 29th September. What is an Elder?

"An Elder is a lay-man or lay-woman appointed by the Diocesan Bishop for service in a

The Church in Suffolk

No. 536   September 1991

DIOCESE OF ST. EDMUNDSBURY AND IPSWICH

New Local Ministry

On the morning of Michaelmas Day, Sunday, 29th September, the Cathedral will be the scene of an ordination unique in the history of this Diocese. One woman and three men will go forward to be ordained Deacon to serve in the Local Non-Stipendiary Ministry.

This will mark a milestone in a three-year course which started two years ago. The local character of the enterprise is emphasised not only by the area in which the new Deacons will minister but also in the place and method of their training. Each candidate has studied together with other lay leaders in their own parish or benefice, the place where they actually live and worship.

The training programme has been 'custom built' for each of the parishes involved by Canon Roger Pallant who, as well as being a Parish Priest is Diocesan Officer for Local Non-Stipendiary Ministry.

The first four to be presented for ordination under this new scheme are:-

Peter Schwier, one of the LNSM Deacons

     Mrs Elisabeth A.T. Arnold and
     Mr Bernard F. Rose, both of St Thomas, Ipswich;
     Mr David L.C. Rutherford of Acton & Great Waldingfield;
     Mr Peter A. Schwier of Fressingfield.

Elisabeth Arnold, though she modestly describes herself as 'housewife' is also a skilled and experienced teacher. As a supply teacher she has worked for a large number of schools in the London Borough of Enfield and she has specialised in remedial work. Bernard Roe is a horticulturist and arboriculturist working for a local firm. David Rutherford, a Master Mariner, has served as Fleet Safety Officer and is a member of the General Council of British Shipping.

The fourth candidate, Peter Schwier, is a Suffolk farmer who has also spent two years of his working life as an Agricultural Missionary in Zaire. We hope to publish Peter's own story in next month's issue.

The new Deacons are to be ordained by Bishop Eric who, on that very day, will be celebrating the 40th anniversary of his own ordination to the diaconate.

At a time when a rural diocese such as ours is hard pressed to offer ministerial cover across its 500 plus scattered parishes, Local Non-Stipendiary Ministry offers an imaginative and exciting approach to the problem. We salute these four pioneers and pray for them and their future ministry.

Bishop John writes on Evangelism . . . See Page 3

WEEKLY IN TERM TIME

SCRAMBLERS	– for 3-5 years old.	– 5.30 to 6.00 pm
CLIMBERS	– 5-7 years old	–)
EXPLORERS	– 8-11 years old	–) 6.00 to 7.00 pm
PATHFINDERS	– 11-14 years old	–)

in the School – Great Waldingfield

A time of Christian education and activity
for all children

WELCOME

to

the Churches of

the Rural Deanery of

SUDBURY

LONG MELFORD

The Christian Community of the
Rural Deanery extends a warm
welcome to you.
We invite you to visit our churches;
to share our pride in the legacy of
our forebears; and, if possible, to
join us in our regular worship.

HAPPY BIRTHDAY TO THE MAGAZINE
10-years old in January

January 1992

We are very pleased to say that the Magazine has successfully reached its 10th birthday and it hasn't cost you a.penny more – still only 10p per copy. This is due to the efforts of the Magazine Committee who collect the contents and the generosity of Mr John Lawrenson and Mr Colin Mitchell who typeset and produce the final copy. From humble beginnings when the distribution just reached 100, the total delivered now nears 400.

Grateful thanks are sent from the Committee to all the Distributors past and present for their hard work and thanks to all readers for their support.

We are enclosing a reprint of our very first edition so that you can see how far we have progressed. It is interesting to note that two groups are now lost from the Village but, of course, we have a considerable number of new ones.

Please note there will be no magazine in January, and all outstanding subscriptions should be paid by the end of the year.

January 1982

Church & Village
News

GREAT
WALDINGFIELD

Wedding Day

MICHAEL Richard Miller, of Bantocks Road, Great Waldingfield and Vivienne Eleanor Calver of 13 Cornflower Close, Stanway, Colchester, who were married at Great Waldingfield. (Picture: Richard Burn)

OCTOBER 1991

Michael Grimwood and Amanda Rowe.

THE wedding took place on September 29 at St John's Methodist church of Amanda M. Rowe, of 56 Lambert Drive, Acton, and Michael Grimwood, of Glebe House, Great Waldingfield. (Picture: Ernest Bateman).

November 7, 1991

THE WEDDING took place at St John's Methodist Church, Sudbury on September 28, of Shirley Bull and Paul Richardson, of 8 Kenyon Drive, Great Waldingfield.

MARRIED at Badwell Ash church were Jonathan Warnock, of Heath Road, Great Waldingfield, and Donna Beales of Badwell Ash. (Pic-

MARRIED at St Lawrence's Church, Great Waldingfield, on May 9 were Nicola Jones, daughter of Mr and Mrs Oliver Jones, of The Wilderness, Great Waldingfield, and John Cawley, of Harrow, London.

1992

THE WEDDING took place at Sudbury Register Office on March 21 of Samantha Jane Baker and Leslie James McKenzie, both of 2 Hardy Court, Grenville Road, Sudbury.
The bride is the daughter of Mr and Mrs B. E. Martin, of 26 Bantocks Road, Great Waldingfield, and the bridegroom is the son of Mr and Mrs E. S. McKenzie of 46 Vicarage Lane, Acton.

THE WEDDING took place at Holy Trinity Church in Ebernoe, near Petworth, West Sussex, on Easter Saturday, of Janet Ruth Wadey, of Kirdford, West Sussex and Jonathan Edward Hills, of Billinghurst, West Sussex.
The bride is the daughter of Mr and Mrs Ron Wadey, of Kirdford, West Sussex and the bridegroom is the son of Mr and Mrs Michael Hills, of Great Waldingfield.

Colin Pinnegar and Jane Higginson

MARRIED at Holy Trinity Church, Long Melford, on Saturday, August 8, were Jane Higginson, of Great Waldingfield, and Colin Pinnegar, of 2 Cordell Cottage, Long Melford.

The bride is the daughter of Tom and Joan Humphreys, of 82 Bantocks Road, Great Waldingfield, and the bridegroom is the son of Colin and Christine Pinnegar, of Plymouth.

Neil Holmes and Joanne Butcher

JOANNE Butcher, daughter of Mr and Mrs A Butcher of Great Waldingfield, and Neil Holmes, son of Mr and Mrs P Holmes, of Haverhill, were married at Suffolk Road Church, Sudbury.

(Picture: Basil Keith)

Nigel Schofield and Jayne Newport

THE WEDDING took place at St Gregory's Church, Sudbury, of Jayne Newport of 38 Cats Lane, Sudbury and Nigel Schofield, of Great Waldingfield.

The bride is the daughter of Ann Newport, of 38 Cats Lane, Sudbury, and the late Jim Newport, and the bridegroom is the son of John and Vanessa Schofield, of Great Waldingfield.

Christopher Canham and Ruth Gilks

MARRIED at Stanstead church were Ruth Lilian Gilks, daughter of Mrs Dorothy Gilks of Cross Street, Sudbury, and Christopher John Canham, of Great Waldingfield, son of Mr and Mrs Neil Canham of Long Melford.

Attendants were Caroline Faircloth, Suzanne Davis, Katie Page and three-year-old Max Norman and the best man was Michael Foster.

APRIL 1993

Mark Harman and Jane Archer

MARK Neil Harman, son of Mr and Mrs F W Harman, of 35 First Avenue, Sudbury, and Jane Helen Archer, daughter of Mr and Mrs J G Archer, of Bancroft, Folly Road, Great Waldingfield, were married at St Lawrence's Church, Gt Waldingfield.

The Rev Lawrence Pizzey officiated. The bride, who was given away by her father, was attended by Mrs Leanne Sanders, Miss Nicky Walton, Miss Samantha Maisey and Miss Natalie Oben.

Best man was Roger McCartney.

The reception was held in a marquee at home. The couple will live in Long Melford.

Paul Hurrell & Deborah Andrews

THE wedding took place at St Gregory's Church, Sudbury, of Deborah Andrews and Paul Hurrell.

The bride is the daughter of Mr and Mrs R Knights, of Chilton Lodge Road, Sudbury, and the bridegroom is the son of Mr and Mrs A Hurrell, of Elm Tree Farm, Great Waldingfield.

Stuart Finch & Wendy Poulson

THE wedding took place at St Mary's Church, Glemsford, of Wendy Poulson and Stuart Finch, of 1 Causeway Close, Glemsford.

The bride is the daughter of Mr and Mrs W Turp, of 19 Coronation Rise, Great Waldingfield, and the bridegroom is the son of Mr and Mrs C Finch, of 19c Shilling Street, Lavenham.

The bride was attended by Zoe Hollocks. The Rev Adrian Mason conducted the service and Graham Davis was best man.

John Maisey & Joanna Davies

THE wedding took place at Sudbury Register Office of Joanna Elizabeth Davies, of 29 Nursery Road, Great Cornard, and John Anthony Maisey, of Cranfield Road, Leicester.

The bride is the daughter of Mr and Mrs G T Davies, of 29 Nursery Road, Great Cornard and the bridegroom is the son of Mr and Mrs J S Maisey, of 103 Folley Road, Gt Waldingfield.

Ancient buildings are often much admired – and hideously expensive to maintain! Our own church of St Lawrence's, and All Saints at Acton both fall into this category. St Lawrence's is about to have the nave roof renewed at a cost in excess of £40,000. The work will probably be done during March and April; and whilst it will still be possible to use part of the church throughout that time, the churchwardens and PCC of All Saints has invited the congregation of St Lawrence's to use that church for worship whilst St Lawrence's is in a state of controlled chaos! Unless you hear differently, all services advertised in this magazine will be in St Lawrence's.

CHURCH LUNCHES

Monthly church lunches in aid of St Lawrence's are held at 73 Bantocks Road. The next will be on Wednesday 19 February. A lunch of home-made soup, rolls and cheese, (optional wine) and coffee will be served between 12 noon and 2 pm. All welcome. Why not come and enjoy a light lunch and good company in a very good cause?

Quiz Night – The quiz night held on 7th March was a huge success. A most welcome £293 was raised towards the cost of some new PE apparatus. As well as raising funds the evening was enjoyed by everyone there.

Thank you to everyone who worked so hard to make the evening so successful and to all the teams for entering – without your support and involvement the evening would have been a flop!

As the event was so popular we will another so keep your eyes open for details. An opportunity to prise the cup away from the Governors perhaps!

1992

ST LAWRENCE'S CHURCH: During May the church was involved with the major fundraising events of the year. A plant sale was held at Whitehall, by permission of Mr M. Oliver.

Many people donated plants and garden equipment and even more people came to buy. A profit of over £1,000 was made for the church restoration fund.

On the Sunday and Monday of Bank Holiday weekend, May 24 and 25, the annual cream teas were held at Brandeston Hall, by permission of Mr and Mrs O. Kiddy.

The organisation for this weekend has grown beyond all recognition. For this year, the sixth, about 40 people were involved at the hall while many more were providers of goods to sell and eat!

Food was provided from 10 am to 6 pm and there were also other stalls and attractions including boat rides on the moat.

Again the profit, which was about £1,800 was for the church for essential upkeep and restoration. The next major fundraising event for the church will be a car boot sale on July 15 in the village, details from the churchwardens.

1993

CHURCH OF ST LAWRENCE: Members of the church were extremely busy during May. The month began with an exhibition in the church of the village, past and present. This was researched and organised by Mr and Mrs R Walter, with contributions from Mr J Misselbrook, the Women's Institute, the school and many parishioners. It was a well supported, popular exhibition.

During the weekend of May 22 and 23 the annual plant sale was held at Whitehall, by kind permission of Mr and Mrs Oliver. Mr and Mrs C Francis and Mr K Phillips had spent many days potting up plants from friends and neighbours, while many people had grown and donated plants. Many people again helped and a special thank-you goes to Mrs M Butcher.

The Whitsun bank holiday saw the ninth annual cream teas weekend. This means four or five days of solid work for the two days of the actual event and many more days disruption for Mr and Mrs O Kiddy and family, who kindly open their house and garden. Neighbouring villages are very helpful and tables and chairs are used from Little Waldingfield, Lavenham, Acton and Kersey village halls. A large number of people serve food and drink all day and a tombola, craft and plant stalls are on site.

As a result of this hard work over £3,000 has been made towards the next stages of church repair and restoration which amounts to over £30,000.

VIOLET ROYE, 1908-1994

Well-established Waldingfieldians, especially those who know or knew the neighbourhood of the church, will vividly remember Violet Roye, who died on 17 June. Violet had lived in Great Waldingfield, mainly at The Lodge as housekeeper to the Darley family, for about sixty years. She was individual, irreplaceable, unforgettable.

Baptisms		**Burials**	
21 Jan	Hayley Jade Bowser	25 Jan	John Steed (49)
18 Apr	Serena Christine Retson	24 Feb	Dorothy May Welsh (70)
15 Aug	Alissa Danielle Benfield	30 Mar	Laurence George Ratcliffe (69)
29 Aug	Nathaniel Adam David Rayner		
3 Oct	Adam Thomas Ratcliffe		
	Rachel Emma Laycock		

Marriages

24 Apr	David Lawrence Gosling and Joanne Catherine Wilson
1 May	Tony Reginald Britton and Joanne Marie Culham
15 May	Mark Neil Harman and Jane Helen Archer

We are saddened to hear of the death of Mrs Grace Parish and we extend our sympathies to her husband and family.

Matthew Warnock & Claire Butcher

MATTHEW Warnock, who was chosen last month as our Super Server 1993, was married at Suffolk Road Church, Sudbury, on October 16, to Claire Ruth Butcher.

The bride is the daughter of Mr and Mrs A E Butcher, of 2 Chestnut Close, Great Waldingfield, and the bridegroom is the son of Mr and Mrs D Warnock, of 10 Heath Way, Great Waldingfield.

Roger Wells & Michelle Cates

THE wedding took place at St Gregory's Church, Sudbury, of Michelle Yvonne Cates, of 12 Heathway, Great Waldingfield and Roger David Wells, of 29 Suffolk Roa

JUNE 1994

Garry Ingram & Andrea Batley

THE wedding took place at St Lawrence's Church, Great Waldingfield, of Andrea Louise Batley, daughter of Mr and Mrs F W Batley, of Bowling Green, Great Waldingfield, and Garry Alan Ingram, son of Mr and Mrs W Ingram, of Quay House, Quay Lane, Sudbury.

The bride, who wore a dupion silk dress edged with Black Watch tartan was attended by Jane Gorham (sister) and Tracey Mansfield and pageboys Adam Ingram and Jack Beckford.

The ceremony was conducted by the Rev Lawrence Pizzey and Graham Ingram was best man.

Christopher King & Tracey Mills

THE wedding took place at St Lawrence's Church, Great Waldingfield, of Christopher King, of 18 Butt Road, Great Waldingfield, and Tracey Jane Mills.

Pat Leathers really put the boot in, winning all three classes in the flower arrangement section.

Entries up at spring flower show

GREAT Waldingfield's 10th spring flower show was held in the village hall on Saturday.

The committee were encouraged by the increase in the number of exhibitors and entries over last year, in spite of the wintry conditions of the last few weeks. There were 54 exhibitors and 194 entries in 31 classes.

The judges were Mr C W S Hurr and Mrs P Kiddy and Mrs J Penrose presented the prizes.

PLANT SALE

The magnificent sum of £1,285 was raised at the plant sale held on 13 May.

Mary Jackson won two classes in the flower section and the prize for the most entries in the show.

Happy birthday to the Church – Whitsunday – 22 May 1994

The Friday Club children and parents will meet at Greenacres at 10am on the morning of Whitsunday. We hope to have a decorated trailer and the children will make banners and flags. We hope as many people as possible will join us on the Green.

We will sing hymns and then go in procession to the church (those able to unable to walk can ride on the trailer). We arrive at the Church in time for a Family Holy communion Service at 11.15am. After the service we are all invited to picnic and continue the birthday celebrations in the garden of Churchgate (by kind permission of Mr & Mrs D Lawrence-Jones). Do join us.

MRS MAUREEN SHINN

Mrs Maureen Shinn having been training over the past four years for Lay Reader ministry, will be licensed by the Diocesan Bishop at a service in the Cathedral, Bury St Edmunds on Saturday 23 October at 11.30 am as a Reader for this benefice of Acton and Gt Waldingfield.

● Musical all-rounder: Penny Statham hit the right note with judges.

Great Waldingfield flower festival organiser Anne Francis admires Kathy Underwood's display.

Villagers show off their flower arranging skills

A TALENTED young musician who started to sing aged five, was the only vocalist to get through to the finals of the West Suffolk Young Musician of the Year.

Great Cornard Upper School student Penny Statham, 17, is something of a musical all-rounder — not only has she passed her Grade eight examination in singing, but she has also reached the same level in piano.

Penny, of Badleys Close, Great Waldingfield, is also a proficient violinist and saxophonist and hopes, one day, to continue her studies at the Guildhall School of Music

in London.

Although she was only a runner-up in West Suffolk Young Musician of the Y contest, she was nevertheless delighted have made it through to the finals.

She admits to being a little nervous her experience of singing at Hengrave H churches, charity concerts, weddings old people's homes helped her deal with situation like a true professional.

Musical talent clearly runs in the Stath family — Penny's mo and her younger sist brother Daniel, seven

A VISUAL feast of colour greeted visitors at Great Waldingfield's flower festival in the village church over the weekend.

The festival, held every two years, is non-competitive and allows villagers to display their flower arranging talents.

This year's theme was harvest abundance and

featured displays depicting various harvests including those of the sea, earth and orchard.

Although the festival is usually for village entrants only, Cavendish flower arranger Kathy Underwood asked if she could enter a display and came up with the magnificent creation in our picture.

"It really was the most colourful display," said festival organiser Anne Francis. "Kathy asked if she could enter a display and although the festival is really for villagers to enter, I wasn't going to turn her away."

Over the weekend £900 was raised for the church roof fund.

Bomb crew veterans return for 50th memorial prayers

■ In memoriam: dignitaries lay wreaths in honour of the 486th Bombardment Group in Sudbury

NOSTALGIA was the order of the day at the special memorial service which marked the 50th anniversary of the arrival of the U.S. Army Air Force 486th Bombardment Group in Suffolk.

During the final years of the Second World War, the 486th flew almost 200 missions from Sudbury airfield, now farmland between Great Waldingfield and Acton.

More than 400 aircrew never returned, but the 54 Americans, including bomb group veterans, their wives and children, gathered yesterday at St Gregory's Church, Sudbury, to remember them.

Since 1983 the 486th Association has been to Sudbury four times, but its Return to England Committee chairman, Charlie MacGill, admitted it could be their last formal visit. "Four days is really too short," he said. "We would love to come back again but I'm afraid attrition is beginning to set in."

Yesterday's memorial service was attended by local dignitaries including the Mayor of Sudbury, Mike Gould, Air Marshal Sir John Kemball, Chief Inspector Bob Lawrence of Sudbury police, Jean Misselbrook, vice-chairman of Great Waldingfield parish council and the chairmen of Acton and Chilton parish councils.

The service was taken by the Rector of St Gregory's, Derrick Stiff, assisted by Paul Lewin, deacon of Sudbury's catholic church, and Laurence Pizzey, rector at Great Waldingfield, who read the lessons.

FLIGHT PLAN

■ The 486th Bombardment Group Association's busy schedule in Sudbury includes visits to the Gainsborough silk weaving company and Lucas Diesel Systems, followed by a tea dance organised by the Sudbury Pensioners' Association today. Tomorrow, the association will unveil a memorial plaque at St Lawrence's Church, Great Waldingfield, which will be followed by a lunch at the village hall, a tour of the airfield and tea at Chilton Hall.

'Dear friends,

We want to thank you for all you did to make our stay in Sudbury so memorable!

The plaque in St Lawrence is such an honour for our 486th bombardier group. I'm sure other members of our families will want to visit in the future to see it.

The dinner and high tea that followed were wonderful too. You have some great cooks there.

Again our sincere thanks and best wishes always.

'As the Chairman of the '50th Mission-Target Sudbury' Committee, may I express our sincerest thanks for your outstanding help in getting the Friendship Plaque in place in St Lawrences, as well as the many 'behind the scenes' details which you both handled so very well for our recent visit. In fact I wrote Mrs Chamberlin that you people of Great Waldingfield did an absolutely unbelievable job of putting the program together, and the day was successful in every way. I wish that you all could have heard the wonderful comments that were made by so many of the 486ers about the day at Great Waldingfield.

Newlyweds have no truck with a limo

BRIDEGROOM Philip Molkenthin normally drives a breakdown truck for his family firm but on Saturday it was given an extra polish and decorated with balloons to carry him to his wedding at Sudbury Register Office.

His bride, Linda Simes (21), also arrived in a Molkenthin breakdown vehicle, a four-wheel drive Discovery – one of the firm's six-strong fleet, driven by her new father-in-law David.

Philip (28) is one of four family members working for the Sudbury-based 24-hour recovery firm and the idea of using their trucks came from his mother Yvonne.

"We weren't paying out for cars when we've got perfectly good vehicles here!" she laughed.

Ex-employee Barry Butters took time off from work especially to make sure Philip and best man Gary Beech reached the register office on time.

And after the ceremony Philip and Linda's special day slipped smoothly into second gear as they left for their reception at Great Waldingfield village hall in an M-registered BMW lent by Colchester dealers Neeps.

The couple have made their home in Acton.

Loser

THIEVES stole garden furniture and electrical tools worth £500 from a shed in Bantocks Road, Great Waldingfield, last week.

1995

Natasha Walmsley (8) found her bonnet quite a weight on her mind at Great Waldingfield Primary School while Zachary Leaf (6) used an egg to provide a new angle on Easter peace at Nayland Primary School.

Council Tax	Waldingfield Great	
BAND A	BAND B	BAND C
380.86	444.34	507.81

Blooming giant in garden

VILLAGERS and tourists at Great Waldingfield are fascinated by a giant which towers over everyone who lives there.

A seven-foot yukka plant in Alf Finch's front garden at 1 Heath Way has been the talk of the village since it shot up over the last couple of months.

Mr Finch (68), who at 5ft 4ins is dwarfed by his prize plant, started growing it eight years ago and he has been amazed by its progress.

"Everybody keeps stopping and looking at it because they are amazed," he said. "We look out and see them talking about it for ages."

A striking cream-coloured flower has sprouted from the plant in the last two months almost doubling the height of the plant.

But Mr Finch has no intention of cutting it down to a normal size.

"It just appears to be getting bigger and bigger but people like looking at it so I'll leave it alone," he said.

● Janet Moss serving up soup lunches, with the help of Betty Headicar, Lawrence Pizzey and Betty Collins.

New man for St Gregory's

THE new priest-in-charge of St Gregory's in Sudbury will be the Rev Lawrence Pizzey, vicar of Acton with Great Waldingfield for the past nine years.

Mr Pizzey (52) has worked in the Diocese of St Edmundsbury and Ipswich since he was ordained in 1967.

Married to Anne with two children, he will succeed the Rev Derrick Stiff, who is now priest-in-charge at St Peter and St Paul, Lavenham.

Mr Pizzey, who does not know yet when he will take over, said: "The parishes of St Gregory's, All Saints and Great Cornard are seeking to work more closely together. And it's nice I shall be able to play an important part in that."

Sand and gravel plan

THE PROSPECT of neighbouring sites at Chilton being used for future sand and gravel extraction has horrified local villagers.

Their worries centre on two areas covering a total of 220 acres on either side of the B1115 which have been earmarked for quarrying in the draft Suffolk Minerals Local Plan.

One site, on the old airfield to the north of the road, also overlaps the parish boundaries of Great Waldingfield and Acton.

The estimated production of sand and gravel from the two would be 5.8 million tonnes to be used in concrete construction.

Chilton Parish Council chairman Veryan Herbert said this week the larger 120-acre site was a quarter of their parish.

"We feel we're under siege here," he said. "Sudbury is encroaching from one end and now we're faced with this. Chilton has been nibbled away at for several years but a quarter is a big chunk.

"At the moment it's agricultural land owned by the county council so they will do well out of it if the plan goes ahead."

YOUNGSTERS from Great Waldingfield Primary School celebrated Mothering Sunday a few days early with a special party for parents and relatives.

● Magic mums: Cathryn Redgewell (left) and Barbara Cole enjoy a spot of pampering from their daughters Carrie and Kathryn at Great Waldingfield School.

Hospital site row

THE long-running wrangle over whether People's Park in Sudbury can be the site for a new town hospital or whether it should be retained as a leisure amenity will be decided in the High Court next month.

West Suffolk Hospitals NHS Trust, who bought the 18-acre site off Waldingfield Road from Sudbury's common lands trustees, planned to build a new £14 million hospital there to replace the Walnuttree and St Leonard's hospitals.

But their plans were held up by Great Waldingfield farmers David and Colin Steed who have campaigned for four years for the site to be kept as parkland as it was bought by the common lands trustees in 1876.

Suffolk County Council refused an application by the Steeds to register the park, also known as Harp Close Meadow, as a town green to protect it from development.

A High Court judge is due to review the decision on April 5, 6 and 7 and the Steeds announced this week they can afford the enormous cost of putting their case in court.

David Steed, who declined to publicise exactly how much cash they are putting up to contest the case, said they were determined to fight the battle to the bitter end.

"It has cost us a lot of money to fight this case and we are hopeful the judge will see our side of it," said Mr Steed, who has offered the health trust his land near the Howlett's roundabout as an alternative hospital site.

"Hopefully the true facts will come out and People's Park will be registered as a town green."

The health trust were disappointed with the hold-up in their plans but they are confident work will begin this year if the judge rules in their favour.

Ruth Finbow is responsible for Lavenham, Thorpe Morieux, Hitcham, Wattisham, Preston St Mary, Kettlebaston, Bildeston, Brent Eleigh, Monks Eleigh, Chelsworth, Nedging, Great and Little Waldingfield.

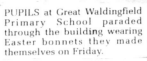

1995

PUPILS at Great Waldingfield Primary School paraded through the building wearing Easter bonnets they made themselves on Friday.

Rianna Smith (9) and her eight-year-old schoolfriend Cathy Page sport their colourfu

17 pupils from Great Waldingfield CEVP School will be saying goodbye to their schoolmates at the end of term

Coronation

A Report of the Coronation Festivities
in this Parish on June 2nd 1953.

At last the great day dawned, the day we had all been preparing for for weeks. All the feverish plannings and counter-plannings, suggestions and decisions of how to celebrate June 2nd were over.

The morning itself was dull and rainy, but nothing could damp our spirits. A large number of people began the day by attending a celebration of Holy Communion in our lovely old Parish Church at 7 o'clock.

Then after a quick breakfast, final touches were given to the tea, which was to come later on. During the morning many people watched the televising of the scene of the Coronation in Westminster Abbey.

After lunch the festivities began. There was a Fancy Dress parade for which many entered - then came Children's and Adults' sports. These were interrupted many times by heavy rain. A television set was fixed in the school for any who wished to view the return journey of our Queen to Buckingham Palace.

A tea was then provided for everyone in the School. It had been hoped to hold this out of doors, but the weather made this impossible.

After tea came the prize-giving for the sports and the presentation to each child of a copy of the New Testament

Willing helpers then converted the School-room into a concert hall complete with stage and curtains.

A very enjoyable evening was arranged, all the items being given by parishioners. During the concert, Her Majesty's speech was heard over the wireless.

At about 10-30 P.M. after a very happy day we all returned to our homes.

Some two weeks after the Coronation all children and all old people were taken to the Cinema in Sudbury to see the coloured film of Elizabeth our Queen.

WALLY LANGRIDGE

WALLY Langridge of Great Waldingfield joined Vauxhall Motors after school as a craft apprentice. He qualified as a draughtsman and went on to become a planning engineer and production forward planner.

Wally joined the sales team at Vauxhall 12 years ago and is now a national account manager for the eastern region.

He is co-ordinator for the Acton and Waldingfields carnival, organises the White Horse fun run every year and takes part, too.

ACTON and Waldingfields carnival queen for the next two years is 18-year-old Penny Statham, of Badleys Close, Great Waldingfield – pictured above.

QUEEN PENNY

BOWLS CLUB

1995

The Annual General Meeting took place on Monday 6 March, present. Officers elected were as follows:

Chairlady	Jean Misselbrook
Vice Chairman	Roy Crisp
Secretary	John Hughes
Treasurer	Roy Willis
Ladies Captain	Lilian Haxell
Gents Captain	John Sparkes

PENSIONERS at Great Waldingfield are on the look-out for vandals who have damaged their property in sporadic attacks over the last two months.

Fred Hessenthaler (79) spoke out on behalf of the mainly elderly residents on the Heath Estate who have become increasingly fed-up with the situation and frustrated that the culprits have not been punished.

Great Waldingfield pensioner Fred Hessenthaler surveys the latest vandalism – on his wall and gate pillar.

PUB regulars at the White Horse, Great Waldingfield, raised £400 for cancer research when they took part in the pub's seventh annual sponsored bike race and fun run.

Fifteen cyclists and half a dozen walkers set off from the White Horse to follow a ten-mile circular route through Sudbury, Long Melford and Acton back to the pub.

The event was organised by landlord Ian Fleming and Wally Langridge, who first ran the route seven years ago when a previous landlord bet him he could not finish in under two hours.

White Horse regulars ready for the start of their charity effort.

THE REV LAWRENCE PIZZEY

The Rev Lawrence Pizzey will conduct his final services as Incumbent of this benefice on Sunday 21 May. He will be licensed as Priest-in-Charge of Sudbury St Gregory with St Peter and Chilton on Monday 5 June at 7.30 pm in St Gregory's Church.

During the interregnum the Churchwardens are legally responsible for seeing that church services are maintained. The Rev David Rutherford, our local non-stipendiary minister, will conduct the majority of these, and will be available to any parishioners who require the services of a priest. All other church matters should be referred to the Churchwardens.

MAUREEN RITA SHINN: More than 200 relatives, friends and colleagues attended the celebration funeral service at the Church of St Lawrence, Great Waldingfield, for Maureen Shinn who died after a short illness, aged 57.

The service was conducted by the rector, the Rev Lawrence Pizzey, whose address highlighted her involvement in so many activities within the village.

"Maureen exercised a tremendous influence on a very large number of people through a great variety of groups and organisations of which she was part, over many years," he said. "The number gathered here in church today bears witness to that fact.

"Although her early years were spent at Grays, Thurrock, Maureen came to live in Glemsford at about the time she went to train as a teacher at Keswick Hall. In both Glemsford (where she met Fred and married him) and subsequently here in Great Waldingfield, Maureen was a teacher in the village school and a prominent attender at the local parish church.

"Professionally, her infinite patience, care and concern for the children in her class, or with whom she had to do, were admired and appreciated by parents and colleagues alike – and of course, by the children themselves.

"Here at St Lawrence's, Maureen's ministry has for long centred on work with children. She inaugurated occasional children's workshops in church – and on each occasion invited, persuaded and cajoled some dozen or more people to help. Having a children's corner in church was her initiative and the Friday Club would never have got off the ground nor grown and continued as it did without Maureen's leadership and enthusiasm.

She asked that instead of flowers, donations should be made to a fund to provide running water to the Church of St Lawrence – a facility long overdue. To date, the fund stands at over £900.

Weekend of gardens

ELEVEN gardens will be open in aid of St Lawrence Church, Great Waldingfield, this weekend, including one property with a Japanese-style garden, which will open on Saturday only.

The weekend will also feature an art show in the church featuring work by a number of local artists, as well as members of the Sudbury Art Club.

100 pc effort

A GIRL Guide is attempting to prove 100 times over she wants to represent Suffolk on a future trip to Sweden.

In order to raise sponsorship, Jo Haynes, of Great Waldingfield, will on June 3 attempt to complete an activity for each letter in the word Sweden, as follows: Swim 100 lengths of a pool; Wink 100 times; Embroider 100 cm of fabric; Do 100 good deeds; Exercise 100 times; Netball 100 shoots.

Aaron Davidson & Charlotte Pask

THE wedding took place at the Church of St Mary the Virgin, Glemsford, of Charlotte Pask and Aaron Davidson, of Windmill Row, Glemsford.

The bride is the daughter of Les and Judy Pask, of Green Acre, Great Waldingfield, and the bridegroom is the son of Rob and Pat Davidson, of School Field, Glemsford.

Simon Cutting & Teresa Grieves

TERESA Louise Grieves of Great Waldingfield, was just about to marry Simon Cutting, of Needham Market, in the exotic surroundings of the Blue Waters Beach Hotel in Antigua, when to her great surprise her father turned up at the last minute to give her away.

Mr P J Grieves had arrived in Antigua only that morning and his presence had been kept secret from his daughter, who thought a family friend, Mr M Bloomfield, was going to give her away.

The bride's mother is Mrs E F Bates, of Great Waldingfield, and the bridegroom is the son of Mrs L Cutting, of Needham Market.

Adam Coleman & Barbara Mullen

THE wedding took place at Our Lady and St John's Church, Sudbury, of Barbara Mullen, of First Avenue, Sudbury, and Adam Coleman, of Bantocks Road, Great Waldingfield.

Haley gets BA degree

A FORMER Sudbury schoolgirl has graduated from university with a BA honours degree.

Haley Ireland (23), of Little Waldingfield, attended Great Waldingfield primary, All Saints Middle and Sudbury Upper schools before moving on to the University of Essex where she studied accounting and financial management for three years.

WE have been asked to point out that ex-serviceman William Green, of Coronation Rise, Great Waldingfield, who recently attended a garden party at Buckingham Palace, served with the Royal Army Observer Corps during the last war.

War veteran William Green, who recently attended a garden party at Buckingham Palace.

Ex-landlady dies

THE former landlady of the White Horse pub at Great Waldingfield, Vera Butcher died on Monday aged 83.

She lived at the pub with her parents and then ran it with her husband Charles for many years until they left in 1976 to move to Sudbury.

The funeral service will be at Colchester Crematorium on Wednesday at noon.

THE death of a dedicated young footballer, who collapsed and died while out jogging, has stunned and saddened friends and colleagues.

Robbie Groom, 23, shared his home at Talbot Road, Sudbury, with his fiancee, Lisa. The couple had met as students at Sudbury Upper School. His parents, Frederick and Diana, live at Braithwaite Drive, Great Waldingfield.

Crash delay for traffic

POLICE had to control traffic for several hours after an accident on the main Sudbury to Newton road on Thursday.

The accident happened on the A134 at the Great Waldingfield turn-off at 1.50pm and involved a lorry and a transit van.

French lorry driver Louay Nizav and van driver Stuart Deacon of Church Lane, Barham, sustained minor injuries and both were treated at West Suffolk Hospital before being discharged.

Parochial Affairs

Mrs. Braithwaite has very generously presented to the Parish the Allotment Lands on the Heath and Mill Field, to be named the Francis, Humphry, and Margaret Braithwaite Trust; and to be used for such educational or social purpose that may seem desirable to the Committee of Management. The Trustees are the Rector; Mr. C. R. Bird, District Councillor; Mrs. Dunnett, Head Teacher; these with Mrs. Alex. Poole, Gen. J. A. Coxhead, Mr. H. Diggins and Mr. Marten Bird, form the Committee.

THE
BRAITHWAITE TRUST.

ALLOTMENTS are let to tenants under the following conditions:

1. That rent is paid at the rate of 4/6 per 20 rods, but such rate may be varied at the discretion of the Trustees, month's notice of such change being given to existing holders.

2. That the rent be paid yearly in advance at Michaelmas.

3. That the decision of the Trustees shall be accepted in any matter of dispute whatever.

4. That the allotment must be kept in a proper state of cultivation.

5. That a holder shall not sublet his plot without permission of the Trustees.

6. That each holder must keep his portion of the fence and the pathway adjoining in order, and the latter at the width of two feet.

A. EDMUND KING, *Chairman.*

J. A. COXHEAD, *Hon. Sec. & Treas.*

GT WALDINGFIELD

Members welcomed June and Bill Raper to the October meeting. They took us on a journey which Moses had embarked upon with the Israelites.

June and Bill have completed various journeys on their boat in the past 9 years and this one took them from Egypt to Petra, via Port Said and the Gulf of Aqaba. By way of slides we visited the pyramids and then went on to St Catherine's monastery. Apparently this was the Catherine who was martyred on a wheel, hence the firework we have today, called the "Catherine Wheel". Within this monastery are a Christian church and a Mosque, virtually side by side. We also saw pictures of Moses' burning bush (although it appeared to have been extinguished when the photo was taken!) This is, by all accounts, a remarkable shrub since all those who have tried to take cuttings from it have failed, including scientists. The plant has always died and yet the bush itself has been growing there for more than 2000 years. The city of Petra, although now in ruins, had a population of about 25,000 at the time of Christ as it was a stop-over point for the trading routes to the east. Petra is also known as The Rose City and we could see why when we were shown the colours in the surrounding rocks. They were the most beautiful pinks, reds and browns.

■ Teresa Grieves, of Great Waldingfield, and Simon Cutting, of Needham Market, after their wedding at the Bluewaters Hotel, Antigua

Richard Whittle and Sally Batt

A FORMER Sudbury man serving in the Metropolitan Police was married at Hemel Hempstead to a fellow police officer.

The bridegroom was Richard Whittle, son of Ken and Jane Whittle, of Great Waldingfield, and the bride

Sally Batt, daughter of Jacky Batt of Hemel Hempstead, and the late Michael Batt.

The couple live at Berkhamsted, Hertfordshire.

The bride was attended by her great niece, Bethany Blackwell and Jonathan Whittle was best man.

Martin Selvester and Moira Bibby

THE wedding took place at Sudbury Baptist Church of Moira Jane Bibby and Martin Stuart Selvester, of Lynns Hall Close, Great Waldingfield.

Howard Yuill & Louise Parker

THE wedding took place at St James' Church, Didsbury, Manchester, of Louise Jane Parker of Great Waldingfield, and Howard Maxwell Yuill, of Didsbury.

Stephen Griffiths & Rowena Diaper

THE wedding took place at Holy Trinity Church, Long Melford, of Stephen John Griffiths, son of Mr and Mrs Glyn Griffiths, of Cockfield, and Rowena Elaine Diaper, daughter of Geoffrey and Beryl Diaper, of Great Waldingfield.

Neil Garrott & Victoria Lingard

THE wedding took place at Foxearth Church of Neil Andrew Garrott, son of Ray and Ilene Garrott, of Hertford, and Victoria Louise Lingard, daughter of Sandie and David Scott, Clay Hall, Great Waldingfield.

Peter & Harriet Hangartner

THE wedding of Harriet Jane Hangartner (née Steed) and Peter Urs Hangartner, who were married in Zimbabwe in September, was blessed by the Rev Lawrence Pizzey at St Lawrence's Church, Great Waldingfield.

The bride is the daughter of David and Joan Steed, of Homelea, Great Waldingfield, and the bridegroom is the son of Rolf and Jennifer Hangartner, of Canon Kopje Farm, Mutorashanga, Zimbabwe.

May 12, 1995

● Wartime songs at Great Waldingfield Primary School.

Pauline East: "Never played the lottery".

tickets," she said.

But not everyone looks forward to Anthea Turner revealing the winning numbers every Saturday evening. People like Pauline East, of Great Waldingfield, are still wondering what all the fuss is about.

She said: "I've never been a gambler so I don't think I shall start playing the lottery now.

Pictures by NICK BUTCHER

GT WALDINGFIELD

SPRING FLOWER SHOW: The Great Waldingfield spring flower show was held in the village hall on Saturday, April 27. This was the 11th spring show organised by the horticultural show committee and attracted 275 exhibits from 112 people. Exhibits were of a high standard and numbers showed an increase over last years, in particular the children's section, thanks to the encouragement of the staff of the village school.

The judges were Mrs P Kiddy, Mrs P Collinson and Mr P Fisk and Mrs Garner presented the prizes.

The shield for the flower section was won jointly by Jean Misselbrook and Ronnie Dawe; flower arranging, Jean Misselbrook; novice flower arranging, Jane Sargeant.

Children's section winners were – pre school age: Lauren Wheeler; 5-8: Elissa Bryant, Emily Taylor, Richard White and Caroline Wilson, 9-12: Anna Marsh.

A prize for most points in show was won by Jean Misselbrook as was the prize for most entries. Finally a new prize this year, for the best exhibit in the show, was won by Anne Francis for a flower arrangment.

The autumn horticultural show will be held in the village hall on September 12.

Keith Smith & Gillian Colquhoun

GILLIAN Colquhoun and Keith Smith, both of Great Waldingfield, were married at Sudbury Register Office.

Stuart Bantock & Michelle Austin

THE wedding took place at St Peter and St Paul's Church, Lavenham, of Michelle Austin of Lavenham, and Stuart Bantock, of Avon Drive, Great Waldingfield

---

VILLAGERS are battening down the hatches in Great Waldingfield after burglars raided 10 homes and stole thousands of pounds worth of property.

Householders in the affected Heath Estate area are understood to be forming a Neighbourhood Watch scheme to prevent it happening again. Homes covered by the existing well-

by NICK RENNIE

supported scheme were not affected.

Police believe the same people committed all of the burglaries, which netted them a haul of cash and jewellery between Wednesday and Friday of last week.

The plight of pensioners Ivan and Maureen Smith, who lost the £300 they had saved for Christmas with the Lucas Diesel Systems club, summed up the

Property worth thousands stolen from ten homes

misery of the victims.

The couple, who have a son and two grandchildren, will only get £50 back in insurance and will struggle to buy the Christmas presents and food they planned to get.

Mrs Smith (59) said her husband was upset that the watch he was presented with on his 65th birthday last year had been stolen.

"We had been saving all year for that Christmas money and we had only just picked it up," she said.

"The worst thing was the way they had been right through the house throwing all our personal possessions over the floor and there was mud and dirt all over the place.

"We've lived here 31 years and never been burgled before. We thought we were safe."

Residents in Bantocks Road, where several of the burglaries took place, used to have a Neighbourhood Watch scheme but it was disbanded some time ago due to apathy.

Brian Brinton, who in 1991 founded the existing scheme covering 50 homes on the other side of the village, said there was now great interest in starting up a similar organisation where the raids were.

He said: "I have warned everyone in my area to be vigilant and I am sure those people living in the area of the burglaries will be in a similar frame of mind.

"One of the biggest problems with Neighbourhood Watch is keeping people's interest but a spate of this kind will I am sure revive any flagging interest."

Parish and district councillor Bill Skinner said the matter was discussed at this week's parish meeting because of local concern.

"The number of burglaries was rather exceptional for the village and a few more people are more interested in Neighbourhood Watch as a result," he said.

Detectives at Sudbury are particularly keen to trace the owner of a car seen parked outside the electricity sub-station in Folly Road, between 5pm and 7pm on the Wednesday.

Anyone who saw the car or anything suspicious when the raids took place is asked to contact Sudbury police on (01284) 774300.

Many people will mourn the death of Maureen Shinn. She was so fully involved with many organisations and groups. At out local school she was the Deputy Head and had won the admiration, respect and love of pupils, staff and parents. Her day at school started early and ended late, she attended many meetings which she felt would help her work at school and she was also a member of the Governing Body. The Friday Club which met in the school every Friday during the term was a time of Christian activity and teaching for children of 3+ to 14+. This was very much Maureen's idea and with her willing band of helpers, the idea became reality and the club thrived.

Her Christian Faith was very strong and an example and help to many people. She, after much work and study, had become a Lay Reader and few people will forget the last sermon she preached in church on healing. Her sense of humour made her great fun to be with, and she certainly enjoyed taking part with her friends in both school and Church concerts.

She was also a member of the Horticultural Club for she loved working in her garden and during the winter made all sorts of craft exhibits. As is mentioned elsewhere she was also a member of the Magazine Committee. We extend to her husband Fred and her sons, and the rest of her family our deepest sympathy.

Former village headteacher dies at 83

FLORENCE Bowers, one of Great Waldingfield's best known residents, died on Thursday at the age of 83.

Headteacher of the village primary school for more than 20 years up to 1972, Miss Bowers lived most of her life in the village.

She loved getting involved in the community as a parish councillor, secretary of the parochial church council, a member of the Womens' Institute and Brown Owl for the village brownies.

Before and during the war she used to ride a motorbike to Bures to teach at the village primary school until petrol began to be rationed.

Her friend Sheila Walter said: "She was wonderful with children. She was always strict in school but she was a lovely lady.

"My two children looked on her as a grandmother."

Miss Bowers spent her last two years in Melford Court nursing home in Long Melford.

She leaves a brother Charles, who lives in Great Walding-field, and a niece.

The funeral service will be held at Great Waldingfield Parish Church on Monday at 10am.

It will be followed by cremation at Bury St Edmunds.

There is a request for no flowers, but donations can be made to Great Waldingfield PCC's fabric fund.

Sudbury rector named as new rural dean

SUDBURY'S new rural dean is the rector of St Gregory's, the Rev Lawrence Pizzey, who took over last week from Canon Lionel Simpkins.

Before coming to Sudbury Mr Pizzey was vicar of Acton and Great Waldingfield for ten years. He was previously at West Stow near Bury St Edmunds.

Canon Simpkins, who is moving to the parish of St Augustine of Hippo in Ipswich, said he was very pleased to be succeeded as rural dean by someone he held in such high regard.

"I know it's going to be a popular appointment with the clergy and lay people in the deanery," he said.

The Rev Lawrence Pizzey outside St Gregory's, where he is the new priest-in-charge.

GT WALDINGFIELD

HORTICULTURAL SHOW: Great Waldingfield show committee brought forward their 13th horticultural show, which is usually held in September, to coincide with Acton and Waldingfields carnival on Saturday, July 6.

In spite of the cold spring and the subsequent dry weather, entries in the fruit, vegetable and flower sections were of a remarkably high standard, reflecting hard work and dedication by the growers.

The handicraft section attracted some excellent entries from some very talented people in the villages, as was also the case for the flower arranging sections.

Exhibitors in the domestic section excelled themselves, showing a high standard and finally, the children showed imagination and flair with entries in their sections. The show attracted 119 exhibitors who entered 353 exhibits.

Mary Jackson (second from left) receives a bouquet from headteacher Philip Illsley watched by, from the left, assistant county catering manager Olive Martin and catering operations manager for Suffolk County Catering Bel Tyler.

THE end of an era will dawn tomorrow at Uplands Middle School, Sudbury, when head school cook Mar, Jackson retires after 19 years service.

Mrs Jackson, who lives in Great Waldingfield with husband Derek, has three children and four grandchildren.

, March 21, 1996

End of an era as cook retires

Villager angry as trees get the chop

Appeal for witnesses

POLICE are appealing for witnesses to an accident in Great Waldingfield on Monday.

A car, believed to be a Volvo, possibly with part index number 525Y, was in collisison with two caravans in Folly Road at 12.45pm, but did not stop.

Anyone with information should contact Hadleigh Police on (01473) 383430.

Safety on call

IT is not often that I disagree with Alan Crumpton, but I think he has got it wrong over communications in the Dedham Vale.

This area is beautiful because it is still farmland and not big housing estates and industrial buildings.

Nevertheless, it is a place of work for those in the agricultural industry. They farm the land, often working alone, in potentially very dangerous conditions. Do they not deserve the same safety conditions that others work in?

Farming, in fact, is one of the most accident-prone industries. The advent of the mobile phone has been a great help to farmers and good reception in the Dedham Vale is a safety necessity.

(Mrs) E F BATES,
Rectory Road,
Great Waldingfield.

THE chopping down of some sycamore trees in the churchyard at Great Waldingfield has angered a villager who says rooks are nesting in them.

But Babergh Council who gave permission to the parochial church council to get the work done on the eight trees have said the work is essential and a matter of safety.

Ilona Northall of The Street, Great Waldingfield, said she was concerned about the birds.

"They are nesting at the moment, I don't know why the trees have to go they are lovely and add to the view."

Babergh's assistant planning chief Richard Watson said the trees are in poor condition and while some would be chopped down, others would remain and be made safer.

"New trees will be replanted so in time there will be mature trees there again but the ones there at the moment are in poor condition."

PARISHONERS in Acton and Great Waldingfield will be welcoming a new vicar in May.

The Rev Peter Liley (35) is currently curate of Exning and some Newmarket parishes. He will be inducted by the Bishop of Dunwich on May 13 at All Saints Church, Acton.

Mr Liley and his wife Sue have four children: Matthias (7) and Bethany, (5), who will both attend Acton Primary School, Simeon (4) and Joshua (2).

Originally from Ipswich, Mr Liley studied music at Liverpool University and did a teacher training course in Oxford.

He then moved back to Ipswich where he spent eight years working with computers for Eastern Electricity.

In 1990 he went to Oak Hill Theological College in North London where he trained for the ministry. He has been in Newmarket for three years.

"I am looking forward to the move, although I will miss the friends I have made in Newmarket," he said. "It will be slightly daunting taking over the parish but nonetheless challenging and I am looking forward to getting to know lots of people."

He succeeds the Rev Lawrence Pizzey, who took over as priest-in-charge of St Gregory and St Peter in Sudbury and St Mary's, Chilton, in June.

Mr Pizzey (52) has worked in the diocese of St Edmundsbury and Ipswich since he was ordained in 1967. He was vicar of Acton and Great Waldingfield for nine years.

The Rev and Mrs Peter Liley with their children, from the left, Matthias (7), Joshua (2), Simeon (4) and Bethany (5).

● *The thatched house in Great Waldingfield, near Sudbury, devastated by fire on Monday*

The blaze was in the hamlet of Upsher Green at Great Waldingfield, near Sudbury, and eight fire crews were backed up by a water bowser unit and mobile control centre as they stayed at the scene for 14 hours.

VICIOUS winds fanned flames which caused an estimated £100,000 worth of damage as a blaze tore through a pair of thatched cottages on Monday.

All is not lost

GREAT Waldingfield's rooks were certainly upset to lose the churchyard sycamores, as reported in your columns, and for artists and the general public this beauty spot is shorn of its beauty.

However, your readers will be glad to know that the rooks have taken no harm. Because of the lateness of spring, only half a dozen eggs were in the lost nests, I understand, and within a day or so the rooks were happily re-nesting.

Although we accept that the trees had to be felled, it is we, the villagers who saw them every day, who will miss those trees more than we can say.

Is there an RSPB for villagers' broken hearts?

(Mrs) SUSAN RANSON,
Lavender Cottage,
Great Waldingfield.

BOWLS CLUB

It is with great sorrow that we all heard of the death of Charles Bowers. He was the greatest character in the Club, having been a member since the Club opened. He was our oldest member, and in spite of reaching the age of 87, he played regularly, thoroughly enjoying every minute. We can all be pleased to say that the Club made the last nine years of Charlies's life very happy. The affection with which he was held was shown in the number of members who attended his funeral. He will be sadly missed and always remembered by those who knew him.

'CRIME WATCH'

Over the past few months, Gt. Waldingfield has been the target for daytime dwelling burglaries. This serves as a reminder to us all to continue to be vigilant and report anything suspicious. Anyone needing crime prevention advice or interested in starting a Neighbourhood Watch are welcome to contact me on the following numbers:

PC1113
Robbie Farrow

PARISH LIAISON OFFICER
NON URGENT ENQUIRIES - 01284 774302

SUDBURY POLICE STATION - 01284 774300

● Splendour for that special occasion: Sudbury Town Hall

Personal gifts

MAY I congratulate you on your series Barsby's Village View, in particular the article on my own village for the past 25 years, Great Waldingfield.

As co-ordinator of the church kneelers project, I would like to point out the following information: of the 80 new kneelers in the church only four of these have been donated by local organisations – bowls club, WI, girl guides and the school.

The remaining 76 were either embrodered or donated (in many cases both) by local folk or friends of the parish, some in memory of a dear one and others for just a personal interest.

ELIZABETH L ELLIS,
Toronto,
Great Waldingfield.

THIS week's Memory Lane picture was taken in Great Waldingfield around 1910 and shows children at the village school preparing for the May Day celebrations and traditional dancing round the maypole.

It was submitted by Graham Peachey, of Swan Street, Boxford.

Mr Peachey has a special reason for treasuring the picture as the May Queen, chosen by a vote in the village, was his mother, then Maggie Bird, later Maggie Peachey.

If you have a photograph that you think would be of interest to our readers send it to Memory Lane, Suffolk Free Press, Borehamgate, Sudbury, CO10 6EE.

TWO brothers are reeling after hearing they must pay up to £150,000 for their unsuccessful fight to prove a proposed hospital site is a town green.

But they refused to accept final defeat in the David and Goliath battle, which has already delayed Sudbury's £8.5 million hospital for four years.

The Appeal Court has ruled an unsuccessful bid by farmers David and Colin Steed to have 15.8 acre People's Park registered as green had been properly considered by Suffolk County Council.

The pair, who have offered alternative edge-of-town land for a hospital, must pay all the costs of the council, plus those of the Department of Health and West Suffolk Hospitals Trust.

The brothers claimed the field had been used for time immemorial by the people of the town for recreation and grazing, and should be retained as open space for the benefit of the public.

● Considering their next move: Farming brothers David and Colin Steed refuse to accept final defeat over the People's Park hospital site.

Church packed for vicar's induction

EXTRA seating had to be brought in to All Saints' Church, Acton, for the service of collation and induction of the Rev Peter Liley as incumbent of the united benefice of Acton and Great Waldingfield.

Mr Liley, his wife Susan and their four children – Matthias (7), Bethany (5), Simeon (4) and Joshua (2) – have moved to Acton from Exning, near Newmarket, where he had served for over three years.

Many of his former parishioners from Exning and Newmarket were at Acton for the service on May 13 which was conducted by the Bishop of Dunwich, the Right Rev Tim Stevens, and the Rural Dean of Sudbury, Canon Lionel Simpkins.

A reception was held afterwards in Acton village hall and the churchwardens of both parishes took the opportunity of welcoming Mr Liley and his family.

They also thanked the Rev David Rutherford and Mrs Jean Rutherford and Canon Charles Payne for serving the parishes so well since the Rev Lawrence Pizzey moved to St Gregory's at Sudbury almost a year ago.

Flower sadness

I WAS appalled to read in the Suffolk Free Press about the flowers being removed from graves at Acton and Waldingfield churches.

I too was very upset and angry on visiting the grave of my mother (who has been dead only 16 months) to find that silk flowers put on her grave for only two weeks had also been removed.

On visiting the vicar's house to discuss this matter, I asked him if he realised the pain and heartache this caused and why his predecessor did not ask for the removal of the flowers. He replied he was not responsible for his predecessor's actions but this was the rule and he would enforce it.

I pointed out that if anyone else had blatantly removed flowers from graves it would be vandalism.

It seems even if you live 70 years in a village, as my mother did – "Acton born and bred", she would say, "and proud of it" – you cannot have a few pretty silk flowers on your grave. Such a sad world.

Mrs KATHY STEELE,
11 Bantocks Road,
Great Waldingfield.

October 31, 1996 **9**

High Thatch, Great Waldingfield, gutted by fire for the second time in recent years.

IN BRIEF
Saddle stolen

THIEVES who broke into a farmhouse in Great Waldingfield last Thursday afternoon stole a leather saddle and bridle worth £500. They threw a breeze block through a window to get in, causing damage put at £50.

Stolen pig butchered

A PIG stolen from a farm was later found butchered in a ditch. Rustlers took the 12-week-old pig from Bantocks Piggery, Folly Road, Great Waldingfield, on Thursday night and butchered the animal and made off with the joints.

ACTON AND GT. WALDINGFIELD FRIENDSHIP CLUB

Unfortunately due to difficulty in finding committee members the above Club has disbanded and all funds distributed to members.

Whose birds?

SUDBURY police are looking after two birds found over the last few days.

A fully grown grey cockatiel was found in Great Waldingfield and a rosella parakeet in Great Cornard.

Anyone who thinks either of the birds might be theirs should contact Sudbury police on (01284) 774100.

Great Waldingfield Primary School. Pic. ref. 219451-10

Great Waldingfield Primary School.

The Rector and the Churchwardens would like to thank everyone who helped our Gift Day to raise over £1,000. This will be an enormous help in maintaining the Parish Church over the coming months. **Thank you.**

GREAT WALDINGFIELD CHURCHYARD

In general, Diocesan rules do not permit artificial flowers in the churchyard. However, after discussion, the following suggestions have been agreed:

Where appropriate, British Legion poppies may be left on graves during the month of November.

Christmas wreaths (comprising natural greenery but incorporating a small number of artificial flowers) may be placed on graves during December and left until the end of January. Please ensure they are removed at the end of this time.

PC **Robbie Farrow** will be responsible for Chilton and will continue to police all the villages. As parish liaison officer, PC Farrow will be responsible for all other parishes in the Sudbury police sector – Great Waldingfield, Acton, Long Melford, Stanstead, Alpheton and Glemsford.

OFF TO SPAIN: Michelle Harris.

FORMER Sudbury women's ruby team player Michelle Harris has recieved a second call up for the national team.

Michelle, 19, of Great Waldingfield, has already been a stalwart of the England students team.

Now she has won an invitation to join to England Ladies A squad for a tour of Spain starting next month.

Great Waldingfield Primary School pupils admiring their work at Sudbury Library. From left, Louise Berry (7), Kimberley King (8), Roxanne Sparkes (8), Laura King (5), Ashley Mansfield (8) and Samwise Wilson (5).

One contestant was in top hat and tails.

Hold the front page!

by RACHEL JENKINS

At the moment she is suffering what might be described as a bit of an uphill battle.

Nevertheless Pat Leathers is determined to make a success of her new role as editor of the village magazine, a post she took up only in January.

An increase in printing costs has trebled the annual subscription rate and the number of readers has dropped accordingly.

Published 10 times a year, the magazine provides an update not only on church news but also records parish council, horticultural society and WI activities, to name but a few.

And although the annual subscription rate has risen to £3 from £1 – the sum charged since the magazine was started 15 years ago – she insists it is still excellent value for money.

Although she comes from nearby Long Melford, Pat has lived in Great Waldingfield for 25 years and describes it as a wonderful place.

And although she admits collecting copy for the magazine is sometimes "a bit of a hassle", her view of the place is untainted.

"This is a wonderful village and a wonderful community," she says, a view echoed by the vicar, the Rev Peter Liley, who joined the benefice a year ago.

"Great Waldingfield has always struck me as a very happy place with a lively lot of people and plenty going on," he says.

His benefice covers both St Lawrence, Waldingfield, and the church at nearby Acton, mirroring a link between the two villages which has grown more apparent in recent years.

"A lot of organisations like the brownies and scouts are joint between the two villages and where they are not – the WI and the primary school, for instance – there are still strong links between them."

Another case in point is the open gardens and church flower festivals which tend to rotate between the two villages, year by year.

Indeed both events point to another facet of village life – its green-fingered contingent as represented by the horticultural club and the allotment holders.

The club is responsible for two annual shows and a major exhibition every five years. Anne Francis, whose husband Chris is club chairman, explained: "We're not a society as such – there's a committee and we generally get together in the run up to our spring and autumn shows to plan the schedule. Our spring show is generally very pretty with its spring flower arrangements and its children's sections. The autumn one is more about domestic produce – vegetables, handicrafts and so on."

Though the number of entries will vary from show to show, there are plenty of classes which are entered by what she describes as "a good cross section of the village".

"The shows are generally good fun and are very well supported locally."

With spring show over and done with for another year – it took place in the village hall last weekend – the next major horticultural event is the plant sale in Butcher's Meadow on May 17. Then there is the Braithwaite Trust, named in honour of two sisters who gave land to the village for use as allotments by local residents.

Under the terms of their bequest, the head of the village school and the vicar of the day must serve as secretary and chairman of the trust respectively.

But the practical business of collecting rents and liaising with the 40 allotment holders from Waldingfield and nearby Acton, falls to the overseer, Frederick Shinn.

The trustees meet twice a year – in June, when their meeting includes a tour of inspection round the various allotments and again in October.

But, according to Mr Shinn, problem tenants are a rarity. "We have to make sure the allotments are left clean and tidy on and the whole it's pretty good."

And while he accepts that the "odd one or two" let the side down and neglect their plot, others, like Tom Nice, are "first class allotment holders".

They're fit for a busy life in the village

WITH 80 bowling members and 60 social members, the Great Waldingfield Bowls Club is probably one of the largest in the village. With only one indoor lane, the club is open throughout the week, allowing its members, particularly the retired, to pop in to its headquarters at Tenterpiece during off-peak times.

Nevertheless, it is a club that spans all age groups, according to its chairman, Jean Misselbrook. "We have lots of inter-club competitions and we've won lots of trophies," she said.

"We visit other clubs occasionally and this year, for the first time, we have taken part in the Sudbury Sunday league."

The social side of things is equally important – the bar is open every evening, the six-weekly whist drives have proved popular and then there are the 10th anniversary celebrations to look forward to next January.

Meanwhile, the WI in Great Waldingfield has been going strong for 77 years, making it one of the longest established in the

county.

Its current president, Mary Jackson, joined the WI in Monks Eleigh as a teenager, transferring to the Great Waldingfield branch when she moved to the village 14 years ago. The group meets in the village hall on the first Wednesday of each month, entering federation competitions and organising the occasional theatre trip or jumble sale.

And more recently, it has launched a keep fit group for the over-50s which meets in the village hall for an hour every Monday morning.

VILLAGE VISIT

BLOOMING WONDERFUL!
Great Waldingfield Horticultural
Association members, above,
with judges at the 13th annual
show and, right, playgroup
leader Pam Wilson with some of
her young charges

WOMAN OF
LETTERS, MEN
OF LAND: Pat
Leathers, editor
of Great
Waldingfield's
Church and

Mum's the word here

Great Waldingfield Primary
School is clearly a source of
pride for the village as a
whole and other
organisations make a point
of forging links with the
youngsters.

The governing body is made
up of village people; many
elderly or retired residents
help out with reading, art and
craft projects and 90 per cent
of its 80 pupils live in
Waldingfield itself.

As a church school, many of
its major events take place at
St Lawrence's including the
annual harvest service and
the end-of-year leavers'
assembly.

But its links with the
community are wider still.
The horticultural club makes
a point of involving the
youngsters in its twice-yearly
shows; the spring event, for
example, had a "design a
family garden" competition
for them. Head teacher Joan
Garner said: "We are very
much part of the community
and the village is generally
very proud of its school."

Within the school itself one
of the latest ventures is the
gardening club, started by
dinner lady Sharon Pritchard.

The young members are
already reaping the benefits –
the daffodils planted last
autumn have just gone over.

Although the nursery unit at
Great Waldingfield Primary
School hives off many
youngsters form the age of
four, there is still room for a
village playgroup. Leader
Pam Wilson and her helpers –
Linda Manning, Eileen Swan
and Claire Dovell – hold three
sessions a week at the village
hall. Pam says: "I would say
we cater for about 30 children
altogether – from birth up to
the age of four. The
playgroup has been running
for about 27 years although
it's been a bit of a struggle in
recent times because of the
nursery voucher scheme
and we can't take
youngsters below the age of
three."

The Mother and Toddler
Group, on the other hand,
caters for younger children
and is thriving. "It's a really
nice group," says Pam. "We
provide free nappies, lotions
and cotton wool – everything
the mothers might need. And,
of course, it's a very
important social outlet for
them."

103

The bride is the daughter of Mr and Mrs K Lock of 67 Highfield Road, Sudbury, and the bridegroom is the son of Mr and Mrs R Coleman of 5 Kenyon Drive, Great Waldingfield.

Anthony Coleman & Kerry Lock

Rules on graves in your garden

AN environmental health manager has said there is no reason why someone can't be buried in their own land following the garden burial of a Great Waldingfield woman.

His comments come after news broke about how reclusive pensioner Irene Hammond (79) was recently laid to rest in a nature garden she helped create with her son Christopher.

She and Christopher lived on the outskirts of the village.

Mike Crisp at Babergh Council's environmental health department said people are not obliged to be buried in a churchyard or cemetery, although being buried in their own land needed consideration.

"Obviously if you have a tiny back garden it may not be the right thing to do, but if you have a reasonable piece of land there's no reason why someone can't be buried in it," he said.

Mr Crisp added a body must be buried at least four feet underground and away from water courses to avoid contamination.

"One thing I would say is that details of the exact position of the grave should be recorded on the property deeds to let future occupants know about it."

He explained no formal approval is needed for such a burial, although planning permission may be needed for a memorial.

"The best thing to do for anyone planning a memorial is to contact Babergh to see if they need planning permission. If it is something substantial it may need planning permission, – but if it is just a few stones and gravel that may be acceptable without permission."

Rose and Bert Witham... "We just enjoy being together."

SELWYN PRIOR

A Conservative member of Suffolk County Council since 1978, Selwyn Prior has served on highways, education, police, arts and libraries, the performance review and the fire and public protection committees. Married with five children, he has lived in Suffolk since 1940 and has also served on Bures parish council.

KEN WATKINS

Ken Watkins, who is standing for the Liberal Democrats is a former editor of the Suffolk Free Press who works in London on the international daily paper Lloyd's List. He has served on Acton Parish Council since 1991 producing the 1994 Acton village guide. Married to Judy, he has two grown up children.

GEOFFREY HULME

Labour's Geoffrey Hulme had a successful career in the higher civil service and has since been involved in research and consultancy on public finance and services. Married with two children, he joined Labour when he retired and is committed to keeping in close touch with the public through meetings and phone-ins.

Couple celebrate 50 years of 'a lovely life' together

FORMER Sudbury police sergeant Bert Witham, who spent 27 years in the Suffolk force, celebrated his golden wedding anniversary with his wife Rose on Saturday.

Albert (71) was a sergeant at Sudbury from 1966 to 1980 and earlier spent six years as Great Waldingfield's policeman.

During their time there he and Rose took such a liking to the police house they bought it when it was for sale in 1979, renaming it Copper House.

GREAT WALDINGFIELD - £165,000

A most attractive period residence enjoying a pleasant position, set back from the road. The property offers considerable charm and character with many exposed timbers. Reception hall/sitting room, attractive drawing room with inglenook fireplace, dining room, kitchen, utility, 2 ground floor cloakrooms, main bedroom with ensuite bathroom, 2 further bedrooms, shower room, gas fired central heating (untested), ample car parking space and garage, timber framed barn with pantiled roof, attractive established gardens.

Douglas Britton and Lisa Charlton

MARRIED at St Lawrence's Church, Great Waldingfield, on August 8, were Lisa Charlton and Douglas John Britton, both of Talbot Road, Sudbury.

The bride is the daughter of Ian and Gillian Charlton, of 7 Mountbatten Close, Sudbury.

The bridegroom is the son of Mr and Mrs D Britton, of 4 Bowling Green, Great Waldingfield.

PUPILS at Great Waldingfield School were pictured in family groups in this week's Memory Lane photo taken in the early thirties.

The photo was brought in by Joyce Day, née Ainger, of Cornard Road, Sudbury, who is fourth from the left in the back row.

Pictured were – back row: Tom Nice, Fred Garrod, Reg Gooday, Joyce Ainger, Phyllis Bowers, Queenie Borley, Sid Borley, Fred Nice and Ernie Weavers; middle row : Douglas Crawford, Dorothy Nice, Mary Peck, Mary Garrod, Lily Garrod, Lily Weavers, Maisie Ainger, Connie Borley, Gladys Gooday and Ethel Nice; front row: Alf Borley, Jack Peck and Doug Borley.

If you have an old photo you think will interest readers, please send it to: Memory Lane, Free Press, Borehamgate, Sudbury, CO10 6EE.

Watch out

FOUR wheels valued at £2,000 have been stolen from a Landrover Discovery parked in Whitehall Close, Great Waldingfield.

Thieves stole a Bailey Cabriolet caravan, valued at £1,000, and a red mountain bike, from Churchgate, Glemsford, last Wednesday.

Thieves broke into a house in Abbas Walk, Great Cornard, and stole a video recorder and compact discs.

Two sets of outdoor Christmas lights, valued at £100, were stolen from trees in Borehamgate Precinct, Sudbury, between December 20 and 22.

● NEXT Tuesday's organ recital at St Peter's, Sudbury, will be given by Patrick Friend, pictured above, organist and director of music at Holy Trinity, Long Melford, and artistic director of Melford Music Society.

WHILE babysitting my very young grandson today, I decided to take him for a walk, pushing the pushchair.

I set out for Great Waldingfield Church, then to Upsher Green and what I thought was a footpath back to Folly Road and then home.

Unfortunately, the footpath I thought I should take had a padlocked gate and so I walked on, and on, and on hoping that there would be another route.

Finally I ended up in Edwardstone and, in desperation knocked on a door to ask for directions. The lady of the house said I couldn't possibly walk all the way back again and insisted on getting out her car and driving me, the baby and the very muddy pushchair home.

Phillip and I thought it must have been our lucky day. Thank you very much unknown lady – you made my day.

MARY SHEPPARD,
Faraway House,
21 Lynn's Hall Close,
Great Waldingfield.

Lung cancer death blamed on asbestos.

A RETIRED company director died of lung cancer caused by breathing in asbestos despite a lifetime of office work..

Kenneth Phillips' widow Joyce told the Bury St Edmunds inquest he must have been exposed to asbestos while working in offices at factories where building work and demolition was taking place.

West Suffolk Coroner Bill Walrond recorded a verdict that Mr Phillips' cancer was an industrial disease caused by exposure to asbestos.

Mr Phillips, 67, of Chapel Close, Great Waldingfield, Sudbury, died at St Nicholas' Hospice, Bury, on March 17 this year.

●GREAT Waldingfie Primary School's Chris mas entertainment i volved the children lots of dressing up – n least this foursome, fro left, Alex May (7), Ro anne Ibbetson (6), Laure Wheeler (6) and Stua Hoggar (6).

Pam Wilson with some of the young members of First Friends at Great Waldingfield.

Pam leaves 'wonderful children' at playgroup for a new challenge

AFTER 15 years amid the paints and Play-doh a playgroup leader has decided to call it a day.

Pam Wilson, of Cornard Tye, said goodbye to the youngsters at First Friends in Great Waldingfield on Thursday morning.

"I have seen lots of faces come and go over the years. They have been so lovely and it's not something you give up lightly but the time is now right to move on and do something different," Mrs Wilson said.

"Things have changed over the years. There are an awful lot of educational things around these days. We have also brought the mothers and toddlers in."

"It is fair to say we have struggled over the years but have got over that by forward thinking."

Mrs Wilson is now to work at the other end of the age range as a carer for the elderly.

"I am looking forward to that but I am really going to miss the children; they are wonderful."

"I always said that the first time one of the children that had been here came back with their child it would be time for me to leave.

"I have to say that hasn't happened – but it can't be far off!"

Join us in our day of prayer

AGAIN I would like to ask your kind co-operation in drawing your readers' attention to the Annual Women's World Day of Prayer, which this year is being held on Friday, March 5 at 2.30pm in the United Reformed Church, School Street, Sudbury. The speaker will be Pat Bush. The evening meeting is at 7.30pm in the Friends Meeting House, Friar Street, Sudbury and the speaker will be Mrs Sue Liley.

Everyone welcome, men, women and young folk at either or both services.

Mrs ELIZABETH L ELLIS, Toronto, Great Waldingfield.

Diana 'hype': more views

MR Richard Mays shows lack of compassion in his pathetic condemnation of Princess Diana. (Letters last week).

"Most children," he writes, "were just not interested in (watching on TV) the funeral and the surrounding baggage" – what's that? And so on and so on.

However, thousands were apparently moved enough to leave their flowers and scribbled messages and teddy bears among the millions of bunches of flowers outside the Palace, as well as at the town hall in Sudbury.

I suppose he is an anti-monarchist. He even adds scornfully: "This woman did nothing more than anyone else in her position has ever done, she just got more publicity."

Happily, this is a blatantly wrong. Months ago I was in personal touch with Lord Deedes – just to quote one example – concerning the abolition of land mines. Now, because of Diana's genuine interest and horror of such dreadful weapons, there is a trust which, since her death, already stands at over £300,000, made up of small contributions of £5 to £20 from ordinary people who admired her and believed in what she was attempting to do. This money goes towards artificial limbs for all those unlucky enough – even children. Mr May – to step on a mine.

One further point: Mother Teresa did have a state funeral and people, including Diana, revered her. Like the princess herself, her body was taken for burial on a gun carriage for all the world to see.

NEVILLE ARMSTRONG,
Old School House,
Great Waldingfield.

MILLIONS of people throughout the world were shocked and very sad over the death of Princess Diana. We cannot all be wrong for loving such a lovely person, who showed so much kindness to people in need.

So I say to Richard May – If you cannot say something nice about any person then please keep quiet.

As regards Mother Teresa, whom my husband has met in person.

She was also much-loved and will be greatly missed. Hopefully she will be given the title of saint in the near future.

That was a very sad week. We lost two wonderful people – may they rest in peace. God bless them both.

K GILES,
Teacher's House,
Great Waldingfield.

ADVENTURE: A couple who met on a blind date more than 60 years ago celebrated their diamond wedding. Harold and Susie Cutts met in London where he worked at a Mayfair butcher's supplying the then Duchess of York — now the Queen Mother and she was in service in a large London house. Paths crossed when Susie's workmate persuaded her to make up a foursome and the couple have never looked back.

More than sixty years later and now in their early 80s, the Cutts live at Coronation Rise, Great Waldingfield, within a mile or two of their son, Roger, their two grand-daughters Wendy and Lorna and their two great-grandchildren, Jenny and Scott.

Picture: KEITH MINDHAM

Excellent care

QUITE frequently, we read in the Press letters of complaint about one or another part of the National Health Service – this is one to the contrary.

Recently, at the age of 72, I have had cause to spend some time in the West Suffolk Hospital, where I underwent a major operation.

The care, comfort and attention I received was excellent and I cannot thank enough my consultant, the doctors and all the nursing staff who looked after me. Nothing was too much trouble; there were clear explanations both before and after the operation, followed by a concise guide given, to help me towards a complete recovery.

I do not forget the high nursing standards of my own training hospital and it was great to find that they still exist in the West Suffolk Hospital today.

JEAN M BUTCHER,
Little Courtleigh,
Upsher Green,
Great Waldingfield.

PS: I do think that the nurses deserve to be supplied with a more attractive uniform!

A GARAGE owner is offering a £1,000 reward after a thief coolly raced off with a BMW car which was being shown to him by a salesman.

Mike Melia, of Great Waldingfield garage, came up with the offer because he said it's time the thief was "put behind bars and the key thrown away".

He believes the thief has tried similar tactics at other local garages and is warning owners and salesmen to be on the lookout for him.

The BMW 528 – registration B919 XUC – was stolen just as garage staff were preparing to close on Thursday.

The thief had already visited the garage the week before to have a look

Great Waldingfield primary school children on a nature walk with their headteacher Joan Garner.

Joyce Phillips and family would like to convey their sincere appreciation to all concerned for their kind sympathies and thoughts on the death of Ken Phillips. He is deeply missed but free from his long, painful suffering.

He is forever with us and especially in St. Lawrence Church.

1997

MESSAGE FROM NORA CLARK AND RON CROW, 11 FOLLY ROAD

We are moving to Thatcham, Berkshire to be near our family and the friends we have made through my daughter and her husband. We have lived in Great Waldingfield for 25½ years. My dear husband died nearly seven years ago. May he rest peacefully. So now we are moving on and would like to say cheerio to all our neighbours and friends. God bless you all.

It is with great regret that we note the death of two people well loved in the village.

Beryl Haclin

Beryl died recently in Norfolk aged 53 after a long illness. Before she moved she lived in Carbonels and was active in many aspects of village life. She supported the playgroup, the Friends of the School and was, for a number of years, letting secretary for the village hall. She was a foster mother, she worked for Mencap, she helped with the toy library and with the playgroup for visitors' children at Stradishall prison. In other words, if help was needed, Beryl was there, cheerful, friendly and generous. We remember her too, for her beautiful soothing Norfolk voice. We send our sympathy to Doug, their children and grandchild.

Fred Hessenthaler

Fred died in St. Nicholas Hospice, after a painful illness, aged 81. His home was in Heathway and for many years he was a familiar sight to us all whizzing along between Sudbury and the village on his racing cycle. Both he and his late wife were keen cyclists. More recently he and his good friend and neighbour Bill Green could be seen out and about on their long country walks. Both lost their wives within months of each other and their friendship became an important part of their lives.

He will be missed and we offer our condolences to his family.

DEATHS

HAXELL: Suddenly and peacefully in hospital, Edward (Ted) beloved husband of Lilian and dear dad of Tricia and father-in-law of Paul and a dear granddad to Rachel and John and a dear brother to Bill. Funeral service at St Lawrence's church, Great Waldingfield, on Friday, March 13, 1998, at 2.30pm, followed by burial. Flowers may be sent c/o Co-operative Funeral Service, Cornard Road, Sudbury.

From the Registers

6th May at 2.30pm — Funeral of William Frederick Hayes

POLICE are warning elderly folk to be on their guard after a 75-year-old woman was harassed into buying £100-worth of fish by a persistent salesman who called at her home in Great Waldingfield.

On being admitted to her home, the man simply refused to take no for an answer, went as far as filling out the pensioner's cheque for her and virtually forced her into adding her signature simply to get rid of him.

The woman, who has not been named, subsequently cancelled the cheque which resulted in a second visit from the man demanding full payment for the fish.

The woman explained that she simply did not want it and told him he could take it back whereupon a second man appeared and demanded to know why she had stopped two cheques – one of which was the one she had signed and a second, which had been stolen.

Yesterday police spokesman PC Roger Depper said the incident served as a timely reminder that elderly people should be on their guard against unsolicited door-to-door salesmen.

"Once again the elderly are being targeted, and our advice would be not to buy things on the doorsteps and certainly don't let people into your home unless they've produced satisfactory identification."

Crash leads to charge

POLICE have charged motorist Brett Doughty of Bantocks Road, Great Waldingfield, with drink-driving following a single-vehicle accident in Braithwaite Road, Great Waldingfield, early on Saturday morning.

A passenger in the Renault car, Brian Martin (19) of the Harlequin pub, Sudbury, was taken to the West Suffolk Hospital, Bury St Edmunds, with serious injuries after being thrown through the windscreen in the crash which happened at 3.40am. His condition was later said to be satisfactory.

DID YOU KNOW?

The Church gets NO direct financial help from the Government or the local Councils. Like all charities we can claim back income tax on covenanted giving and Acton Parish Council maintain the "closed" part of the Churchyard, but otherwise all the running costs of the Church (some £1,200 a month, not including repairs to the building) have to be raised by giving.

BOTTOM RIGHT: Great Waldingfield youngsters dress-up for Science Week.

GREAT WALDINGFIELD

SPRING FLOWER SHOW RESULTS: The 14th Spring Flower Show, organised by the Horticultural Show Committee, was held in the school on Saturday, April 18. The show attracted 203 exhibits from 100 exhibitors, many of the public visiting the show in the afternoon were pleasantly surprised at the high standard, bearing in mind the early warm spell followed by prolonged rain and cold winds, conditions definitely not conducive to good quality blooms.

RESULTS: **Class winners:** Anne Francis, Edna Allen, Tom Nice, Chris Francis, Mandy McCullum, Pat Highton, Doris Hamilton, Oliver Haynes, Sally Brinton, Bill Whittaker, Pat Leathers, Joan Curtis, Sheila Mead, Phoebe Heffer, Joshua Liley, Verity Butcher, Bethamy Liley, Roxanne Ibbetson, A. Sowman.

Hunt for 'funeral' raiders

THIEVES got away with around £6,000 worth of jewellery last week when they raided an elderly couple's home while they were attending a friend's funeral.

Hazel and Jim Leggett left their home in Great Waldingfield last Wednesday morning to attend the funeral in nearby Stanstead. When they arrived back at just after 2pm they were horrified to find the place had been ransacked.

Mrs Leggett said: "I was upset anyway and to find this mess was miserable. They went through every room and turned everything over.

"At first I was very angry but there is nothing you can do about it. It is the hands of the police now.

"It is not so much what was taken. It is worse that somebody has been into my home uninvited which is an absolute intrusion."

It is believed the thieves got into the house at around 12noon after breaking a downstairs window.

The perils of passive smoking

HOPEFULLY the year is still young enough for us to be thinking of new beginnings and new year resolutions. May I suggest that this year we put the issue of passive smoking high on the agenda?

The medical evidence that passive smoking is extremely bad for our health is now proven. No-one should therefore be put in the position of having to work in an indoor environment whilst inhaling other people's cigarette smoke.

The question of smoke-free areas in public places such as restaurants, clubs etc, is not so simple to resolve, but I urge everyone to campaign for more no-smoking areas.

An easy, positive way to start is to designate your own home as a no smoking house. This policy I have operated, without complications, for five years. I, personally, do not condemn smokers.

Indeed, there are many dangerous hobbies, but passive smoking must be eliminated for those who do not wish to participate.

A happy and healthy 1998 to your readers and staff.

MRS E F BATES,
"Ramla",
Rectory Road,
Great Waldingfield,
Sudbury.

Drill theft

AN electric drill, valued at £25, has been stolen from a garage in Lavenham Road, Great Waldingfield.

Thieves empty handed

THIEVES left empty handed after a spree of break-ins last Saturday night at an industrial area in Great Waldingfield.

Among the premises attacked was the bowls club in Tentree Road. Member of the club John Sparkes, who lives opposite the club, said: "At about 1.30am I saw the security light come on which I thought was a bit strange. A little later it did it again and then the alarm went off.

"Whoever it was got in by smashing a window in the ladies toilet before going into the main area of the building where the sensor must have picked them up. Luckily they didn't get away with anything because the alarm scared them off."

The would-be thieves also attempted to break into business units further up the road.

George Millings, part owner of Sudbury Tooling and Sudbury Components, said: "They tried to break into our shed where we keep heavy machinery so they would have had a hard job trying to get it away.

Joan Bell introduced Great Waldingfield to life behind the scenes in haute couture. After training she was taken on by a London fashion house just before the end of the Second World War with all work being hand done and two or three fittings for a single garment.

Regards from Mo

A WOMAN from Great Waldingfield received a personally signed letter from Northern Ireland minister Mo Mowlem.

Ann Holloway, from Holbrook Close, who is a Quaker and the secretary of Churches Together in Sudbury and District, wrote to Dr Mowlam to congratulate her on her efforts for peace in the Northern Ireland talks..

The return letter thanked Mrs Holloway for her support and encouragement. It was also personally signed "Marjorie."

Mrs Holloway said: "I wrote to Mo Mowlam because I feel she has done more than anyone to create peace in Northern Ireland.

"People have been saying that Tony Blair should get the Nobel Peace Prize but I feel it should go to her."

110

ROWING CHAMP: Peter Gostling

The Steed brothers: Were they right all along?

Open

THE GARDEN of a 16th century moated house, Chilton Hall between Sudbury and Great Waldingfield, will be open in aid of the Red Cross from 2pm on Sunday.

The home of Mr and Mrs Veryan Herbert, the house has a listed walled garden and large herbaceous borders. There will be a plant stall and teas.

Admission is £2 for adults, accompanied children free.

May 14, 1998

Never mind the quality

PROTESTERS battling to stop further quarrying in their villages are hoping poor quality of materials will stop any activity.

Villagers in Great Waldingfield, Chilton and Cornard Tye opposed the scheme which was the subject of a five-month long enquiry last year.

A report from the public inquiry described the land between the three villages as "only marginally viable".

Chilton Parish Council chairman Veryan Herbert said the minerals could not be extracted without a lot of money being spent on crushing and washing stone.

AFTER refusing to give a breath test, a Great Waldingfield man was banned by Sudbury magistrates from driving for three years.

At court on Friday, Keith Leslie Frost (50), of Alexander Drive, was also fined £160 for failing to provide a specimen of breath on September 5 after pleading guilty to the offence at an earlier hearing.

Frost was fined £250 for having no insurance as well and his licence was endorsed.

THIEVES targeted four cars parked in Great Waldingfield overnight on June 15 and 16.

Ten gallons of petrol was siphoned from a Ford Sierra parked in Badleys Close, power tools worth £1,350 were taken from a Vauxhall Astra in Coronation Rise, £50 damage was caused to the rear window of a Vauxhall Corsa van in Bantocks Road and a £500 CD-radio player was stolen from a Vauxhall Astra in Alexander Drive.

Police believe the incidents are linked.

SUDBURY'S new hospital could be back to square one after a landmark legal ruling which leaves the way open for People's Park to be registered as a town green.

A four-year battle was fought by Great Waldingfield farming brothers David and Colin Steed in a bid to keep the area as open space.

They appeared to have lost when the Court of Appeal ruled in 1996 that it could not be registered as a green but now five Law Lords have said that ruling was "wrongly decided".

AN antique wrought iron bench, valued at £200, was stolen from Red House Farm, Lavenham Road, Great Waldingfield, between midnight on Friday and 10am on Saturday.

VW haul

A £200 bumper was stolen from a black Volkswagen Golf GTi at Carnation Garage, Great Waldingfield on Sunday evening. Thieves also got away with a VW badge, Volkswagen silver lettering and a spare tyre part.

FROM THE CHURCH REGISTERS:

Baptism:

4th January at 11.15am - Matthew James Dereve

Blessing of Marriage:

28th December at 2.00pm - Simon and Norah Graves

Funerals:

23rd December at 2.00pm - Fred Borley (Burial)
17th February at 2.00pm - Roy Crisp (Cremation)
19th February at 2.00pm - Madeleine Bateman (Burial)

WOMEN'S WORLD DAY OF PRAYER

This takes place on Friday March 6th and has the theme "Who is my neighbour?" (the material has been prepared this year by Christian women from Madagascar). Services are at 2.30pm Sudbury Baptist Church (speaker, Mrs P Hulford) and 7.30pm at The Friends' Meeting House (speaker, Mrs Jean Russell).

Everyone (women, men and young people) is most welcome.

'Natural causes' verdict for former textiles worker

YEARS of working in textiles may have contributed to the heart and lung problems of a pensioner from Great Waldingfield, an inquest heard last week.

Ronald Crisp (74) of Whitehall Close, Great Waldingfield, died in February of natural causes including severe hardening of the arteries contributed to by emphysema with fibrosis.

During the inquest, West Suffolk coroner Bill Walrond heard from Mr Crisp's widow Kathleen who said doctors, who first diagnosed problems when the couple lived in London before they moved to Great Waldingfield seven years ago, suggested the silicone vapours and dust from the cloth could have contributed to her husband's poor health.

Towards the end of his life Mr Crisp had to have oxygen for up to 15 hours a day to help with his breathing and he died in West Suffolk Hospital on February 4.

Recording a verdict of death by natural causes, Mr Walrond offered Mrs Crisp his condolences. "You have my deepest sympathy. No matter how many times I do this it doesn't harden me to it." he said.

Fuel gone

THIEVES stole 200 litres of diesel fuel valued at £120 from a Volvo articulated lorry on Chilton airfield, Great Waldingfield, between 4.30pm last Wednesday and 6.30am Thursday.

Body found

THE BODY of Steven Victor Bugg (32) of Nayland was found at a house in Francis Road, Great Waldingfield, last Wednesday morning.

Police said there were no suspicious circumstances. The coroner has been informed.

Woman given oxygen

AN ELDERLY woman was given oxygen by firemen following a small fire in her bedroom in the early hours of Sunday.

Two appliances from Sudbury attended after receiving a call to Brandeston Hall, Great Waldingfield, at 12.25am.

Four firefighters used breathing apparatus to tackle the first floor bedroom blaze which left the rest of the house full of smoke.

The incident took two hours to bring under control and the woman was given oxygen after inhaling smoke.

A night to remember for Rev Lawrence

A RECTOR is "still on cloud nine" after more than 150 people turned up for a special service to celebrate his 30th year as a priest.

The two hour service, for the Rev Lawrence Pizzey, who was ordained at Bramford, near Ipswich, in 1968, was held at St Gregory's Church, Sudbury, on Tuesday evening.

Clergy from all over the country attended the service to pay tribute to Mr Pizzey. Other guests included the town mayor and councillors, and members of his congregations past and present.

Hymns were sung by St Gregory's Church Choir and by the Sudbury Choral Society.

Churchwarden Ray Smith said: "People from all the other local churches have come here tonight and so have people from all over the country. Rev Pizzey has been here three years and has become as great a friend to each and everyone of us.

"We couldn't ask for a better rector."

After a spell in teaching Mr Pizzey became a rector in West Stow in 1978. In 1985 he took over the parishes of Acton and Great Waldingfield before moving to St Gregory's in 1995.

"Coming to Sudbury was very different because my other parishes were extremely rural but it's a wonderful place to work. The people are so willing to help. I have a very supportive congregation," said Mr Pizzey.

He takes much pride in his work and says he couldn't imagine getting as much satisfaction from anything else.

He was also very pleased with the celebrations.

He said: "It was just a wonderful night, one I will never forget. I am still on cloud nine."

After the service Mr Pizzey was presented with a communal chalice and an antique clock.

Rev Lawrence Pizzey, centre, at the service to celebrate his 30th year as a priest.

LEFT: Kerrie Scott (8) and Sandra Scott (6) hand flowers to mum Morag Scott during the Mother's Day celebration at Great Waldingfield school.

MOVING ON FROM GREAT WALDINGFIELD

IN BRIEF
RSPCA charge

A FARMER from Great Waldingfield has pleaded not guilty to 19 charges of causing unnecessary suffering to a herd of cattle.

Quentin Ship, of The Heath, also denied three breaches of welfare regulations when he appeared before Bury St Edmunds magistrates last Friday.

It is alleged that Ship (57) failed to feed the livestock a wholesome diet and kept them in a building with sharp edges and without proper lighting.

The RSPCA, which has brought the prosecution, allege that Mr Ship committed the offences between autumn 1998 and February this year.

Ship will return to court for a pre-trial review on August 6.

I WOULD like to say a very sincere thankyou to all those who voted for me in the recent local elections. Although I did not secure a place on Babergh District Council, I very much enjoyed meeting people and admiring the lovely gardens at this time of year.

E FRANCES BATES,
"Ramla,"
Rectory Road,
Great Waldingfield.

Why are they rabbiting on?

IT is amazing that Great Cornard Parish Council may agree to a rabbit cull in their country park "reluctantly and under protest." Occupiers of land have certain legal responsibilities and one of these is to keep the wild rabbit population under control (by an order made under section one of the Pests Act 1954).

The order is designed to help farmers and others in their efforts to protect their crops from damage by wild rabbits. A hundred years ago the parish council would have appreciated that rabbit damaged crops could affect Cornard's bread supply. Fifty years hence we may all frighteningly be very aware of the connection between farming and food. The country park is indeed a beautiful asset to this area but if it is such a haven for wildlife, why do the rabbits venture onto neighbouring farmland? Maybe because there are too many rabbits and not enough food. If the parish council were to employ a professional pest control firm the park could be patrolled regularly and rabbits kept to sustainable numbers.

Alternatively, the parish council could at vast expense provide rabbit proof fencing around the whole of the park. For a short while this would be fine, but soon the park's flora would be depleted and the rabbits longing to get away from this particular haven to somewhere where they could get a square meal.

Mrs E F BATES,
"Ramla",
Rectory Road,
Great Waldingfield.

Cash snatch

A BURGLAR made an untidy search of a house in Great Waldingfield after getting in through an unlocked rear door.

The burglar struck between 10.20am and 12 noon last Wednesday and escaped with about £5 cash.

Brian Martin, of Braithwaite Drive, Great Waldingfield, pleaded guilty to threatening behaviour and possessing 5.7 grammes of cannabis resin worth £24.

Martin John Morris (23), Kenyon Drive, Great Waldingfield. Used a vehicle in Bantocks Road, Great Waldingfield, with no insurance. Fine £150, costs £35, banned from driving for three months, licence endorsed. Did not wear a seatbelt. No separate penalty.

Benjamin Ian Newman (18), Coronation Rise, Great Waldingfield. In Sudbury, used threatening, abusive or insulting words or behaviour. Fine £200.

Jermena Bradley (24), Chapel Close, Great Waldingfield. Used untaxed vehicle in Suffolk Road, Sudbury. Fined £20, £30 costs, back duty £62.50.

Simon James Matthews (18), Garrison Lane, Great Waldingfield. At Bantocks Road, drove vehicle having consumed excess alcohol (52 microgrammes of alcohol per 100 millilitres of breath). Disqualified for 12 months, fined £100, costs £55.

"Jack" was the Chairman of the Parish Council of Great Waldingfield for over 25 years. It was during this time that so much of the post-war development and expansion of the village took place. Heath Estate was being built at the time Jack moved into Babergh Place Farm and he saw the completion as Chairman. Subsequently, Greenacres was built together with Chestnut and Chapel Closes and Bantocks Road. It was Jack's eye as a farmer and countryman which helped the council in its deliberations over these and other planning matters.

His enthusiasm for so many village projects, his help to so many organisations and parishioners means that his memory lives on with all he helped.

My personal memories of Jack are of a kind, courteous man whom it was a pleasure to serve under and to call a friend. His sense of humour at "harvest horkeys" dressed in a countryman's smock, telling jokes and stories in a broad dialect will never be eclipsed.

Funeral and Burial

12th May: Reginald Thomas Jarvis (79 years) of Badleys Close and former Churchwarden of the Parish for over 25 years

Reg Jarvis

The following is an extract of the address given by the Rector at Reg's funeral:

Although Reg wasn't born in Gt. Waldingfield, all of us thought of him as one of the village's "Old Residents" who remembered the time before the new estate, the new school, the new Post Office, the time before the airfield changed not only the landscape but the village's outlook, the time when this Church had its own Rector resident across the way.

Actually he came here in 1940 when he married Marjorie and he'd lived here ever since; here they brought up their daughter Monica; and he chose to stay here amidst the familiar surroundings after Marjorie's death some fifteen years ago.

Reg worked all his life at Weldon's the fruit farmers and I'm told that there was not much he didn't know about apples and pears, particularly the traditional English varieties; this was a reserved occupation during the war of course, but Reg did his bit in the Home Guard.

And he contributed to the life of the village in many other ways too: for many years he was a school governor, both when it was next-door here and after it moved into the new building; he was a trustee of the Braithwaite Trust (in which capacity I first met him, as we made our annual tour of the allotments) - he was a keen gardener of course and had an allotment himself for many years; and, of course, for over twenty-five years he was a Churchwarden of this parish, seeing it through the unsettling process of being merged into the United Benefice with Acton and (at that time) Little Waldingfield; he would chime the bells before services

Good for us all

THE article on Natural Neighbours and last week's letter from Valerie Waters highlights what appears to be a very sensible idea. There must be millions of acres of garden in England and for these to be wildlife friendly enables everyone to make a positive contribution towards our environment. It is so easy to criticise the farming community for the demise of just about every living creature!

I hope people will contact Sudbury Town Council to find out more about this scheme.

Mrs E.F.Bates
Ramla
Rectory Rd
Gt. Waldingfield

Francis - Harvey

MARRIED at St Lawrence's Church in Great Waldingfield were Naomi Ellen Harvey and Glenn Edward Francis, both of Hughwoods, Colchester.

The bride, who was given away by her father, is the daughter of Len Harvey of Buxhall and Sue Ayres of Sudbury.

The bridegroom is the son of Mr and Mrs Chris Francis of Great Waldingfield.

The ceremony was conducted by the Rev Peter Liley and the bride was attended by Kerry Francis, Jenny Harvey and Emily Coulthard and the best man was David Locke.

Holy Matrimony

22nd May: Sophie Patricia Lawrenson (of the Old Rectory) and Mark William Little (of Wyck Rissington, Gloucestershire)

Ince-Hill

THE wedding took place at St Lawrence's church in Great Waldingfield of Emma Louise Hill and Lloyd Ince. The bride is the daughter of Mr and Mrs D J Hill, of Bantocks Road, Great Waldingfield, and the bridegroom is the son of Mr and Mrs R Ince of Hunts Hill, Glemsford.

The bride was attended by Emma Hobin, Amanda Jane Ring and Marc Longhurst. The best man was Philip Longhurst and Andrew Peter Hill was the usher.

Given away by her father, the bride wore a dress of heavy duchesse satin in ivory and carried a bouquet of pink and ivory roses.

(Photograph: Mike Arnold)

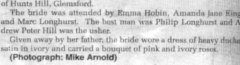

THE UNITED BENEFICE OF
ALL SAINTS, ACTON AND ST. LAWRENCE, GREAT WALDINGFIELD

VICAR / RECTOR
Rev'd Peter James Liley, BA (Hons) Dip HE
The Vicarage,
Melford Road,
Acton,
Sudbury,
Suffolk CO10 0BA

Tel. (& fax by arrangement): 01787 377287

St. Lawrence Church Gift Day - Saturday 23rd October 1999

BOWLS & SOCIAL CLUB

Chairlady	Jean Misselbrook	
Secretary	John Hughes	
Treasurer	Ron Highton	
Committee	Basil Radley	(Gents Captain)
	Mary Jackson	(Ladies Captain)
	Fred Shinn	(Social Representative)
	Kath Crisp	(Membership Representative)
	Charles Mallett	
	Pat Highton	
	Fred Smith	
	Lilian Haxell	

Habel – Chatters

Glenn Habel and Hayley Chatters were married at Great Waldingfield Church.

LAND ADJOINING RECTORY ROAD – GT WALDINGFIELD

As owners of the above field which includes the area of the proposed byway, we would like to inform local people of our feelings regarding the proposed byway No.15.

Originally we left an access at each end of the field to allow people across. Unfortunately, people have been walking with their dogs off leads allowing them to run across the field, some barking at ourselves and the horses. This alerted us to a potentially unpleasant situation occurring. We have now closed off the access awaiting the Public Inquiry, which we are advised, will be held within the next few months determining the exact location and nature of the proposed byway.

We are keen to see the proposed byway opened as Public Right of Way and placed on the definitive map, all we ask is that people exercise a little patience for an early conclusion to the current situation and whilst we realise not everyone will be happy, we hope most will.

Barry & Pat
8/2/99

The cast of Great Waldingfield Primary School's nativity play.

1999

A STEEPLEJACK has been making
emergency repairs to a village
church tower to save hav-
ing to close part of the
churchyard.

CLOSER TO HEAVEN: Steeplejack Reg Dosell scales great heights to repair
the tower of Great Waldingfield Church.
Picture ANDY ABBOTT

Poppy seller
Bill Green.

LIGHT: Mayor Nick Irwin receives his candle from Chris Martin and Ann Holloway   Photograph: ANDY ABBOTT

Light to lighten the new century

A MAYOR yesterday saw the light of the new Millennium when he received one of 4,000 candles being distributed to local homes by church workers.

A team of 70 volunteers are delivering the candles to all properties in Sudbury and Great Cornard, having raised £2,300 to cover the cost of the exercise.

Town mayor Nick Irwin was handed a candle by Chris Martin, chairman of Churches Together in Sudbury, and Ann Holloway, secretary. The initiative is part of a nationwide exercise by churches, and recipients of the candles are invited to light them in their windows just before midnight on December 31.

Each candle is accompanied with a print-out of the resolution: "Let there be respect for the earth, peace for its people, love in our lives, delight in the good, forgiveness of past wrongs and, from now, a new start." Candle packs are being given to all homes.

Churches choice

GREAT Waldingfield woman Ann Holloway has been selected to chair meetings for Suffolk Churches Together.

Mrs Holloway, who is the Quaker representative and secretary of the group's Sudbury branch, was chosen by the leaders of eight other denominations.

"As one of seven brothers and sisters who all married into different denominations, I have grown up knowing that churches do things differently," she says.

"But we can work and pray together and I believe that as fellow Christians we should not do apart things we can do together."

Peter Mark Berry, Braithwaite Drive, Great Waldingfield. Kept an untaxed vehicle in Braithwaite Drive, Great Waldingfield. Fine £100, costs £30, back duty

Allotment veteran dies

TOM Nice, a veteran of the allotments in Great Waldingfield, will be remembered by most people in the village for his kindness, cheerfulness and dedication. He died peacefully in Walnuttree Hospital on October 29, after the rapid onset of cancer, at the age of 81.

As guardian of the allotments he cycled nearly every day to tend his crops, discuss matters, advise his fellow allotment holders and say whether he agreed with the weather forecast.

He grew mammoth crops of pumpkins, cabbages, carrots, onions, lettuce and beans, and his annual hedge of sweet peas was a joy to behold.

Between 1990 and 1997 he won the challenge cup for vegetables at the annual horticultural show.

A member of an old local family, he lived all his life in the village, and worked till retirement on the farm of

Stephen Cobbold at Acton. His brother, Fred Nice, who helped devotedly to keep the village well trimmed and tidy, died in June at the age of 83.

We miss them both, and honour their service to the community.   *Bill Skinner*

A DISABLED swimmer taken seriously ill at a Sudbury gala has given Kingfisher staff and club helpers his grateful thanks for bringing him back from the brink of death.

Len Wimshurst (83), who has one leg, swam a length-long race at the Station Road pool at the yearly Avocet disabled swimming club competition on Saturday and afterwards complained of breathlessness.

Club helpers Steve Macey and Phil Moore saw he was in difficulty and helped him into the changing room.

by Jim Henderson

Len, pictured right, of Heath Estate, Great Waldingfield, said: "I was out of breath and felt dizzy and they helped me into a changing room. I don't remember much after that."

Club helper Steve (41) said: "Len had looked in trouble in the water and when he got out he looked vacant.

"In the changing room he seemed a blueish colour and he lost consciousness. We took him by wheelchair to a cubicle.

"We checked his pulse and we couldn't find it for a whole minute. Phil and I gave him three rounds of chest pressure resuscitation.

"We were so relieved when he came round. He was sick and still confused but at least he was conscious."

Pool staff backed up the pair and administered oxygen to Len and shortly afterwards Sudbury-based paramedic Andy Barlow arrived from the town's ambulance station and placed him on a monitor.

Len was taken by ambulance to West Suffolk Hospital, Bury St Edmunds, where he was kept in for observation until Tuesday.

Speaking form his home, widower Len, a keen lifelong swimmer, said: "I'm so grateful to Phil and Steve. If it wasn't for them I wouldn't be here now.

"The doctors suspect I may have had mild heart attack. I'm afraid my swimming days are over but I'll be going to see my many friends at the club every Sunday to keep in touch."

Kingfisher Leisure Pool manager Dan Lawrence said: "We are all relieved to hear Len is recovering. Our emergency medical procedures all worked well in the circumstances and I would like to thank the staff and helpers."

Recovering: Len Wimshurst

MARGARET King from Great Waldingfield has successfully completed several information technology classes at the Sudbury local learning centre of West Suffolk College.

What a gesture

A GREAT Waldingfield woman is a lot happier this week after an ornament stolen from her father's grave was replaced.

Three weeks ago the Free Press reported how Andrea Hodgkinson, of Badleys Close, had discovered a small dog-shaped ornament had been stolen from her father's grave at St Lawrence's Church.

After reading the report Chris and Tina Wiggett, of C & T Stone Ornaments, of Alpheton, offered to replace the labrador figurine.

Mrs Hodgkinson said: "My mother and me are so pleased and grateful that it has been replaced.

"They are the same people who ordered the original ornament for us. They phoned the day after the piece in the paper and asked if they could give us another one."

Tina Wiggett said: "The story touched me and I thought it would be a nice gesture to replace it."

MILLENNIUM HORTI-CULTURAL SHOW: An excellent show and was well supported by the villagers with 155 entrants.

Considering the weather the flowers, fruit and vegetables were of a good standard.

Organisers reported it was good to see the domestic section so well supported – the best ever.

Flower arranging was excellent and the number of entries was very good. The village can boast so much talent – the craft items were exceptional.

Cup winners:

David Riley for vegetables and fruit, Ronnie Dawe for flowers, Mandy Harvey for fuschias, Anne Francis for flower arranging.

Paula Barry for novice flower arranging, Mandy Harvey for handicraft, Jean Misselbrook for domestic, Jean Misselbrook for home-made wine.

Mandy Harvey for most points in handicraft, Derek Jackson G W Resident with points in vegetables and fruit, David Riley for most points in show.

Mary Jackson for best rose in show, Pat Leathers for best exhibit in show (childrens 9-12 years), Verity Butcher for The Shinn Cup (5-8 years), Ella Crawford for The Misselbrook Cup (up to 5 years).

Elizabeth Anderson for The Misselbrook Cup. Lewis Cawtheray for Best Handwriting (Geoff Chatters Cup)

The cups were presented by David Floyd, chairman of the parish council.

The barn dance in the evening went with a swing. All enjoyed a fish and chip supper and the staff of the local, the White Horse, provided the bar.

ALEXANDRA ROSE DAY

Frances Bates is pleased to report that the collection in the village raised £142. She would like to thank all who donated and especially the collectors, Jenny Haynes, Sheila Green, Janet Elmer, Helen Page, Joyce Kaye, Molly Blackwell and Mandy Harvey.

St Lawrence Church

50/50 AUCTION SALE

Saturday, 30th October

at

Gt Waldingfield Village Hall

Viewing from - 10.00 am
Sale starts - 2.00pm

May 23

Gillian Elizabeth Denman (52), of Heath Estate, Great Waldingfield. At Northern Road, Sudbury, used vehicle without necessary insurance. Fined £140, costs £35, licence endorsed six points. Used vehicle with no test certificate, fined £25. Failed to produce driving licence, fined £10.

Judith Ann Cutler (54), of Plough Cottage, Belchamp St Paul. On B1115 at Great Waldingfield, drove vehicle without due care and attention. Fined £120, costs £55, licence endorsed four points.

From the Registers

1999

Funerals 10th June: Marjorie Raine Stoker of Badleys Close
(followed by cremation at West Suffolk)
22nd June: Frederick Nice of Coronation Rise
(followed by burial in the Churchyard)
22nd June: Doris Morgan of Heath Estate
(at West Suffolk Crematorium)

NEWS FROM THE PARISH COUNCIL

meeting on 23 May 2000

Election of officers:	Chairman	Mr D J Floyd
	Vice-Chairman	Mrs J M Misselbrook
Playing field committee:	Mr R S Hogg	Mrs K A May
	Mr G C Ball	Mr W Skinner
Village Hall committee	Mr D J Floyd	Mrs J M Misselbrook
	Mr J Steele	

THE Kaye family like to do things together – especially if it involves jumping off tall buildings.

2000 will be a leap year in every sense of the word for Graham Kaye, his wife Joyce, and daughters Phillipa (15) and Robyn (14), pictured left.

The family adventure kicks off in July – nine storeys up on the roof of the maternity block at Ipswich Hospital.

All four plan to abseil down the side of the building to raise money for sufferers of cancer and Huntington's Disease.

CHILDREN'S MILLENNIUM PARTY

Saturday, 24th June 2000
2.30pm - 5.00pm

To celebrate the Millennium, Great Waldingfield Parish Council invites all children aged 13yrs and under, living in the parish of Gt Waldingfield or attending the village school, to a party on the village playing field, on Saturday 24th June. There will be free food and entertainment for the afternoon, with children's' entertainer, Uncle Ted, a bouncy castle, a disco and electric Go-Karts, plus a ball pond for the smallest children.

DEATHS

MAGUIRE - MICHAEL JOHN "Mick" aged 48 years. Passed away peacefully on May 31, 2000. Devoted Husband to Glenda and loving Father to Amy also a much loved Brother to Maureen, Colleen, Roger and Philip. Mick will be sadly missed by all who know him. Service to take place on Friday, June 9, St. Lawrence Church, Gt. Waldingfield, followed by Interment service at 2.00pm.

HAYES - NORA, peacefully on July 4 at Walnuttree Hospital, Mother of June and Pauline, devoted Grandma and Great Grandma. Funeral service on Friday July 14 at St. Lawrence Church, Gt. Waldingfield at 1pm. Family flowers only please, if desired, donations for St. Lawrence Church may be left at the Church or sent to W. A. Deacon, Funeral Services, Norman Way, Lavenham. CO10 9PY.

CARTER - DAISY passed away peacefully on September 9, 2000 aged 78 years. Dearly beloved Wife of Donald much loved Mum of Glen. Funeral Service to take place at Great Waldingfield Church on Friday September 15, 2000 at 2.30pm followed by cremation at the West Suffolk Crematorium. No flowers by request please but donations if desired to the volunteer association of the Blind (Sudbury Branch) c/o Co-Operative Funeral Service, Cornard Road, Sudbury.

WHITTAKER ALAN (Bill)

Aged 65 years Passed away unexpectedly on Tuesday, September 26, 2000. A very much loved Husband, Dad and Grandad. Funeral service to take place at Great Waldingfield Church on Friday, October 6. 2000 at 2.00pm followed by interment. Family flowers only please, but donations if desired to Papworth Hospital may be sent c/o Co-operative Funeral Service, Cornard Road, Sudbury.

St Lawrence Church

Annual Plant Sale

Saturday 13th May
Gt Waldingfield Village Hall
From 8.30am

Chance to own gift sent by Queen Mother

A VILLAGE flower festival will be a regal occasion after a personal donation from the Queen Mother.

A vase given by the Queen Mum will be a major feature of Great Waldingfield Flower Festival.

The event is being held to raise funds for a £240,000 restoration scheme at the village's St Lawrence Church.

St Lawrence Church

Flower Festival

Saturday 23rd, Sunday 24th September
in St Lawrence Church
from 10.00am each day

GIFT FROM THE QUEEN MOTHER: Jean Misselbrook with the engraved crystal vase, which will go to help the Great Waldingfield church tower appeal
Photograph: KEITH MINDHAM

BARN DANCE

in the Marquee

Dancing to the "BONNY MILLER BAND"
Saturday 15th July 2000
8 pm

Licensed Bar applied for
Tickets £5 ~ to include a Fish & Chip Supper
[Children under 14 years ~ £2.50]

Saw point

A MAKITA chainsaw, valued at £200, was stolen from a barn in Badley Road, Great Waldingfield, overnight on Saturday.

C O Munson, Folly Road, Great Waldingfield. Failed to pay income tax, year 1998-99. Ordered to pay £504.86.

Paul Denman (19), Heath Estate, Great Waldingfield. Drove on Prospect Hill, Great Cornard, without due care and attention. Fine £150, costs £200, licence endorsed 8 points.

Stacey Kenneth Brewster (23), 2 Badleys Close, Great Waldingfield. Drove a car in Great Eastern Road, Sudbury, having drunk excess alcohol – 58 microgrammes of alcohol per 100 millilitres of breath, when the legal limit is 35 microgrammes. Fine £135, costs £55.

Melissa Ann Frost (25), Bantocks Road, Great Waldingfield. In Gregory Street, Sudbury, used a vehicle without insurance. Fine £175, costs £35, licence endorsed six points. Failed to produce driving licence. No separate penalty.

Zoe McPherson (25), of Lynns Hall Close, Great Waldingfield. No TV licence. Fined £90, costs £45.

Marella Parker (24), Folly Road, Great Waldingfield. Failed to notify change of vehicle keeper. Fine £50, costs £45.

Shaun Anthony Jacobs (19), of Bantocks Road, Great Waldingfield. At Sudbury, assaulted Gary Rose by beating. Dismissed – no evidence offered. Bound over in the sum of £250 for 12 months to keep the peace.

Reverend Peter Liley writes ...

Just a note to thank everyone who contributed to the "farewell" presents and parties we were given before we left at the end of July. The picture of Sproughton Mill by Winnie Hannrahan is gorgeous, the book-tokens will be most useful and some of the money has already been used to buy one of the robes I need for services in my new Church. It was lovely to see so many friends both at the evening party in Gt Waldingfield and at the afternoon Tea in Acton. We greatly appreciated your kindness - once again, thank you.

The Parish Council and St Lawrence Church invite all Senior Citizens to the

MILLENNIUM CHRISTMAS PARTY
Sunday 3rd December
4.00pm
Village Hall

There will be good food and entertainment.

Forms will be sent round soon for you to fill in and return to the post office

Festival stalwart dies

FRIENDS, colleagues and ex-pupils will be saddened to learn of the death of Tom Wells on the August 20, aged 90. He was buried at Holywell Row Methodist Church, not far from Isleham, where he was born and brought up.

Tom will be remembered for a life dedicated to education and furthering the musical abilities of children in the Clare and Sudbury area. He was headmaster of Clare Primary school in the days before the three-tier system of schooling in Suffolk. While living in Great Waldingfield, he also directed the parish church choir there for many years.

Together with Joy, his wife, and a small group of Clare people, the Clare Music Festival was formed. Forty-four years later, this has now become the Sudbury Festival of Music, Speech and Dance, an annual event.

From 1981-1991, Tom was president of the Festival and on moving from the area, he became President Emeritus. He retained a lively interest and donated the Joy Wells Piano Trophy in memory of his late wife.

Many young people have benefited from competing in the Festival over the years and Tom was always interested in the progress of those prizewinners who went on to a musical career.

For the last few years, Tom Wells was a resident of Charterhouse in London (his son Robin is Director of Music at Charterhouse School), living in the community of Brothers. Here he pursued his love of history, researching the life of Charterhouse. He always welcomed visitors from the Sudbury area to talk about people and places he had known.

Representatives from the Clare area and the Festival were present at the funeral.

Golden Jubilee Celebrations

We, as a lane, did celebrate the Jubilee Bank Holiday. We had a barbecue and music on June 4th. Everyone in the lane who was in residence on the day and had family and friends staying was made welcome at the party in Garrison Lane. There was a real feeling of community. We all supplied dishes of food, wine and beer and of course food for the barbecue.

We had a 'Guess the Baby' photo challenge. We also held a raffle and raised £50 for Barnardo's.

M Harvey

The really bad news is that we are going to lose Chris and Stuart from the village shop to Woodbridge. They have given us nearly eight years of splendid service. We on the newsletter are grateful for their support. They have helped our income by advertising and provided us with the opportunity to sell the magazine in the shop. If there was any way they could help us they did. We shall miss them. Good luck Chris and Stuart.

David and Norma Chambers will be celebrating their Ruby Wedding on March 11th. We hear there will be a blessing and re-taking of their vows at our church with a reception afterwards. Sincere congratulations you both and to **Reverend David and Jean Rutherford** who will celebrate fifty years of marriage with a thanksgiving service on 24th March at Acton parish church.

Weekend Thought
by Godfrey C Miller

WHEN people are held hostage, they are saved from despair by hope. Hope that a deal will be done or that they will be rescued.

Others handle serious illness, great loss or deep sadness, in the hope that science, or, someone out there, will come along with the answers.

It is heart-rending to occasionally meet people who have lost all hope and nothing seems to comfort them any longer.

Christians speak of their hope in the living God. They use the word hope not in the sense of uncertainty, but in that reality not yet realised. For example, the pioneers in America heading west in the 19th century could say that their hope was California... they did not mean they hoped the place existed, only that it was a reality yet to be experienced.

Hope beats eternal in the heart of every Christian. He knows that the God of miracles can step into his situation at any time and bring help. Then with eternity in mind, the best is yet to be.

"May the God of hope fill you with all joy and peace in believing so that by the power of the Holy Spirit, you may abound in hope." (St Paul)

St Lawrence Church

50/50 Auction Sale

Saturday 20th October
Viewing from 10.00am
Sale 2.00pm
Ploughman's lunches

If you have anything to put in the sale, we must have items by 10th October at the latest, to give us time to lot and catalogue them. Please come along and enjoy the day - it's very interesting and exciting

---

Consider the alternative

EVERYONE in Sudbury and the surrounding villages wants a new, adequate and well-sited hospital.

Many peole are not happy about the use of Harp Close Meadow as a suitable site. Too many of the green spaces in the town are being swallowed up into intensive housing.

There is already an increasing traffic problem from Waldingfield Road into Sudbury. This will be aggravated by the proposed building programme on the Chilton Estate, and the subsequent increased number of commuters by rail to London. Local residents resent losing the peace or People's Park.

The Steed brothers have spent over £200,000 trying to save the park for the amenity of the people in Sudbury. Their free offer of land as an alternative site should be considered.

The health authority has already recovered the £850,000 they have paid for Harp Close Meadow by selling it for luxury housing unwanted by Sudbury citizens. It is a tragedy that the health authority cannot afford to finance the new hospital, limited though are the facilities it will offer. Time may be lost waiting for private capital to turn up.

Perhaps it would speed the hospital building if the health authority accepted the generous offer from the Steed brothers for the proposed site off Newton Road.

This would avoid the traffic implications of People's Park, and be more accessible to the road system. It would also be a more peaceful and environmentally healthy scene, and need set no precedent for more development in Cornard.

Stop the delay, accept the Steeds' offer, get the planning permission, transfer the plans and cut the bureaucracy. Let us have the hospital, with room to expand if necessary.

People's Park can be developed into a Millennium Park, of which Sudbury could be proud.

BILL SKINNER
Garrison Cottage
Great Waldingfield

The Steed brothers, Colin and David.

JOHN EGGBY

Passed away after a brief fight against cancer on 5th November 2001 in St Nicholas Hospice.

Much loved husband of Pam and father of Jason and Matt. He will be greatly missed by family and friends.

Funeral service at the church of St. Lawrence, Great Waldingfield, on Monday 12th November at 2pm, followed by cremation at West Suffolk crematorium.

Flowers or donations for 'St Nicholas Hospice' may be sent to W A Deacon Funeral Services, Norman Way, Lavenham, CO10 9PY.

ALAN WHITTAKER (Bill)

In loving memory of a dear Husband, Dad and Grandad Who died on September 26, 2000

Always in our thoughts. Forever in our hearts

From your Wife Shirley and Children Graham, Nigel, Janet and Partners. Grandchildren James, Dawn and William

BULLARD - ALFRED REGINALD (Alf). Suddenly at home on February 16, 2001, aged 69 years. Sadly missed by his Wife Bet and his children John, Kath, Margaret and James. Father-in-Law of Sarah, Ken, Jane and Michael, dearly loved Grandad and Great Grandad. Funeral service at St. Lawrence Church, Gt. Waldingfield at 3.00pm on Friday, February 23, 2001. Family flowers only, donations, if desired to Ward F7 West Suffolk Hospital c/o Brown, Fenn and Parker, 37 North Street, Sudbury CO10 6RD.

Youth thanks

I WANT to congratulate a large group of young people who, during the summer holidays, worked long and hard to redecorate and refurbish the Eden's Youth Project premises.

Led by Vron Shears and Paul Tamsett they stripped, scrubbed, painted and shifted furniture achieving a different look to the cafebars and cellar.

It is, I know, a really cool place to be!

Many hours of hard work and planning have gone into this facelift and it is good to report on sterling work done by young people — well done to all concerned.

ANN HOLLOWAY
8 Holbrook Close
Great Waldingfield

Leisure.

"Leisure is sweet when it follows work well done" - so said the caption on my bingo card. Bingo is a means of leisure, but how did our forebears make use of their free time - Did they have any? It seems to me that their days were fully occupied with their employment, (sometimes as serfs and slaves) their homes, families and small patches of land, the spinning and the weaving of cloth and the dying of the same cloth. Garments had to be made, for there were no shops and money as we know it to-day. Food had to be hunted for and predators kept from the door. Kindling had to be found to warm their caves and later their huts. Perhaps some of these chores were their way of spending their leisure time!

Let me leave our ancient forebears and delve a little into the the leisure of the Tudors - the Regency period, the Victorians the Edwardians, and on to the present day.

The Tudors had little leisure at Court although most of the day was spent in leisurely pursuit. During the afternoon they would hunt and joust and during the evening they would attend balls and pageants. Dancing was not as it is to-day. The Pavane and Courante were graceful and gliding, with controlled movement and then later - the Italian Galliarde - lively, and the only one of the Tudor period, danced bareheaded.

Ladies of the Court spent their days sewing or attending the Queen and leisure time was limited to a very short morning period. Servants had long days. After putting "masters" and "mistresses" to bed in the small hours, their work commenced again at cock-crow. Poorer folk toiled all day with perhaps an evening "break" at the local town.

With little change, during the Regency period rich people visited Bath and Harrogate to partake of the waters, and Brighton became famous because of its association with the Prince Regent.

The Victoria era produced other "leisure time" ideas. My mother — a town mouse — worked as a bookbinder, but the tales relating to her free time used to fascinate my brothers sisters and myself. She was an excellent seamstress but above this she loved to walk out and watch the folk entering Drury Lane Theatre and The Opera House in Covent Garden. Many hours she spent strolling through the Strand to Charing Cross, and to the Thames Embankment. Like a good many town and provincial people she was able to visit the music-hall, which at that time was coming in to its own.

And now the countryfolk of the Victorian-Edwardian era? Farmworkers laboured long even when work commenced at 8 years of age. There were many destitute children, perhaps leisure time was spent in stealing. Travel was by horse and coach, the coach stopping at some fine hostelry. The railways were beginning to spread their network, and many people could not afford the fares. Many plodded miles to one or the other of the ancient chartered fairs. Others visited the taverns. Harvest horkeys provided the social occasion.

Countryfolk gathered wood for fuel, picked fruits and nuts from the hedgerows. They gathered sheeps wool for spinning and weaving into cloth. They collected lichens and other (natural) ingredients for dye making.

The well-to-do would have spent their leisure time at parties, hunt balls, musical evenings and perhaps poetry reading. The daughters of the house learnt fine sewing and household management.

How do we, the new Elizabethans enjoy our leisure? Working hours are shorter. Some people even manage two jobs. From those around us we can deduct how they use their free time - Let me go back a little in time - As a teenager in the late thirties I learned to ride a bicycle, and found that cycling was an excellent way of enjoying my leisure time - With friends I was able to explore much of the Surrey countryside - alas the war stopped a lot of this. We did not dare venture too far for fear of being caught in an air-raid. Then free time was spent knitting for ourselves and the troops, firewatching and other voluntary work that was available.

Coming back to to-day - we still have the cinema, which, although in the decline for several years can still attract an audience. The theatres are thriving, but gone are the days when a theatre outing was great fun - one had to queue for a gallery seat or hire a seat on the pavement, whilst awaiting the theatre to open.

Perhaps one of the greatest inventions of our time is the motorcar. Many families own a car. A trip to the seaside or the country is their way of spending their leisure time. Do they really enjoy it? Roads are full of vehicles fuming to get to their destination, and instead of a leisurely drive it becomes one of frustration.

The youngsters seem able to fill up leisure time - Youngsters always did! They have a freedom unknown ever before. Their kind of music does not appeal to all but they adore it. It is heartening to see many enjoying the works of the great composers. Many join youth organizations and spend happy hours learning fresh skills and aiding people. Sport is appreciated by nearly all – live or televised!

Older people probably still work at leisurely skills that they learned in their youth. I still enjoy walking, cycling and working on my patchwork, a craft I learned as a small girl.

What of to-morrow? Working hours will be shorter. Will we carry on much the same as to-day? Who knows?

Oct
1972

Keep mum about this lot, boys!

GET a load of these Legs XI! They are mums of youngsters who played for Great Waldingfield Under 11s in October, 1972.

The mums played the boys for fun but Mrs Shirley Whittaker – who loaned us the picture and is circled third from left – cannot remember the score.

12

Delegates at the West Suffolk Women's Institutes seen at their annual meeting in the Athenaeum, Bury St. Edmunds, yesterday.

Bring back the death penalty call by WI

EAST ANGLIAN DAILY TIMES 4·5·72

MURDERERS who plan their crime should suffer the death penalty, West Suffolk WI members agreed yesterday at the county's annual meeting in Bury St. Edmunds.

Mrs. Sybil Lucking, also from Bures WI, disagreed, saying capital punishment was too final a solution. She suggested longer and more severe prison sentences.

● A resolution by Mrs. Jean Gibbs for compulsory chicken inspection was carried.

Speaking for Stanton WI, she claimed that Bury — one of the few authorities which inspects poultry—had condemned 139,000 birds as unfit for human consumption in the past two years.

Also passed was a resolution to stamp the date on prepacked perishable goods and that the Government should reconsider abolishing the need to print the country of origin on goods.

Members also urged that water boards should de-salt sea water rather than flood land with reservoirs.

● Women's Institute members must campaign for West Suffolk's conservation, urged county chairman Mrs. Mary Wheeler at the county group's annual meeting yesterday.

Damage was being done by "enormous container vehicles hurtling through on roads originally built for the horse and cart."

She urged members to take stock of what must be saved or recorded — a village green or pond, a footpath or a flint wall, local crafts or customs, or a rubbish dump cleared.

"Prison alone is not sufficient deterrent," claimed the proposer, Mrs. Margaret Hitchcock of Bures.

"The aim of this resolution is to try to make the world a little safer to get about in."

Mrs. Hitchcock suggested euthanasia as a possible substitute for hanging. Capital punishment should be brought back for such armed crimes as kidnapping or hi-jacking, she said.

"Are not light sentences an incentive to potential murderers?" she asked.

"Is there more sympathy for murderers than for their victims? Did we do away with the death penalty too soon?"

UPSHER GREEN £235,000

A SUBSTANTIAL DETACHED BUNGALOW IN SWEEPING GARDENS WITH
POTENTIAL SELF-CONTAINED ANNEXE

Comprising 2 halls, sitting room, dining room, kitchen,
up to 5 bedrooms, 2 bathrooms, double garage, double glazing.

GREAT WALDINGFIELD £225,000

A WELL PRESENTED DETACHED BUNGALOW WITH GOOD SIZED
GARDENS, AND A COMMERCIAL BUILDING AND YARD WITH
ESTABLISHED MOTOR GARAGE/VEHICLE RECOVERY USE

Bungalow with porch, hall, sitting room, kitchen/dining room, utility,
2 bedrooms, bathroom, UPVC windows, gas c/h, garden. Office building
workshops with office cloakroom, with extensive apparecage vehicle compound.

OLD GREAT WALDINGFIELD £299,000

A LARGE GRADE II LISTED DETACHED HOUSE, AT THE END OF A TINY
COUNTRY LANE IN 0.5 ACRES

Entrance lobby, 19' sitting room, garden room, 21' dining room, 21' x 20', kitchen/breakfast
room, pantry, cloakroom, potential further room, six large bedrooms, garage and parking,
wonderful English country garden, stunning views.

2001

GREAT WALDINGFIELD £119,000

A PLEASANT AND WELL SITED DETACHED BUNGALOW, OPPOSITE A
SMALL GREEN AWAY FROM BUSY TRAFFIC

Covered porchway, hall, sitting/dining room, kitchen/breakfast
room, conservatory, 2 bedrooms, bathroom, garage and further
parking, uPVC windows, gas c/h, private south facing garden.

GT WALDINGFIELD

Sudbury 3 miles

A superb character house of considerable style. 2 receptions, 28ft kitchen/living room and utility/cloaks.
4 bedrooms, 2 with en-suites and family bathroom.
In all 0.47 acres.

£325,000

Solving problems

IF your garden is posing a thorny problem you could find the answer in Great Waldingfield next week.

A panel of local experts will be on hand to help at a gardeners' question time session in the village hall on Friday, February 22.

Waldingfield's horticultural show committee will be answering queries from 8pm. Tickets cost £5 and include wine and nibbles.

Proceeds will go to the village's Jubilee show on August 10. Further details are available from John Hughes on (01787) 378342.

March 1

Mandy Louise McGin (27), Bantocks Road, Great Waldingfield. At Sudbury Post Office, for the purposes of obtaining benefit, falsely claimed that she had done no work – paid or unpaid – when she was working for Catchpole Court nursing home. Twelve similar offences admitted and asked to be taken into consideration. Fined £200.

Court, July 7

points.
George Barr (32), Bantocks Road, Great Waldingfield. At B1115 road, Monks Eleigh, drove a motor vehicle without insurance. Fined £75, six penalty points.

Sharon Barr (36) of Bantocks Road, Great Waldingfield. Assaulted PC Gary Skinner at Great Waldingfield, a constable in the execution of his duty. Community order for 18 months with supervision requirement. Ordered to pay £50 compensation and £50 costs.

Council says sorry over tax demand for THREE pence

0108-299-8

LAST REMINDER
UNPAID COUNCIL TAX

This notice relates to:

Heath Estate Great Waldingfield Sudbury

At close of business on 16/08/2001 your Council Tax account was in arrears by £0.03

You now need to pay that amount by 31/08/01. If you do not, you may lose your right to pay by instalments.

Please read the notes below, they explain what happens if you do not pay on time. We must by law give you this information.

by Steve McKenna

BABERGH Council has said sorry after accidentally sending a letter to a pensioner warning her that she owed THREE pence in council tax.

When Sheila Mead (65) received the two-page "final warning" telling her to pay up, she called the Free Press to complain, labelling it as "stupid, petty and ridiculous".

After we alerted Babergh to the case, the council moved to apologise and said it usually operated a common-sense policy where tiny payments are concerned.

Mrs Mead, who lives with her husband Derek on the Heath Estate in Great Waldingfield, pays her council tax bill in monthly instalments, either by cheque or over the counter at Babergh's offices in Hadleigh.

"I pay the same amount every month so I couldn't see how I owed anything," she said. "But even if I did, is it really worth sending out letters telling people they've got to pay such a tiny amount?

"A computer may have found this error but it would have taken staff time to print the letter, put it in an envelope, put a stamp on it and post it.

"This all takes time and money and I want to bring this to people's attention. I'm probably not the only one who's got a letter like this."

After investigating the matter, a Babergh spokesman said: "Our computer system normally sifts through payments and any overdue bills are printed out to be looked at manually.

"We operate a common-sense policy on lower limits where amounts which fall below a particular watershed are not pursued.

"This case should have been spotted, but it was missed and we are sorry for this."

Mrs Mead said: "Babergh offered us an apology and we are happy to accept it. Hopefully this sort of thing won't happen again."

Paperwork: Sheila and Derek Mead with their final demand for three pence council tax.

GREAT WALDINGFIELD WI

At our first meeting of the year we were given an insight into what will surely be our last ceremony - Mrs Melanie Hunnibal, funeral director, gave a talk about her career entitled 'It's a funny job for a woman'. Perhaps you thought of them as undertakers, but nowadays their functions include arranging the appropriate type of funeral for each person, counselling, floral tributes and more. There are more aspects to the business than we realised with many more people requesting green burials, incorporating modern music into the services and other religious requirements to be observed.

Next month on Wednesday 6th February at 2.00pm we will welcome Mr David Floyd, Chairman of Great Waldingfield Parish Council to talk about the workings of the Council which should be of interest of everyone.

What about waste?

RECENTLY a group of us visited the recycling unit at Great Blakenham run by Viridor.

After the initial shock of realising how much rubbish we humans do produce we then concentrated on the sophisticated, expensive machinery used for sorting.

We saw the materials suitable for recycling reduced in size and stored in square, moveable blocks.

Plastic containers and plastic bags are sent to China to be made into plastic bags.

We saw our pink plastic bags but realised that many are wasted because of the system of collection.

It would greatly help Viridor and Babergh to reach the recommended 20 per cent recycling target if these bags could be collected separately.

This would probably require an extra vehicle to be on the road but it must be worth the cost in the long run.

We cannot continue to bury so much rubbish.

The arrival of Sort It through our letterbox helped us understand the problems even more, so thank you to Babergh for producing this newsletter.

MRS FRANCES BATES
Ramla
Rectory Road
Great Waldingfield

TOT SAVED

Rescued: Natalie Roberts.

by Nick Wells

A HEROIC father plunged into icy cold waters to save his four-year-old daughter from drowning, after a day out turned into a nightmare.

Quick-thinking Les Roberts leapt into action after daughter Natalie fell into six feet of water during a day out in Norfolk.

His move prevented a possible tragedy, but now the Roberts family from Alexandra Drive, Great Waldingfield, want to warn other parents of the potential dangers.

The furious family is demanding that immediate safety measures be taken to ensure no-one else is put at risk in future.

It was on Sunday when Les and Liza Roberts took their three daughters Jessika (7), Natalie (4) and Lucy (1), on what was supposed to be a relaxing day out in Norfolk.

After hiring a boat in Wroxham they went to see the Broadland Conservation Centre in nearby Ranworth and on their return the drama unfolded.

Mrs Roberts explained: "Jessika and Natalie were slightly in front of us and went out of view for literally seconds.

"We were just coming around the corner when we heard Jessika shout that Natalie was in the water and we could see her hanging onto a branch.

The spot where the incident happened.

"My husband ran down and jumped off the jetty into the water.

"He only expected to get wet upto his knees, but it was six feet deep. Les dragged her out of the water but needed help to get out himself.

"It was absolutely terrifying. I just can't get the look on Jessika's face out of my head when I first saw her in the water.

"I really thought I had come out with three daughters and would be going home with two."

She said Natalie was terrified at the time but was feeling better and saw it as a bit of an adventure.

But her husband was still very bitter and angry that it had happened at all.

The Roberts family now want to warn other families of the potential dangers of the area, and want to see safety measures taken to prevent any similar incidents.

David John Muddimer (26), Brandeston Close, Great Waldingfield. At the school fields by Acton Lane, Sudbury, was in possession of a lump of cannabis resin and a joint containing cannabis resin. Conditionally discharged for 12 months, costs £55. Magistrates also ordered that the drugs be destroyed.

WALDINGFIELD'S HEAVY PRICE
THE VILLAGE CONTRIBUTION TO THE GREAT WAR

St Vitus day, 28th June 1914. Events that happened many miles away in the Bosnian capital of Sarajevo would be the "first domino" in the chain of events that would catapult Europe into the war. The bloody murder of Archduke Franz Ferdinand and his wife had fearful consequences for the men of our village.

In that bright morning I wonder if a shiver ran down the spine of the farm labourers on their walk to work. Perhaps the crowd that strolled out from Upsher Green were a little quieter than usual. Young men like Albert Day and the King brothers, Walter and Peter. Charles Bird, a smallholder who lived at the Compasses public house, may have sat up in bed and rubbed his aching neck after a night of broken sleep. In Owl Cottage, the home of the Eadys, the old lady had noticed an unusual silence from her sons as they sat for breakfast. Further down the "Street" from Gooday, the blacksmith, to Lean, the wheelwright, people felt a little uneasy, as if something was on the horizon. The Reverend Francis Braithwaite had the rare opportunity of having three of his eldest children staying with him that week and for an inexplicable reason found himself standing at their bedroom doors and watching them sleeping. Mary Ann Bowers of the Heath, whilst cleaning her range, sat back for a moment and thought of her sons, Fosker and Nicholsen, rapidly now growing from boys to men. A big Waldingfield family, the Bowers, with cousins, uncles and aunts scattered throughout the village, and old Elijah Bowers, the head of the family, still alive and going strong down at Upsher; yes, a big family those Bowers.

Of the eight lads who served, five were killed, one was captured and Norris was reported missing on 21st March 1918. Other families suffered too. The Day boys, Albert, killed in action, Belgium, 21st August 1917, aged 28. His brother, Alfred, killed seven months later in France, aged 28. He was wounded and then just got swallowed up by the mud, along with thousands of others who have no known grave and are now commemorated on the Arras Memorial, Pas de Calais.

Readers, over the next few months I hope to tell you of our World War One campaign. I shall dramatise the events, tell you their individual stories and let you know everything I have discovered about their lives. I admit some of it won't be cheerful bedtime reading but the tales must be told. Just eighty-two years after the conclusion of this terrible war the mists of time are already starting to cloud over these events. Various families have moved away. Sometimes the surname has just died out in the locality. An appeal for information in the local papers brought a very poor response with leads on only four of the names mentioned on our memorial. But if there is one thing I've learned from my other hobby of metal-detecting, it's that perseverance pays.

FOOTPATH FOCUS

Action - The Glebe Footpath   For several months now, the Old Way/Roman Road (between Rectory Road and the lane to Upsher Green) has been open - thanks in no small way to those who filled in user evidence forms to support the reopening of this old cart-track.

Last summer the first step was taken in starting the same procedure for the higher and drier footpath on the former Glebe field, a few yards away along the north side of the Old Way: we sent the formal application for this path to be declared public in to the County Council. Now we need all former users of the path, if they generously would, to fill in an evidence form as before. The more the years of usage described, the stronger the case will be, so long-term and very long-term use is highly important, in fact indispensable. However, in addition, a large number of replies, even if shorter-term, will also be proof of past public use. All completed forms will be valuable.

Copies of the forms are with me now. Please ring me or write to me and I will send you one, together with a map of the exact path we are defending this time. Also included will be a stamped return envelope - the village needs your help in this.

P.S. You have far-flung or even not so far-flung family or friends who may not see this page? Send them a photocopy or give them my phone number and they may want to help too. Thanks.

Susan Ranson   (Tel. 01787 372471)
Lavender Cottage, Great Waldingfield, Sudbury. CQ10 0TN

Gladys Snell

At her funeral the Rector said the following:

It seems to me that, over the last couple of years we have buried most of the "Old Villagers" who were born here and lived here and remembered the place before the Second War, the Airfield and the more recent housing developments (Ted, Fred, Tom and now Gladys): and it is sad that a whole block of memories of those days and those ways are slipping away.

For Gladys was born in Gt. Waldingfield - her father was the last village Smith, and had the old forge just around the corner from the Church; and she lived most of her life in the parish, (here, in a prefab, in Upsher Green) until she took the difficult decision to move to a more suitable home, which was more conveniently located in Sudbury, some fifteen years ago.

During the War Gladys served in the R.A.F. and was a telephonist with the "Dambusters" squadron; and whilst in the Air Force she met and married Robert. They had four sons (Les, Derek, Ray and Gordon). Sadly, Robert died somewhat prematurely and left Gladys with two of the boys still at school, so she had to work part-time as a cleaner to make ends meet.

Gladys attended the old school next-door to the Church as a child, and later in life would play the piano at concerts there

Remembering Fred Nice

Fred died in the West Suffolk Hospital on Saturday, 12th June, aged 83. He had suffered ill health for nearly four years.

Born in Gt Waldingfield in 1916, he lived here all his life and was only away doing army service. In his younger days he was a very fit man and did a lot of long distance running for the army as well as boxing. He always said his happiest times were in pre-war India. He served and saw action in many countries during the war and, because of his fitness, was transferred to the elite Parachute Regiment where he reached the rank of sergeant. While in Burma he was captured by the Japanese, but made a daring escape into the jungle. He found his way back to the British lines after several days. This was an experience that left him with nightmares many years after the war.

He came home to Waldingfield with his wife, Florence, whom he met during the evacuation of Malta. He leaves his wife, three sons and two daughters. When Fred died a part of old Waldingfield went with him, the likes of which we will never see again. We will miss him.

GREAT WALDINGFIELD

In October we visited Wattisham Air Base where we learned some of the difficulties involved in the everyday running of the bases and rescues performed. How exciting also to be on the Base when one of the Sea Kings returned from a call-out, although we were certainly deafened and windswept! Later in the month Mr Barry Wall gave us a fascinating talk on the history of the village and surroundings. All sorts of information was revealed and in fact I am sure we have all got even more questions to put to him. We were particularly intrigued by all the bunting that was produced in the homes of Great Waldingfield to be exported all over the world.

June 28
Colin Bracewell (68), Lavenham Road, Great Waldingfield. At Tudor Road, Sudbury, exceeded drink-drive limit, having 92 milligrammes of alcohol in 100 millilitres of blood when the legal limit is 80 milligrammes.
Banned from driving for three years, fined £145, costs £55. Magistrates ordered that ban be reduced by nine months if defendant successfully completes a rehabilitation course.

July 31
Terrence Peter Fletcher (28), Greenleaves Bungalow, Great Waldingfield. At Assington, dishonestly obtained from Pizza Town, Sudbury, various pizzas to the value of £47.
Fined £50, ordered to pay £47 compensation to Pizza Town.
Also at Assington, dishonestly obtained from Saamrat Tandoori restaurant, Sudbury, various meals to the value of £54.65. Fined £50, ordered to pay £54.65 compensation to Saamrat Tandoori.
Also at Assington, dishonestly obtained from Saamrat Tandoori restaurant, Sudbury, various meals to the value of £47. Fined £50, ordered to pay £47 compensation to Saamrat Tandoori.
At Sudbury, was caught in possession of cannabis. Fined £50.
Also at Sudbury, fraudulently used a tax disc. Fined £50.

September 18
Terrence Peter Fletcher (28), Badley's Road, Great Waldingfield. At Gainsborough Street, Sudbury, used a motor vehicle with no insurance. Banned from driving for four months, fined £70.
Also at Gainsborough Street, used a vehicle with no test certificate. No separate penalty.
Also at Gainsborough Street, drove otherwise in accordance with a licence. No separate penalty.

BARN DANCE

in the Marquee

Dancing to the "BONNY MILLER BAND"
Saturday 15th July 2000
8 pm

Licensed Bar applied for
Tickets £5 ~ to include a Fish & Chip Supper
[Children under 14 years ~ £2.50]

GREAT WALDINGFIELD PARISH COUNCIL

A vacancy exists to represent the village as a
Parish Council appointed School Governor for
Great Waldingfield CEVCP School

If you are interested and would like to discuss
this further, please contact Parish Councillor
Mrs Jean Misselbrook (Tel: 373837)

NEWS FROM SCHOOL

Staff and governors were absolutely delighted to be told this month that the school has won a DfEE School Achievement Award. These are for schools that substantially improved their results between 1997 and 2000. The hard work and dedication of teaching and support staff are crucial to a school's success. School Achievement Awards are intended to celebrate and reward these efforts --- we are particularly pleased to be one of the first schools in the country to win the award.

On Red Nose Day the children paid 50p for the privilege of dressing in red instead of school uniform. They were also able to spend their pennies at stalls organised by James Kiely, Sam Wilson and Class 2, with a contribution from Mrs. Scott of her famous 'tablet'! James and Sam worked very hard making everything for their stalls at home. Altogether the children raised £78 for Comic Relief, with £30 of that coming from James and Sam's stalls. Well done everyone!

FREDERICK AND HELEN FULKER

Happy Diamond Anniversary
All our love
Pat and John,
Susannah, Robert,
Samantha xxx

Peter Dagger, Lynns Hall Close, Great Waldingfield. Failed to provide information on person responsible for vehicle. Fined £100, costs £40.

Daniel Bull (23), Kenyon Drive, Great Waldingfield. At Northern Road, Sudbury, used unlicensed vehicle. Fined £50, back duty £106.67.

Terry Fletcher (28), Badley Road, Great Waldingfield. At Market Hill, Sudbury, used unlicensed vehicle. Fined £100, costs £50, back duty £53.34.

Henry George Mayhew (41), Folly Road, Great Waldingfield. Used an untaxed vehicle in Springlands Way, Sudbury. Fined £50, costs £50, back duty £10.

Peter James Dagger (36), Lynns Hall Close, Great Waldingfield. At A134 Sudbury, used a motor vehicle with no insurance. Fined £65, costs £35, six penalty points.
Also at Sudbury, failed to produce licence to police constable. Fined £10.

Peter James Dagger (36), Lynns Hall Close, Great Waldingfield. At Springlands Way, Sudbury, used an unlicensed vehicle. Fined £80, costs £50, back duty £40.

Linda Lutz (51), Nutwood Cottage, Lavenham Road, Great Waldingfield. On the B1078 at Bildeston, drove without due care and attention. Fined £300, costs £35, six penalty points.

July 8
Peter Doughty (19), Girling Street, Sudbury. Breached 14 month probation order. Order revoked. Re-sentenced for original offences.
At Bantocks Road, Great Waldingfield, had in his possession an air rifle, causing Christopher Smart to believe that unlawful violence would be used against him.
At Great Waldingfield, assaulted Christopher Smart causing actual bodily harm.
Jointly with Luke Twiklett, stole cash and a cash box to the value of £365 after trespassing a property in Bantocks Road, Great Waldingfield.
At Sudbury Magistrates Court, failed to surrender to custody after being bailed.
For all these offences, magistrates decided to impose a three month curfew on the defendant, which will be in effect between 8pm and 6am daily.

SEPT 2003

Great Waldingfield Primary School

David Floyd, chairman of Great Waldingfield parish council, married to Anne, two sons, two grandchildren

Lived in the village how long?:   41 and a half years
What do you like best about the village?:   It's a friendly place where most people try to help each other overcome life's difficulties
What do you like least about it?:   The mindless vandalism
Where were you born?:   London
What's your favourite holiday destination?:   France
What's your favourite past-time ?:   Woodturning
Which living person do you most admire?:   H.M.The Queen
Which historical figure do you most admire?:   I.K.Brunel
What is your pet hate?:   Cruelty to animals
What is your favourite book?:   Anything by Dorothy L.Sayers
Your favourite TV programme?:   Fred Dibnah
Favourite colour?:   Green
Favourite flower?:   Dahlia
Favourite music?:   Ally Bain
Favourite film?:   Genevieve
Have you a joke you can share with us?:   I don't do jokes

Pupils from Great Waldingfield Primary School pay tribute to their mums.

0503-30-7

Shivering Scouts get back to nature

SCOUTS braved the cold and snow to take part in a camp with an environmental theme.

Members of 1st Acton and Waldingfield Scouts stayed at the Bradfield Park Scout camp and spent their time building and putting up bird boxes as well as planting shrubs and trees around the site.

The work, which counts towards various awards, was sponsored by the Environment Agency's Action Earth project, which supplied the materials.

● The group is always looking for new members. For more information contact Cliff Dark on (01787) 378071.

Boxing clever ... Members of Ist Acton and Waldingfield Scouts with the bird boxes they made at camp.

Ist Acton and Great Waldingfield Scouts give the churchyard a facelift.

Clean-up team in action

SCOUTS worked hard at wildlife and conservation work in Great Waldingfield churchyard.

Helped by the churchwarden, members of 1st Acton and Great Waldingfield spent an afternoon cutting back brambles, removing molehills and clearing weeds and nettles. They also put up two bird boxes.

Their work was sponsored by the Environment Agency's Action Earth project, which provided tools and materials.

● The Scout group is still looking for new members. For more information contact Cliff Dark on (01787) 378071.

Thanks for your votes

I WOULD like to thank all those who voted for me in the Babergh district elections and I am very pleased to be one of the two elected members for the Waldingfield ward (Acton, Chilton, Great and Little Waldingfield).

Meeting people and seeing the beautiful gardens of the area has once again been a real pleasure. My best wishes to you all.

FRANCES BATES
Ramla, Rectory Road
Great Waldingfield

Great Waldingfield
14th Century Village Inn

Flashback ... Edna Allen and the mystery plant taking over her garden.

Press readers name Edna's space invader

KEEN gardeners from all over the area have been trying to identify a giant plant which is taking over a garden in Great Waldingfield.

Most think the invader in Edna Allen's flowerbed is either a squash or a gourd.

Suggestions included a gourd, a butternut squash, and a custard marrow.

As one person put it: "It's obviously successful at squashing other plants to get its way!"

The trailing monster which at the last count was 20 feet long and still growing appeared as a tiny seedling in the back garden of Mrs Allen's home at Heath Estate.

Among the gardeners who contacted the *Free Press* was Ted Wright of Brent Eleigh Road, Lavenham, who thought it was a butternut squash.

"I grew some myself this year for the first time and it just ran riot like the one in Waldingfield."

Lucy Brebner of Great Cornard thought it looked like an edible squash, and David Watts plumped for a marrow squash.

Valerie Craig and Ken Drury agreed on a custard marrow – known in America as a patty pan squash.

Another caller believed it was an ornamental gourd. "The fruits can be varnished after they've dried out and make excellent Christmas decorations."

But the last word goes to professional gardener Ken Jolly who, after inspecting one of the fruits and consulting his reference books, identified it as a Crown of Thorns gourd.

Mrs Allen said this week that the plant was now bigger than ever.

"Several people have been round to look at it, and someone else said it was a Crown of Thorns, so I think that's probably right.

"I'll have to get rid of it eventually, but I'm going to leave it until I have to cut the lawn," she said.

Suffolk Constabulary - Community Beat Update

12.09.03 Bantocks Road, trees uprooted in the garden of private house.

20.09.03 Theft from motor vehicle left unattended in Braithwaite Drive
CD player & CDs stolen.

!!! IMPORTANT NOTICE !!!

PARISH COUNCIL MEETING
on
MONDAY - 21 MARCH
Village Hall at 7.30pm

The main item for discussion will be the planning application for a

Waste Recycling Facility

proposed to be sited on the airfield behind Green Acre, near the industrial units.
This is an extremely unwelcome proposal which, if brought to fruition,
will have many unpleasant consequences for our village.

Please come to this meeting and air your views.
SPREAD THE WORD to your friends and neighbours.
Make sure all the village knows!

THE PARISH COUNCIL

There was no election for the parish council as there were insufficient
nominations to warrant one. The seven serving councillors were nominated
and will now serve again.

They are: Sheila Dunnett
David Floyd
Vince Humphries
Linda Lutz
Jean Misselbrook
Bill Skinner
John Steele

Suffolk Constabulary - Community Beat Update

Between
06.03.03 & Sometime overnight some tools were taken from a garage in
07.03.03   Garrison Lane.

07.03.03   In the early hours of the morning a house burglary occurred in
            Garrison Lane.

Between
12.03.03 & A burglary occurred overnight at a house in Lavenham Road
13.03.03   and antiques were stolen.

PLANT SALE

The annual plant sale which was held on 11 and 12 May at White Hall Farm, by kind permission of Mr & Mrs M Oliver, was once again a great success. We had a great many plants of all kinds for sale, and crowds of people, not only from the village but from far afield, came to buy. A profit of about £1000 was made, which will go towards putting a new roof on the Church.

Queen's speech to the WI

The Queen's speech to the the National Federation of Women's Institutes at the Royal Albert Hall, June 7, 1990.

"I AM very pleased to be with you today to share in celebrating the 75th Anniversary of the National Federation of Women's Institutes. Both my mother and I are long-standing members, and I am sure our Institute at Sandringham will be joining in the many special events and activities planned for this birthday year, as will more than 9,000 other Institutes throughout England, Wales, the Channel Islands and the Isle of Man. I know that your programme in 1990 is not only one of celebration but also one of re-dedication and renewal of the aims and ideals of the movement.

"The pioneers who helped to establish the movement in 1915 and steered it through a World War from Government sponsorship to full independence can hardly have envisaged the success of their enterprise. The world they lived in was very different from that of today. Yet the foundations they laid and the principles they established not only survived, but have assumed even greater relevance for today's membership.

"Over the past 75 years, the Women's Institutes have been active in improving the quality of rural life and have often campaigned on issues long before it became fashionable to do so. It is worth remembering that in the 1920s, not long after the movement began, the Women's Institutes were already talking about oil pollution, about health services in rural areas and about adult education and how the voluntary movement could contribute. That set the tone for the Institutes' long record of public service and for the keen awareness that they have always shown for developments which might adversely affect rural areas and the women and families who live in them.

"The Federation of Women's Institutes has a history of which to be proud. It is unique in having its own adult education establishment at Denman College, which I so much enjoyed visiting some years ago. It is also responsible for over 500 co-operative markets countrywide, which provide thousands of small rural producers with weekly outlets for their produce, their crafts and their home-cooked food.

"As the organisation looks ahead to its Centenary. I know it is pledged to continue its work to nurture and maintain those values on which it was founded. The Women's Institutes are renowned in all they do for their high standards, for the balance and commonsense of their comments on matters of public debate and, perhaps above all, for their commitment and concern for the countryside, for families and for the lonely and disadvantaged. I wish you every success in your plans to live up to that reputation in the future.

THREE VILLAGER CARNIVAL QUEEN

Float Procession starts 12.30 p.m.

The Acton & Waldingfields CARNIVAL 1991

Look out for Wally's Angels

Three Villages' Carnival Queen Larissa King, *pictured right*, with her Princesses Sally Baldwin' and Jackie Parker will lead the Carnival procession around Great Waldingfield in an open topped veteran car.

Larissa will then open the grand fete at 1.30pm.

Meanwhile other carnival queen entrants, nicknamed 'Wally's Angels' and dressed in distinctive costume, will be selling programmes in the ground.

Jackie Parker, 15.

Sally Baldwin, 17.

the Grand Carnival site in Folly Road, Great Walding-field will make it easy for the expected 2,000 visitors to enjoy an afternoon of fun for all the family.

Over 40 local organisations are participating, plus trade and craft stalls.

A very special arena event, combining excitement and danger, is being kept secret until the last moment.

At least eight teams will be taking part in the Tug'o'War contest, including entrants from the two local pubs, cricket clubs, police, firemen and the RAF.

Nine pewter tankards for the winning team have been donated by Vauxhall Motors.

Local sponsors have been absolutely magnificent, said carnival organiser Wally Langridge, above all Dave Holland of Laser Art who has produced all the publicity material for the event.

If you are lucky, you could win a colour television, donated by Solar Garages, with your lucky programme number.

Programme sellers in distinctive costume, nicknamed 'Wally's Angels', will include carnival queen contest entrants.

More than £300 worth of prizes have been donated for the the Grand Draw to be held at 5pm.

The annual horticultural show in the school building will give the green-fingered a chance to show off the fruits of their labours — and fill the rest of us with envy!

Children will enjoy the funfair, Scalextric marquee, junior go-kart and pony and trap rides.

They can enter on the day for the decorated bike contest (under 15's) and children's fancy dress (under 12's).

The Friendship Dancers (who perform East European folk dances), a display of pristine classic cars organised by Martin Blaake, and a dog obedience display will all entertain visitors.

A barbecue, beer tent and refreshment stalls will fortify the inner man.

Go along and enjoy a fun-packed programme of events.

PART TIME CLERK TO THE COUNCIL

Applications are invited from persons for the above post which will be at a salary of £2938 pa. Applicants should preferably have Local Government experience.

Grand Carnival Programme

50p

The Acton & Waldingfields

CARNIVAL 1991

Saturday September 21st 1991
The School Field – Gt Waldingfield

Lucky Programme Colour Television
Donated by

SOLAR GARAGE

VAUXHALL
Main Dealer

Retain your programme. Winner announced on Carnival Day

Your LUCKY NUMBER is   2191

GRAND CARNIVAL, 1991   N⁰ 1716

Promoter: J Sears,
'Stomer', Valley Road, Great Waldingfield

GRAND DRAW

First Prize £150
Second Prize £75
Third Prize £50 - Fourth Prize £25
Plus Various Other Prizes

To be drawn at Great Waldingfield School Field
on Saturday, 21st September, 1991

Printed to conform with the Lotteries & Amusements   Ticket 20p.
Act. 1976 Reg. with Babergh District Council   Book of 5 - £1
Hogshead Press, Lt. Waldingfield, Tel: Lavenham (0787) 247784

ACTON got together with Great and Little Waldingfield on Saturday for a three-village carnival which brought about 2,000 visitors pouring into the area.

The first combined event of its kind, it was a major success and is expected to make a substantial profit for local organisations.

Proceeds will also help fund the next carnival, to be held at Acton in two years' time.

"Rats" from Great Waldingfield's school block their ears to the sound of the Pied Piper.

Above, wizard capers for Great Waldingfield Playgroup in the carnival procession on Saturday.
Left, fairy tale time for the 1st Acton and Great Waldingfield Guides.

First class

A GREAT Waldingfield man has been awarded a first class honours degree in computing and electronics by the University of Hertfordshire.

Steven Bacon, of Lavenham Road, is a former pupil of Uplands Middle and Sudbury Upper schools.

David Floyd of Great Waldingfield, Ray Seymour of Little Waldingfield and Chris Moss of Acton, who judged the floats.

Best exhibit was Great Waldingfield Playgroup's Wizard of Oz who took the Oliver Cup. The primary school float, Pied Piper, was second and Acton and Great Waldingfield Guides third with Book at Bedtime.

FROG RACING EVENING

In aid of St Lawrence Church Funds

Saturday, 25th March 2000

at

Gt Waldingfield Village Hall

7.00 pm

Entrance: £3.00 adult & £1.50 children

Includes a Buffet Supper
(Bring your own drink and glasses)

Raffle

This event proved a great success last year, with much fun and laughter had by all. There will be 8 races with super prizes, so please come along and enjoy a happy family evening.

144

1991

Suffolk Constabulary - Community Beat Update

Between 02.12.02 & 03.12.02	Theft from motor vehicle in Bantocks Road
13.12.02	Vehicle in Public House car park had its tyre slashed.
19.12.02	Badleys Close. Petrol siphoned from unattended vehicle.
29.12.02	Bantocks Road. Person arrested for being Drunk & Disorderly.
Between 29.12.02 & 30.12.02	Coronation Rise. Damage to Christmas decorations at locus by unknown persons.
26.12.02	House sign from Lavenham Road stolen.

GREAT WALDINGFIELD HORTICULTURAL SHOW

The eighth autumn horticultural show was held on Saturday 21st September. This year it was held in the village School hall as part of the Three Villages Carnival held on the nearby playing field.

Louise Eady, former pupil of Great Waldingfield Primary School, has continued with her career in Law by being taken on as a salaried partner at her present workplace, Blocks of Ipswich & Felixstowe.

Louise, after leaving the Sudbury Upper School where she became Head Girl, continued her education at the University of Teesside, where she graduated in her chosen profession, Law.

expressed requests include:—
Keep Fit at Gt. Waldingfield

1993

WI President Ann Holloway presents a plaque to parish council chairman David Floyd to mark unveiling the new village hall sign.

GREAT WALDINGFIELD WOMEN'S INSTITUTE
1918-1993

This sign marking the entrance to the Village Hall was the idea of the members of the WI who paid for the lettering to commemorate the 75th Anniversary of the Institute

On 2 June we are celebrating our Anniversary and invite everyone in the village to come to the Village Hall for tea and biscuits between 2.30 and 4.30 pm. No charge – we just want you to come!

AN INVITATION TO THE VILLAGE PEOPLE – in the evening the members, past and present, are having a birthday party and, dressed in the style of 1918, will enjoy an Old Time Music Hall when members of surrounding WIs are coming as our guests.

A HOLIDAY in Portugal cost Richard Clarke (20) of Lynns Hall Close, Great Waldingfield, a £25 fine at Sudbury Magistrates Court on Tuesday.

Unemployed Clarke, who is charged with assaulting David Binstead and damaging his Ford Sierra at Sudbury on February 15, pleaded guilty to failing to surrender to custody on April 5.

Gerry & Gladys Ball from Carbonels celebrated their Diamond Wedding on 27th February. Mr Ball is a member of Gt Waldingfield parish council and Mrs Ball was a former President of Gt Waldingfield WI. Congratulations to you both and we hope you enjoyed your special day with your daughter and family.

JULY 10 1993

● Actor Paul Eddington opening the Three Villages Carnival at Great Waldingfield.

Carnival queen chosen

Winners for the second year running were Great Waldingfield playgroup with their Peter Pan float.

THE winner of the 1993 Three Villages Carnival Queen competition will be proving she is not just a pretty face during her year of office.

Alison Bale, 19, of Great Waldingfield, *above*, is planning to take part in a ten-mile charity bike ride on July 18 as part of the Sudbury and District Celebration.

Her duties as carnival queen for Acton, Great Waldingfield and Little Waldingfield include leading the carnival procession on July 10 in an open-topped vintage car with her two princesses, Samantha Jacobs of Little Waldingfield and Jessica West of Acton.

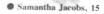

● Samantha Jacobs, 15   ● Jessica West, 15

Weekend Thought
by Ann Holloway

A 1,000 piece jigsaw lies on my table, some of it is completed, some pieces have dropped on the floor and a great number of blue sky pieces have been put to one side as too difficult to do this morning!

I began optimistically enough, the edge pieces fitted together very easily followed by the bright coloured middle of the picture – so far, so good.

Then came the more difficult bit.

The picture on the box provides me with a pattern to follow but, nevertheless,

I keep putting pieces in the wrong place and, when they don't match up, I have to take them out and try them again somewhere else.

Eventually, the whole picture will emerge piece by piece, and I will be able to see just how all the tiny pieces have fitted together.

I can look back over the jigsaw of my life so far and see that in many times. I have put pieces of it in the wrong place!

I can see how the people I have met and been influenced by have given me some of the pieces, things I

have done (or not done) have altered the ever growing picture of my life.

Only God has the whole picture of my life but he has left me to place the pieces.

He also sees the much bigger picture of how we, as pieces, fit into his plan.

Yes, we keep putting pieces in the wrong places but he gives each of us a special place and asks us to use our special skills to fit into the big picture.

Try reading Romans 12: 4-9, and use your own special talents as part of God's jigsaw.

Gordon Aldridge with the 1921 Fowler BBI he drove at the rally.

Rally was a record-breaker

TRACTION engines, tractors, steam engines, motorcycles and classic cars were among the 300 exhibits on show when the Farm Machinery Preservation Society held a record-breaking rally at the weekend.

Sunday's sunshine drew an estimated crowd of 3,000 to the Great Waldingfield show site giving the organisers their best-ever event.

"It was a very successful weekend," said chairman Ron Mansfield. "We had the largest number of exhibits and the largest attendance we've ever had."

Spectators were able to browse round the vehicles dating from 1916 to the 1950s, and there were plenty of other attractions.

The Southern Hellraisers gun-fighters, Sudbury's Tudor Archers and a Bernese mountain dog team all gave displays.

Working machinery exhibits included a number of traction engines with threshing outfits and a model straw baling machine producing its own mini bales.

"Interest in the society continues to grow," said Mr Mansfield. "We have about 350 members mainly from Suffolk and Essex and about 15 people wanted to join at the weekend."

Steam power ... an enthusiast drives a scaled-down traction engine at Great Waldingfield.

Between 02/10/03 & St Lawrence church entered and chairs stolen two of which were later recovered nearby

WI member Edna Allen with Thomas Emmins and Sandra Scott in front of the WI display.

VILLAGE organisations and parents joined pupils at Great Waldingfield Primary School in devising displays of materials for a time capsule.

Headteacher Joan Garner explained the children had been planning an art exhibition for some weeks and they wanted to involve the whole village.

"We decided to widen it to include parents and to give it a millennium twist we asked them and village organisations either to design a logo or

by Pat Bray

assemble a time capsule. They all went for the time capsule.

"In the end we had the church, parish council, women's institute, bowls club, post office and several parents putting in their ideas and they all approached it in a different way.

"Some had collections of photographs and artefacts and the WI had all sorts of things including jars of jam and chutney, a mixing bowl, photos and lists of members and meetings.

"The school's time capsule contents covered the last 100 years and parents were fascinated looking at old attendance and punishment books."

GRAND MILLENNIUM DANCE

Friday 31st December 1999
8.00pm - 1.00am
The Village Hall
Dancing to Chomp & Stomp Disco

Tickets £14.00 each
Contact 373837, 375691, 373265

Buffet Supper - Bar

Come and enjoy celebrating in the Millennium

The first of the village's millennium celebrations has now taken place. Around sixty of us gathered in the village hall to welcome in the New Year. After the traditional Auld Lang Syne, we finished the evening by standing in a circle and all singing Cliff Richard's "Lord's Prayer". This seemed a very fitting way to start the New Millennium. We hope the other village events taking place during the year will be just as enjoyable and successful.

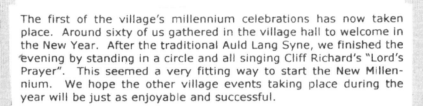

24 February 2000,			
	BAND A £	BAND B £	BAND C £
Waldingfield Great	557.01	649.84	742.68
Waldingfield Little	529.59	617.85	706.12

St Lawrence Church

Annual Plant Sale

Saturday 13th May
Gt Waldingfield Village Hall
From 8.30am

Please note the change of venue.

Once again we are asking for help to make this event a great success. If you have any plants that are surplus to requirements or can be split up, we would be most grateful for them. Also, any pots, garden equipment or any cakes for the cake stall, please bring them to:

81 Bantocks Road or ring 370734 if you need anything collected.

Pictured: How the lightning blaze spread in seconds

The Armstrong family were yesterday looking for temporary accommodation while their home is assessed for damage.

From blast to blaze: dramatic pictures taken by neighbour Mary Adams show how the roof of the Great Waldingfield house became a fireball within seconds of being struck by lightning in Monday's thunderstorm. The picture on the left was taken shortly after the thunderbolt struck. In the centre picture flames are licking around the roof edge. The picture on the right shows the moment the flames burst through the roof.

Annual Church Meeting

At the Annual Church Meeting on 12th April the following were elected to office: Churchwardens, Mr. Chris Francis and Mr. David Lawrence Jones; Parochial Church Council members, Mrs. Anne Francis and Mrs. Margaret Graves (with one outstanding vacancy). Thanks were expressed to all who have served as officers or P.C.C. members over the last year and special mention was made of Mrs. Pat Leathers who has now retired from the P.C.C.

THE CHURCH OF ST LAWRENCE

Rector	Rev John Fieldgate The Vicarage, Melford Road, Acton CO10 0BA	Tel 01787 377287
Retired Priest	Rev David Rutherford 18 Gotsfield Close, Acton CO10 0AS	Tel 01787 374169
Readers	Mrs Jill Fieldgate The Vicarage, Melford Road, Acton CO10 0BA	Tel 01787 377287
	Mr Derek Thompson 6 Chilton Corner Cottages, Gt Waldingfield	Tel 01787 312081
Churchwardens	Mrs Norma Chambers Woodruff, Newmans Green, Acton CO10 0AB	Tel 01787 370117
	Mr C Francis The Waldings, 81 Bantocks Road Gt Waldingfield	Tel 01787 370734

IMPORTANT NOTICE

The induction of the Reverend John Fieldgate will take place in St. Lawrence church, Great Waldingfield, on Monday, 14th May at 7.30pm.

2001

GT WALDINGFIELD
WI by Linda Lutz

WE were pleased to welcome Mr David Floyd, chairman of Great Waldingfield parish council to talk at our February meeting. He was able to explain some of the history of the council, its duties and explain the way the work is budgeted for in the precept – basically where our money is spent. There was lively discussion afterwards and lots of interest in the topics raised. We were delighted to welcome some new faces at our meeting and would love to see even more, so if you're wondering about coming, just pop in, you'll soon be made welcome.

Our next meeting on Wednesday March 6 at 2pm has as its subject The Button Lady, with Ms Sigrud Jurefowski.

On Wednesday, March 20, Barry Wall will again be giving one of his fascinating history evenings, again in the village hall at 7.30pm.

● Cornard captain Terry Bacon with the Quinton Bowl at Halesworth

Rev'd David Rutherford BA (Hons.)

Congratulations to Rev'd David Rutherford who has recently been awarded an Honours Degree in Theology following five-year's part-time study. Well done David!

Great Waldingfield Primary School's reception class.

0110-319-65

SUFFOLK CONSTABULARY COMMUNITY BEAT UPDATE

04.5.01	Child's scooter stolen from playground whilst unattended.
Between 07.5.01 & 08.5.01	Burglary, dwelling Badleys Road. Access gained via french doors. Antiques and silver stolen.
19.5.01	Three mountain bikes stolen from garage in Chapel Close. Pink Amoco girl's MTB; blue Raleigh Fusion boy's MTB and a black/ red Man.Utd boy's MTB
26.5.01	Damage to fence in Garrison Lane. Young offenders dealt with
27.5.01	Mountain bike stolen, Bantocks Road

SUFFOLK CONSTABULARY - COMMUNITY BEAT UPDATE
Great Waldingfield

Between 06.01.01 & 07.01.01	Damage to garden wall, Bantocks Road, Gt Waldingfield.
Between 13.01.01 & 15.01.01	Theft of heating oil from Bowling Club, Tentrees Road.
21.01.91	At 2.45pm offenders stole items from unattended car. It is believed they drove off in a red Mercedes.
29.01.01	Theft from motor vehicle, Kenyon Drive.

Village's Jubilee show

THE village of Great Waldingfield came out to celebrate the Queen's jubilee year on Saturday with a horticultural show.

0208-90-16

Mary Jackson with a fine collection of produce.

0208-90-11

Anne Francis and flowers.

0208-90-19

Mandy Harves with a tasty tea.

Time to praise young people

AT the recent Summer Policing Forum held at the Sudbury Town Hall, the theme of the day was "Perception of Crime" and included both young people and the elderly. I was there in the latter category!

I was enormously impressed by the young people who were there.

They were articulate and courteous and presented their views with a maturity I found extremely helpful and informative.

I was not, however, quite so impressed with the way in which some older people made sweeping generalisations about "young people nowadays."

It was particularly salutary to hear about the manners of some elderly people towards the young.

Since the Forum I have been observing shoppers in Sudbury and have seen instances of OAPs pushing young people out of the way, not saying thank-you when young people hold the door open, of standing in doorways talking with our friends and being cross with young people who ask politely to get by.

To see ourselves as others see us is not always comfortable.

Treat others as you would like to be treated yourself – manners and courtesy should cut across all age groups.

ANN HOLLOWAY
8 Holbrook Close
Great Waldingfield

John is a Winner!

Congratulations to John Hughes who has won the best allotment prize in the Sudbury-in-Bloom competition. He also won the best small garden in the novice section.

20.02.03   A charity box was taken from the pub containing approximately £50.

2002

GREAT WALDINGFIELD PARISH COUNCIL
Annual Parish Meeting

The meeting was not that well attended but proved to be interesting and lively. The following organisations gave their reports:

Parish Council : Mr Floyd, chairman, said that 25 planning applications had been received, some of them not well presented. The council was keeping its eye on a recent Government green paper which may have a detrimental effect on parish councils' planning responsibilities.

Public attendance at parish council meetings had been encouraging. At the September meeting the public outnumbered the councillors! New and refurbished seats were in place. Thanks were due to Mr & Mrs Hogg and the WI for their support in this.

Police: PC Seager said that criminal offences in the village had increased slightly to 64 cases compared with 52 in the previous year. Fifty per cent of the crime was committed between April and July and, as it turned out, by one family of 8 from Great Cornard. Unfortunately in February and March this year there were 16 crimes on the airfield industrial estate; this period coincided with the presence of the travellers on the airfield. PC Seager would be leaving his post soon and was thanked by the chairman.

Village People

Congratulations to **Heidi** (nee Carsbolt) and **Jim Mayhew** on the birth of their new baby son 8lbs 7ozs. A welcome brother for **Chrissy** and **Matt**.

We were pleased to hear that **Ron Leeks** was home from hospital after being seriously ill for several months. He is making slow progress and we wish him well.

Thankfully **Barbara Leeks** has fully recovered from a nasty fall sustained last month in Sudbury.

Congratulations to **Briar and Bill Skinner** on the birth of their third grandchild.

Congratulations to **John Hughes**, Secretary of Gt Waldingfield Horticultural Show Committee, on getting an award from the National Blood Transfusion Service for giving 75 pints of blood over a number of years.

Our thoughts are with **John Eggby**, who is seriously ill, and with his family.

We send good wishes to **Ron Highton** for his continuing recovery.

SUFFOLK CONSTABULARY - COMMUNITY BEAT UPDATE

Great Waldingfield

01.03.02	Theft of a lady's pedal cycle from Braithwaite Drive.
08.04.02	Theft from Babergh Place Farm overnight. Power washer and generator stolen.
12.04.02	Theft of purse from motor vehicle parked in Chapel Close. This occurred during daylight hours.
23-25.04.02	Theft of ride-on lawn mower and other items from Brook House Farm.
16.10.02	Assault at Bantocks Road. Offender to be arrested.
Between 13.10.02 - 14.10.02	Vehicle had 4 tyres punctured in Bantocks Road.
Between 17.10.02 - 18.10.02	Large quantity of diesel fuel stolen from the Street
23.10.02	Sundial stolen from a front garden in Lavenham Road

JOHN LEEKS

Happy 60th Birthday John on July 19th 2002
You haven't changed a bit.
Lots of love
Mary, Colin & Danny
xxx

LAWRENCE - JONES - On the October 25 2002, GWYNNE (nee Logan), dearly beloved wife of David for 53 happy years. Mother of John, William and Robert and Grandmother of seven. At home after a short illness. Family cremation. A Memorial Service will be held at The Church of St. Lawrence, Great Waldingfield at 12 noon on Monday November 4. Donations in her memory, if wished, to the Motor Neurone Disease Association, PO Box 246, Northampton NN1 2PR.

SUMMER CONCERT

It is with great pleasure that we proudly present our first *"Summer Concert"* at St Lawrence Church on 22nd June 2002. With our very own Mark Saberton and from Sudbury, Elaine Henson, who both kindly agreed to give us the pleasure of hearing their superb talents. We also have the benefit of the musical gifts of Patrick Friend who will be accompanying them for their *"Midsummer Feast of Music"*.

The concert will start at 7.45pm, so make sure you are in your seats in plenty of time; you can bring a cushion if you feel it necessary. There will be refreshments served in the interval and tea and coffee at the end of the concert.

The ticket price is - £6 for one *or* £10 for two.

They will be on sale at the Post Office and from any of the members of the Friends and the PCC. We encourage you to invite friends and family as we are sure it will be a night to remember.

BOWLS & SOCIAL CLUB

Officers elected:	Chairlady:	Jean Misselbrook
	Vice-Chairman:	Charles Mallett
	Secretary:	Roy Willis
	Treasurer:	Pat Highton

Committee:	Kath Crisp	Maureen Game	Mary Jackson
	Brian Eady	Noel Game	Ron Highton
	Basil Radley		

Ladies' Captain: Mary Jackson
Men's Captain:· Brian Eady

Sarah Douglas (née Gant)

Sarah died, from cancer, at West Suffolk Hospital on March 13th aged 37. She leaves a husband and a young son. Sarah, who was brought up in Acton, attended All Saints Middle School and Sudbury Upper where she will be remembered as a sunny natured, bright pupil with excellent musical ability. She played the clarinet in school and county orchestras. She taught for several years at Great Waldingfield School where she was great fun and well-loved by her pupils, many of whom went to Acton church with their parents to see her married in her mother's wedding dress, on a sweltering summer day. The news of her death has shocked and saddened many people and we send our heartfelt condolences to her husband, Iain, and son, Charlie, her mother and the rest of her family.

care at hospital

I READ with interest letters in the *Free Press* on West Suffolk Hospital and patients' views on care received and whether they would recommend it to their nearest and dearest.

My husband was in West Suffolk Hospital recovering from a serious illness. The care that John has received has been fantastic and I will always be grateful to everyone concerned. He is now home.

It is not only John that has received care, but myself and my family during some very traumatic hours.

West Suffolk Hospital is a good hospital and I certainly will be recommending it to my nearest and dearest.

JEAN MISSELBROOK
Great Waldingfield

BULB SALE
specially imported
TOP QUALITY DUTCH BULBS

Great Waldingfield Village Hall
Saturday, September 21st
9.00am - 3.00pm

"and then my heart with pleasure fills,
and dances with the daffodils"
(also tulips, crocus and hyacinths!)

Great Waldingfield Revisited

With the arrival of Autumn we will have lived in the centre of Sudbury for nearly a year. Although we are happy with our new home we miss the spirit of living in a village such as Great Waldingfield. Thus we were very pleased to return to the Horticultural Show last Saturday and to be asked to present our Photographic Trophy to the winner. It was great to see many old friends from twenty-five years of living in Upsher Green. Our thanks to the Committee and all concerned for making us so welcome.

Jean and Hugh Butcher

The Mobile Library

Did you know that the library van visits Waldingfield on alternate Thursdays? I have never used it but I am going to give it a go. If we don't use it, we may lose it. Check it out!

The van stops on Heath Estate at the Coronation Rise turn for 20 minutes 1.45-2.05pm. It then goes to the church where it stops from 2.10-2.30pm. It arrives on alternate Thursdays. The next visits are:

November 14th, 28th and December 12th

Bowls Club

September 21st saw the final of the Geoff Daw Cup. This is a mixed pairs competition. Finalists were Carol Leeder and Luke Batley against Pat Edmeades and Brian Eady. Some excellent bowling on both sides and the final score did not reflect the game. Winners were Pat and Brian.

Competitions now in progress are the Captain's Challenge. This is a competition with a difference which is much enjoyed. Also in progress is the Ladies Singles.

Best wishes go to Arthur Faiers, Edna Allen, Ron Highton and John Misselbrook who have all had a spell in hospital recently.

The Bowls Club is primarily a village club and we do rely on local support, so if you are interested please come along and 'have a go at bowling'. You could enjoy it!

We send our deepest sympathy to **Mr Lawrence-Jones** and his family on the death of **Mrs Lawrence-Jones**.

5

Community Achievement Awards - Edna Allen

We are delighted to hear that Edna Allen of Heath Estate is to be a recipient, having had her name put forward by the parish council who received her nomination from two villagers.

Edna has lived in the village for many years and has been active, without any fuss, in many fields. She was a pillar of the Acton-Waldingfield Friendship Club for the over sixties. Even though the club has disbanded, Edna continued to befriend the elderly of the village in every way she could. She is a Meals-on-Wheels driver/deliverer, she is active in the church and the WI

Miscellaneous

It was decided that this Village History Book should be in the charge of a small committe always For this charge officers elected are :—

Mrs Butcher :— President.

Mrs G. Maxell (Representing Womens Institute)

Canon T.C. Alexander (Rector) & Mr D. Abbott.

until further notice.

July 14th 1959

Owing to the departure of Canon T.C. Alexander and the resignation of Mr Abbott, the Committee was reconstituted as under :—

Mrs Butcher :- President

Mrs G. Maxell (Representing Women's Inst.)

Rev. Francis Kenyon-Kenyon

Mr. R. Leeks.

VILLAGE ORGANISATIONS

Parochial Church Council
Mrs S Brinton
Tel 01787 881804

Parish Council

Mr M Murkin (Clerk)
Tel 01787 312605

Mr David Floyd (Chairman)
Tel 01787 373265

Village Hall Committee
Mrs J Baldwin (Letting Secretary)
Tel 01787 374973

District Councillors
Mr C Spence
22 Rochester Way, Sudbury
Tel 01787 378184

Mr L Stedman
78 Bantocks Road, Gt Waldingfield
Tel 01787 370087

Tree Warden & Chairman of Branchlines
David Taylor
Tel 01787 373541

Acton & Gt Waldingfield Conservative Assoc
Mr L Stedman
78 Bantocks Road, Gt Waldingfield
Tel 01787 370087

Horticultural Show Committee
Chairman - Chris Francis Tel 01787 370734
Secretary - Mr J Hughes Tel 01787 378342

Friends of St Lawrence Church
Chairman - John Lawrenson
The Old Rectory, Gt Waldingfield CO10 0TL
Tel 01787 372428

Women's Institute
Molly Blackwell - Secretary
Tel 01787 371452

Gt Waldingfield Primary School
Folly Road
Tel 01787 374055

First Friends Pre-School
Ann Stone
01787 373606

1st Acton & Waldingfield Scout Group - For enquiries about Beavers, Cubs & Scouts contact:

Group Scout Leader
Mr M Poulter
Tel 01787 375833

Guides
Mrs A Wimms
Tel 01787 370245

Bowls Club
Mr Roy Willis - Secretary
Tel 01206 854008

Braithwaite Allotment Trust
Mr David Floyd
Tel 01787 373265

Sudbury Police Station
Tel 01284 774300

Neighbourhood Watch
Co-ordinator
Brian Rose
01787 376499

Church chairs stolen

POLICE are searching for thieves who took four chairs from a church in Great Waldingfield.

One of them was recovered, having been dumped in a hedge near to St Lawrence's Church where they were taken from.

The thieves entered the church between noon on Thursday, October 2, and 7.20am on Sunday, October 5.

● Anyone with any information should call PC Shaun Beck at Sudbury Police on (01284) 774300.

Tributes to Briar Skinner
who died on November 5th aged 74

2002

From the Free Press who kindly gave permission for us to use Ken Watkins' article, below

Briar, who had lived in Great Waldingfield since 1976, was married to well-known local Labour politician and organic grower Bill Skinner.

As well as being a loyal member of the Women's Institute for 25 years, and a governor at Sudbury Upper School for ten years, she was involved in a voluntary capacity with a number of local and international charities.

Briar worked for Oxfam's Hungry for Change movement, organised the village collection for Christian Aid, played an active part in the local Amnesty International branch, was a dedicated member of the United Nations Association, collecting for UNA's recent flag day, and more recently was involved with the Refugee Support Group.

She had recently been appointed secretary of Sudbury's Churches Together group.

She was a lifelong member of the Labour Party, one grandfather - HD Wilson - being a Sheffield MP. Briar was a Quaker for more than 30 years, she and Bill joining the Society of Friends because they were both pacifists.

Chilton Estate 'not the right spot for Homebase store'

AM I the only person to be upset about the siting of the Homebase store on the Chilton Industrial Estate? Did anyone raise any objections during the planning process, and was there an alternative site available? Let's hope damage limiting landscaping will lessen the visual shock when travelling into Sudbury along the B1115.

FRANCES BATES
Ramla
Rectory Road
Gt Waldingfield

top oarsman

HORTICULTURAL SHOW: The show committee staged the 20th village horticultural show in the village hall.

The show attracted 312 exhibits from 52 exhibitors.

"The numbers of exhibitors and entries were up on last year's show, which is encouraging. When talking to the judges there appears to be a general downward trend in support for the traditional show," said show secretary John Hughes.

"Our gardens and allotments have been suffering from the long dry summer, just getting produce to the showbench was an achievement.

"The flower arrangers excelled themselves once again and individual talents were displayed in the handicraft and domestic sections."

Mr Hughes added the winemaking section was very well supported with 36 entries and to a high standard, as was the new section for photography with 25 entries.

Unfortunately, this year the children's section was poorly supported with only 10 entries.

After the prizegiving and raffle draw, the show committee chairman Chris Francis, thanked Edna Allen for presenting the prizes, all the exhibitors without whose entries there would not have been a show, the committee for their hard work in putting on the show, the visitors for their support in the afternoon, Ronnie Dawe, the auctioneer, and the show judges.

2003

Prizewinners:

Braithwaite Cup – John Hughes. Horticultural Committee Salver – Ronnie Dawe. Bowls Club Cup – Jean Misselbrook. Comminity Council Cup – Anne Francis. St Lawrence Cup – Christine Hutton.

Parisg Council Cup – Claire Kiely. Cagienard Cup – Mary Jackson. Blackburn Cup – Paddy O'Brien.

The Shinn and Misselbrook Cups for Children – Charlotte Rayner, Nathaniel Rayner, Bronwen Berry.

The Goeff Chatters Cup for Children's Handwriting – Ella Crawford.

The Maureen Shinn Memorial Salver for Handicraft – Janet Van Dyk. The Great Waldingfield Residents' Challenge Cup – Christine Hutton.

Francis Cup for most points in Show, Village Hall Cup for Most Entries, WI Cup for the Best Rose – Ronnie Dawe.

The Magazine Cup for Best Exhibit – Alan Scott.

ABOVE: 2 Green Acres, Great Waldingfield

THIS link-detached family home is in Great Waldingfield, near Sudbury and is on the market with Bradford & Bingley (01787 881442) at a price of £225,000.

I MUST thank K Risley for the letter in last week's edition of the *Free Press*, which gives me a chance to write more about the Ballingdon depot.

When the Babergh councillors were asked to comment on the Twin Bin scheme we were limited to 50 words!

The depot is mostly for larger recyclable waste (including car batteries and fridges) but there are a few skips for household waste.

I have driven into the site twice now in my 4x4 and didn't knock down the 5' 9" barrier. Higher vehicles can park to the far side of the site and enter by a pedestrian gate.

The staff on site are helpful and will, if needed, assist people to unload their cars. A very impressive JCB bin compactor is in residence which reduces the bulk of materials.

There have certainly been some teething problems with the Twin Bin scheme and some changes will need to be made. The residents of Alexandra Road (near dustcart storage) seem to have a valid complaint and I hope Cleanaway can address this in some way.

FRANCES BATES
(Babergh ouncillor for Waldingfield)
Ramla
Rectory Road
Gt Waldingfield

Gerry and Gladys Ball: 60 years of marriage.

ple

IT was a midnight song that brought the two of them together and more than 60 years on they are still side by side.

Gerry and Gladys Ball celebrate their diamond wedding today at their home in Carbonels, Great Waldingfield, with friends and family, including their daughter, son-in-law and two grandchildren.

gratulations to **Fred** and **Helen Fulker** of Chapel Close on their diamond ding (5th December 2002)

IN COURT

2003

Paul Denman (22) of Heath Estate, Great Waldingfield. Drove a Transit van in York Road, Sudbury, without due care and attention. Fined £120, costs £40. Licence endorsed with five points. Failed to stop after an accident. Fined £120.

George Barr of Bantocks Road, Great Waldingfield. Failed to give information to identify the person responsible for a motor vehicle. Fined £150 with £50 costs.

George Barr of Bantocks Road, Great Waldingfield. Fined £50 with £50 costs for failing to give information to identify person responsible for a vehicle.

Sharon Barr, Bantocks Road, Great Waldingfield. Found drunk in Bantocks Road. Community rehabilitation order for 12 months. Costs £25.

Thomas David Sagon of Badley Road, Great Waldingfield. Being the keeper of a vehicle whose driver was alleged to have been guilty of a road traffic offence at North Street, Sudbury, failed to give information to identify the driver. Fined £130 with £35 costs and licence endorsed with three penalty points.

St Edmundsbury Magistrates' Court, September 7

Nathan Goodwin (18) of Bantocks Road, Great Waldingfield. Drove a motor vehicle in First Avenue, Sudbury otherwise than in accordance with li-

Deborah Lait (35), of Lynns Hall Close, Great Waldingfield. For the purpose of obtaining council tax benefit, made a false statement or representation which she knew to be false, by failing to declare the income from child maintenance paid for her son and daughter. Fine £200. Costs £225.

Wendy Louise Berry of Braithwaite Drive, Great Waldingfield. Failed to identify person responsible for car. Fined £50, costs £50.

Sudbury Court, July 11

Sally-Anne Hoskyns (38) of Windrush Cottage, Great Waldingfield. Permitted a motor vehicle to wait in North Street, Sudbury, where waiting is prohibited. Fined £40 with £35 costs.

Sudbury Magistrates' Court, May 25

Shaun Anthony Jacobs (23) of Bantocks Road, Great Waldingfield. Drove a car without due care and attention at Ten Tree Road, Great Waldingfield. Fined £160 with £70 costs. Licence endorsed with five penalty points.

Sudbury Magistrates' Court, August 18

Joseph Mitchell (35) of Bantocks Road, Great Waldingfield. Used a motor vehicle on the A134 at Leavenheath with no test certificate. Fined £100 with £35 costs.

Charles Langford Steed (36) of Badleys Cottage, Great Waldingfield. Drove a Ford Transit van in Lavenham Road after consuming excess alcohol, 79 microgrammes of alcohol per 100 millilitres of breath. The legal limit is 35 microgrammes. Fined £200, £55 costs and disqualified for 24 months. Disqualification may be reduced if defendant satisfactorily completes rehabilitation course.

Mark George LaFord of Alexander Drive, Great Waldingfield. Kept an unlicensed vehicle in Ballingdon Street, Sudbury. Fined £100 with £50 and ordered to pay £13.34 back duty.

Gareth Claude Gipp (22) of Alexander Drive, Great Waldingfield. Used or threatened unlawful violence. Community punishment order for 80 hours. Order for forfeiture and destruction of

The following were fined for unlawfully using a colour television set without a licence:
Mark Barnard (42) of Shelley Avenue, Great Cornard, fined £120 with £45 costs.
Peter Berry (31) of Braithwaite Drive, Great Waldingfield, fined £120 with £45 costs.

Emily Kirwan (33) of Upsher Green, Great Waldingfield. Used an unlicensed motor vehicle on the A134 at Sudbury. Fined £220 with £50 costs and ordered to pay £41.25 back duty.

St Edmundsbury Magistrates' Court, June 25

George Barr of Bantocks Road, Great Waldingfield, Sudbury. Being the owner of a Ford Mondeo failed to give information in writing to St Edmundsbury Borough Council identifying the driver. Fined £60 and ordered to pay £46.89 costs.

Sudbury Magistrates' Court, June 16

David Donald Steed (68) of Badley Road, Great Waldingfield. Drove a Peugeot in Waldingfield Road, Sudbury, after consuming alcohol exceeding the prescribed limit, 91 milligrammes in 100 millilitres of blood. Disqualified for three years and licence endorsed. Fined £50. Ban may be reduced by nine months if defendant satisfactorily completes rehabilitation course. No test certificate, no separate penalty.

Peter Douglas Mayhew (50) of Lynns Hall Close, Great Waldingfield. Drove a motor car at Parkway, Bury St Edmunds, with no insurance. Fined £100 with £30 costs and licence endorsed with six penalty points. No test certificate and drove otherwise than in accordance with licence, no separate penalty.

A TEENAGER was ordered to pay £500 compensation after destroying property in a drunken rage.

Peter Williams (18) of Brandeston Close, Great Waldingfield, admitted destroying plant pots and damaging the door of a house in Great Cornard after rowing with a friend following a drinking session.

Prosecutor Anita Addison told Sudbury Magistrates' Court on Friday how Williams had been drinking with friends before committing criminal damage, on December 22 last year. Shortly after mid-

HAXELL William James (Bill). Passed away peacefully in the West Suffolk Hospital on Wednesday 4th June 2003 aged 80 years. Sadly missed uncle to Trish and great uncle to Rachael and John. Brother in law to Lilian. Bill will be greatly missed by all his family and friends. Funeral service to take place at the Church of St. Lawrence, Great Waldingfield on Monday 16th June at 10.30am.

FULKER, HELEN MAY At home on 5th September, beloved wife of Frederick, Mother of Patricia and the late Robert, Grandmother of Susannah, Robert and Samantha. The funeral service will take place at St Lawrence Church, Great Waldingfield on Monday September 15th at 12.30am. Family flowers only please. Donations if desired to Marie Curie Cancer Care Nurses

WELSH. Mr Henry Welsh died at the West Suffolk Hospital on 12th June 2003. The funeral will take place at Great Waldingfield Church, Monday June 23rd at 11.30

RADLEY Freda Joyce (formerly Hasler) aged 80 years, passed away peacefully at Mellish House on Friday 3rd October. Much loved wife of Basil and mother of John and Stephen Hasler. Mother-in-law to Rosemary and the late Valerie, grandmother to Daniel, Patrick, James and Tony. Funeral service 10am on Monday 13th October at St. Mary's Church, Gestingthorpe. Flowers or, if desired, donations for The Alzheimer's Society

HAXELL Lilian Ada passed away peacefully on Saturday 26th February 2004 aged 81 years. A much loved wife to the late Ted, mother to Trish, mother in law to Paul and Grandma to Rachel and John. The funeral is to take place at Great Waldingfield Church on Wednesday 10th March 2004 at 11.00am. Flowers or donations if desired to Cancer Research UK may be sent in memory of Lilian c/o Co-operative Funeral Service, Cornard Road, Sudbury.

STEED David Donald of the Badleys, Gt. Waldingfield. Eldest son of Donald and Joyce Steed passed away at home Saturday 25th September. Funeral service Great Waldingfield Church, Thursday 7th October 2.30pm. Flowers optional or donations to Cancer Research.

Douglas Harry East

1930 - 2005

A GREAT Waldingfield couple celebrated 50 years of marriage this week, joined by almost every guest who was at their wedding.

Great Waldingfield Primary School

Harvest Gifts

Rev John Fieldgate and Edna Allen took gifts from the Harvest Festival at the church to elderly people in the village. Their thoughtfulness was greatly appreciated and much enjoyed, not only for the gifts but for the opportunity of a little chat and, for some, a first meeting with the Rector.

A TERRIFIED teenager fought desperately to control a car after her mother collapsed and died at the wheel.

Melanie King's 18-year-old daughter Sarah grabbed the steering wheel and hand-brake in a bid to prevent a crash. The car eventually came to rest against a bank.

Poignant reminder ... Flowers laid at the spot where Melanie King's car came to rest in Great Waldingfield after she collapsed and died at the wheel.

Melanie King, with daughters Sarah, right, and Alison, pictured on a family holiday.

Gemma: a model in the making

FASHION'S newest supermodel glided down the catwalk and paused to take in the admiring glances.

Then, as the audience burst into applause, she gently wagged her tail.

It was her first time on the runway but with her toy blue elephant clamped firmly in her mouth, she took to it like a duck to water – or, well, a dog to a marrowbone.

Guide dog Gemma was helping her partially-sighted owner Mandy Cunnington model in a fashion show organised by Edinburgh Woollen Mills in Sudbury.

Mandy and the four year-old yellow labrador made four trips down the catwalk at the town centre shop during the show in aid of Guide Dogs for the Blind on Monday.

Jane Jones, a friend of Mandy who is also registered blind but does not used a guide dog, also modelled four outfits in front of around 70 people.

Mandy, from Great Waldingfield, said: "Gemma is a lovely dog. I've had her for two and a half years now.

"She did really well and carried her favourite toy in her mouth up and down the catwalk. She was tired by the end, though, because of all the excitement.

Special service will remember loved ones

TWO village churches will be holding a special service on Sunday for people wishing to remember relatives and friends they have lost.

Tuesday, November 2, is All Souls' Day, the day on which Christians remember the souls of those who have died.

For the second year Acton and Great Waldingfield churches, All Saints and St Lawrence, will each be holding special services on the Sunday before at 3pm.

Extending an invitation to people to join together in this act of remembrance, the Rev John Fieldgate, said: "The service will provide the opportunity to share with others in celebrating the life of our loved ones. There will be a memory tree for us to write the name of loved ones on a leaf and hang it on the tree.

"There will be an opportunity to chat with one another over a cup of tea after the service. Many people found the service helpful last year and I hope it will prove to be the same this year.

"Everyone will be welcome."

n Poppy Appeal award certificates were awarded to: Hazel Batley, Alan Brockbank, Betty Bullard, Jack downs and Bill Shirley for five years; Stuart Carpenter and Caron Downs for ten years; Beverley Smith for 15 years; Barbara Gardiner for 20 years; Pauline Bartrop for 25 years; Gwen Stearns for 30 years and Peggy Pell for 55 years.

New rural beat officer will be patrolling familiar ground

● His 12 parishes are: Lavenham, Cockfield, Thorpe Morieux, Preston St Mary, Brettenham, Little Waldingfield, Great Waldingfield, Acton, Chilton, Newton Green, Bures St Mary and Little Cornard.

Born and bred ... PC Darren Marshall is taking on 12 Suffolk parishes – including the one where he was born.

Picture: Phil Morley

0311-189-30

● Tools worth £1,000 were stolen by thieves who broke into a van in a driveway in Folly Road, Great Waldingfield, between 8pm last Wednesday and 7am last Thursday.

Police ask anyone who saw anything suspicious to call PC Jason Rice on (01284) 774300.

Police want your help

POLICE are appealing for information after a home was broken into in Great Waldingfield.

The home in Bowling Green was entered between noon on Thursday and noon on Friday.

It is not known what items, if any, have been stolen.

Peter Berry (37) of Braithwaite Drive, Great Waldingfield. Used an unlicensed vehicle in Windham Road, Sudbury.

Proved in absence. Fined £50 with £50 costs and ordered to pay £9.17 back duty.

Nick wins international award

Seeing is believing ... Nick Oliver of Waldingfield has won a top photographic award.

Happy landing for crash pilot

A PILOT who was forced to eject from his burning jet fighter over Great Waldingfield in the 1970s returned to the area for the first time to catch up with some old friends.

RAF Flt Lieut George Fenton bailed out when his Lightning XP700 caught fire shortly after take-off from RAF Wattisham in 1972.

The reunion was organised by Ken Hayward, of Chilton Lodge Road, Sudbury, who was a fireman stationed at RAF Wattisham for 10 years.

While researching the history of the crash, he had the idea of getting the pilot and others involved in the incident together for the first time.

He said: "A lot of people have asked me about the accident, and I realised that many people were confused about what had actually happened.

"These days some people say that the fighter plane, which crashed in Waldingfield, came down during the Second World War. I wanted to research the events and come up with the definitive version of what happened.

"I got more interested in the idea as I went along, and in the end came up with the idea of getting in touch with the pilot and inviting him back."

Flt Lieut Fenton was taking part in a rehearsal for an air display, which involved a team of pilots taking off one after the other at intervals of three seconds.

As his Lightning Interceptor aircraft left the runway, he became caught in the slipstream of the previous jet to take off and touched the runway with the underside of the plane.

A member of the ground crew noticed flames coming from a fuel tank and contacted the pilot to tell him he had to bail out.

Luckily Flt Lieut Fenton was able to climb to 2,000 feet – a safe height to launch the ejector seat – before the flames took hold.

He came down in Milden, where he was picked up by farmer Philip Morley, who looked after him until a USAAF helicopter picked him up and took him to hospital. He had no serious injuries.

After the pilot ejected, the plane carried on towards Sudbury and eventually crashed into a holly tree at Valley Farm, Great Waldingfield, much to the astonishment of farm workers harvesting nearby.

On Saturday Flt Lieut Fenton, who how lives in Holyhead, Wales, met Mr Morley as well as others who had witnessed or played a part in the events of 32 years ago.

Also present were members of the Suffolk Military Aviation Group and representatives of Wattisham Aircraft Museum.

Mr Hayward gave a short talk about the events of the crash, before presenting the pilot with a framed photo of his Lightning XP700 as well as parts recovered from the crash site.

He said: "The reunion went very well. George was very pleased to have been invited back to the area, and seemed very happy to meet up with everyone who was involved at the time."

Looking back ... Onlookers pose with the tail section of the crashed jet at Valley Farm, Great Waldingfield.

Jumble cash

A JUMBLE sale in Great Waldingfield Village Hall last month raised £970 for the Rainbow Ward at West Suffolk Hospital.

Organisers Garry and Tina Farthing thank everyone who helped them.

THE garden party held by Mr and Mrs Paul Martland at their home on August 4 raised £396.73 for arc (Arthritis Research Campaign).

This amount will be doubled by Barclays. The committee of the Sudbury branch of arc would like to thank Mr and Mrs Martland and all those who supported this event.

SHIRLEY ROSE
Sudbury chairman, arc
Chestnut Close
Great Waldingfield

Harvest blaze

SUDBURY firefighters were called to Badley Road, Great Waldingfield, where they dealt with a blaze involving a combine harvester last Wednesday afternoon.

KYTE Madeline May passed away peacefully at Laxfield House Nursing Home on Monday March 28th 2005. Aged 91 years. Wife of the late John. Dear Mother to Godfrey. Nana to Thomas. Sister to Betty and a dear Mother-In-Law to Carolyn. The funeral service will take place at Our Lady And Saint John Catholic Church, Sudbury on Tuesday April12th at 12.30 followed by cremation at Colchester Crematorium. Flowers or donations if desired payable to Brown, Fenn & Parker and send to 37, North Street, Sudbury. CO10 1RD. To be donated to local charities.

Sudbury courthouse.

Great Waldingfield man admits nightclub assault

A GREAT Waldingfield man has been warned he may face jail after a nightclub wounding incident in Sudbury.

Adam Bull (21), of Kenyon Drive, appeared at Ipswich Crown Court on Monday, when he pleaded guilty to unlawful wounding of Mark Batten (24) in the early hours of February 29 this year at Eastern's nightclub.

Recorder Rex Bryan postponed sentencing to July 30 for a report from the probation service.

Mr Bryan bailed him to the sentencing date.

Stuart Roscoe (31) of Badleys Close, Great Waldingfield. Used a colour television without a licence. Fined £120, ordered to pay £45 costs.

Thomas David Sagen (18) of Badleys Road, Great Waldingfield. At Weavers Lane, Sudbury, drove a car with disfunctional lights. Fined £80 with £35 costs. Credit given for guilty plea.

The following were dealt with for using a colour television set without a licence:
Wendy Berry (34) of Braithwaite Drive, Great Waldingfield, fined £120 with £45 costs.

House burgled

A BURGULARY took place at a house in Alexander Road, Great Waldingfield.

The house was entered on Sunday, January 25, between 6.45am and 9am, and a handbag stolen.

George Barr (35) of Bantocks Road, Great Waldingfield. Kept an unlicensed vehicle on a road. Fined £100, ordered to pay £50 costs and back duty of £68.75.

April 4

George Barr (35) of Bantocks Road, Great Waldingfield, Stole one can of Red Bull value £1.30 belonging to Gainsborough Service Station. Stole spanners value £399.95 belonging to Halfords. Community punishment order for 40 hours, 12 month period, and £60 costs. Ordered to pay £1.30 compensation to Gainsborough Service Station and £399.95 to Halfords.

Sharon Barr (36) of Bantocks Road, Great Waldingfield. Drove a motor vehicle on a restricted road, the B1071 at Lavenham, at a speed exceeding 30 miles per hour. Fined £80 with £35 costs. Licence endorsed with four penalty points.

James Barr of Lynns Hall Close, Great Waldingfield. Kept an unlicensed vehicles in Bantocks Road, Great Waldingfield. Proved in absence. Fined £200 with £50 costs and ordered to pay £9.17 back duty.

Magistrates' Court, June 14

Peter Mark Berry (37) of Braithwaite Drive, Great Waldingfield. Used a motor vehicle at Windham Road, Sudbury, with no insurance. Fined £240 with £35 costs and licence endorsed with seven penalty points. No test certificate, fined £110. Both proved in absence.

Andrew James Sagon (19), 117 Folly Road, Great Waldingfield. Used a vehicle which was untaxed. Fine £435, costs £50, back duty £217.50.

Alan Norman Perry (31) of Holbrook Close, Great Waldingfield.
Assaulted Emma-Jane Perry by beating at Great Waldingfield. Community order with supervision for 12 months. No order for costs or compensation in view of lack of means.

Robert Leeks (40) of Tentree Road, Great Waldingfield. Drove a Ford Mondeo in Waldingfield Road after consuming alcohol which exceeded the legal limit, 77 microgrammes in 100 millilitres of breath. The limit is 35 microgrammes. Disqualified from driving for 20 months and fined £200 with £43 costs. Disqualification may be reduced by five months if defendant satisfactorily completes rehabilitation course. Drove without due care and attention, fined £100. No test certificate and no insurance, remanded until July 9 to produce documents.

Robert Leeks (40) of Tentree Road, Great Waldingfield. Failed to surrender to bail. Fined £50.

John Kevin Cook (53) of Alexander Drive, Great Waldingfield. Drove a motor vehicle on a restricted road, the A1092 at Cavendish, at a speed exceeding 30mph. Fined £60 and licence endorsed with three penalty points. Pleaded not guilty to driving a motor vehicle on the A134 at Newton Green at a speed exceeding 30mph. Case dismissed, no evidence offered.

IN COURT

Sudbury Magistrates' Court, April 5
Basil Jack Brett, 49, of Lavenham Road, Great Waldingfield. Drove on the A14 at Rougham at a speed exceeding the 70mph limit. Fined £250 with £35 costs. Licence endorsed with four penalty points.

Christmas story goes walkabout

A PROCESSION depicting the true story of Christmas made its way through Great Waldingfield on Tuesday.

Children from the village primary school, dressed as the key figures from the Nativity started their journey at school and travelled through the village.

Jane Hatton and Jane Crawford led the way as Mary and Joseph on a pony and they stopped at houses along the way, asking if there was anywhere for them to stay.

They then made their way to the church for their Bethlehem "census", and filled in their census forms along with fellow pupils.

Later, the procession made its way to a nearby stable where shepherds and real sheep visited Mary and Joseph and baby Jesus.

The procession was then led back to the school by an illuminated star and the three wise men.

Teacher Faith Marsden said: "The day was wonderful and went very well."

"We've never done anything like this before but a lot of people were interested in it and the children did very well."

Stable mates ... Mary (Jane Hatton), Joseph (Jane Crawford), baby Jesus and a four-footed friend. 0312-150-2

Snowdrop Weekend

We are hoping that there will soon be a magnificent show of snowdrops in the churchyard once again this year. On **22nd February** we will be providing refreshments in church between **2-4pm**. So please come along to enjoy the snowdrops and join us for a cuppa.

Curtis-Clark

MICHAEL Curtis and Michelle Clark of Lynn Hall Close, Great Waldingfield, were married at the Olympic Lagoon Resort in Cyprus.

Warburton – Harris

David Warburton, of Hitcham, and Jaimie Harris, of Great Waldingfield, were married at St Lawrence's Church, Great Waldingfield.

Grieves – Chapman

John Grieves, of Great Waldingfield, and Melanie Chapman, of Darlington, County Durham, were married at St Lawrence Church, Great Waldingfield.

Lt Colonel Arthur Claverley Hordern

Lt. Col. A. C. Hordern passed away on September 19th 2004 at the " Claremont" residential home, Corsham, Wiltshire at the age of 97.

The "colonel" as most of us neighbours knew him, but generally " Mike" to his close family and friends was born in 1907 to a church/military family, spending his early years in Cheshire. His father was a Chaplin General and he told me it was inevitable that he would follow the family tradition and go into the army. He studied at Oxford University obtaining an honours degree in history but also represented his university at rugby, cricket, rowing and cross-country. Following his time at Oxford he joined the army in 1931 as a commissioned officer, rising through the ranks to Lt Colonel. He served through the conflicts in Burma and Malaya commanding the 1st Royal Warwickshire Regiment and later the 3rd Malay Regiment. He held other staff appointments in many parts of the world before retiring from the army in the 1950s. He was awarded the OBE before leaving the army for his services, something that he did not refer to or use very often. Only recently when this cropped up in conversation he explained to me that OBE stood for " Others B—— Efforts" and that as the recipient he had been awarded the honour not only due to his own achievements but also to the achievements, courage and bravery of the men he had commanded. Modesty in the extreme.

Regal trio ... The Three Wise Men, Vince Humphries Paul Harvey and John Fieldgate outside Great Waldingfield Church. 0312-1

Special guest launches new guide

THE annual church fete in Great Waldingfield welcomed a special guest for the launch of a new church guide.

Rose Braithwaite (90), grandaughter of one of the village's best known vicars, signed copies of the guide which gives a history of St Lawrence Church, built in the 14th century.

Her grandfather was Francis Joseph Braithwaite who led the congregation in Victorian times and who is buried in the churchyard.

He has a road named after him in the village – Braithwaite Drive - and was a popular and generous man.

Churchwarden Chris Francis contributed to the guide along with other villagers and the current rector, the Rev John Fieldgate, who also opened the fete.

Miss Braithwaite had travelled from her home in London for the fete which raised more than £600 for church funds.

Mr Francis said: "We sold 30 guides and thought it fitting to invite Rose to help us launch it.

"Her grandfather was very highly thought of when he was vicar here and did much for the village.

"There is a lot of local history connected with the church and the guide reflects this."

om left, the Rev John Fieldgate, Rose Braithwaite and Chris Francis unch the new guide to Great Waldingfield Church.
Picture: Phil Morley. 0407-109-130

16   Free Press, Thursday, May 26, 2005

Hymn writer honoured at village church

A SPECIAL service is being held to celebrate the life of a 16th century rector who helped write some of Britain's favourite hymns.

John Hopkins, rector of Great Waldingfield from 1561 to his death in 1570, was co-author with Thomas Sternhold of the first national English hymn book.

Sunday's service at Waldingfield's St Lawrence's Church will feature some of the book's best known hymns – including *All People That On Earth Do Dwell*.

Susan Ranson, author of a book on John Hopkins, said the 16th century-style service which starts at 11am would be followed by refreshments.

Freelance proof reader Mrs Ranson, from Norwich, lived in Great Waldingfield for 35 years and used to sing in the church choir.

2005

Playgroup leader Ann Stone said: "We had the opportunity to move and decided it would be nice to be a part of the school.

"It is very useful to have everything under one roof – it means we can join in with some of the activities which the older children do, while still keeping our independence.

"We are now right in the centre of the village which makes it easier for people to get here."

Celebrating ... pupils and staff from First Friends playgroup in their new home at Great Waldingfield primary school.   0502-225-4

A HEARTBROKEN couple is facing a court showdown with Babergh District Council after the authority decided to go ahead with legal moves to throw them off their own land.

Not only do they face possible eviction from their treasured smallholding but also a fine of up to £20,000 following the outcome of a meeting held last week.

Eric and Christine Hazell have lived in a caravan at Folly Farm, in Great Waldingfield, for the past four years - where they have enjoyed a secluded existence tending to their livestock.

Unseen from Folly Road their temporary home has not drawn a single complaint from neighbours and the couple enjoy the full support of Great Waldingfield Parish Council for their unconventional lifestyle.

Good wishes and congratulations to **Kathy Crisp** who is recovering from a hip operation and will be celebrating her 80th birthday on 21st July.

Good wishes too to **Luke Batley** who is receiving further treatment after having had two operations

Condolences to the families of **Bill Haxell, Henry Welsh** and **Mrs Riches** who have sadly died recently.

Always someone to cheer you up ... Mrs Garner (left) and Mrs Middleton with children at Great Waldingfield Primary School. 0407-188-6

JOAN Garner will miss her pupils desperately when she retires this week as head of Great Waldingfield primary school.

But two special children in her own life will be seeing a lot more of her ... grandchildren Emily (10) and Oliver (6).

Spending a lot more time with them is a top priority among her retirement plans.

Mrs Garner has retired after nine years as head of the 80-pupil village school.

Village People

Congratulations to **Anne Francis** on her community achievement award.

Anne Francis was given a Community Achievement Award for her voluntary work with the "Success after Stroke" group at Bradbury Courtyard in Sudbury. The group meets every Tuesday morning, and has an hour of physiotherapy exercise, followed by social time and then speech therapy. The award was presented at Stoke by Nayland Golf Club on Wednesday, 23rd February 2005.

Musical youth ... From left, Jamie Hunt (9), Gabby Pars (8) and Kate Hann try their hand at playing the didgeridoo during Great Waldingfield Primary School's Creative Earth Arts festival.
www.photostoday.co.uk 0506-57-95

Standard bearer on parade at Sudbury. 0511-120-

SCHOOL GOVENOR

World art in the spotlight

We send our condolences to **Betty Tegg** on the recent death of her husband, **Eddie**.

Mike Stone, who runs his business in the building next to the shop (the building is called Hopkin) called out to me the other day as I was walking from the bus and invited me in to see (no, not his etchings!) but the mural depicting the village that is on the wall of his back room. It was painted by Mick Culham who is a self-taught artist, but obviously with loads of talent. It is amazingly colourful and lively with lots of surprising features, which children will love. It combines the main features of life in this village and deserves to be seen by many people. Mike has asked me to tell you about it and to emphasise that you are truly welcome to call in to look at it when you are passing, in normal business hours of course.

Inspired ... Author Michael Stone and artist Michael Cullum pictured in front of the mural showing aspects of Great Waldingfield.

0503-225-292
Picture:

MEMORIES and pictures of a Suffolk village are wanted for a new book on the history of Great Waldingfield.

And to celebrate the launch of the community project, artist Michael Cullum has painted a mural of the village in the office of author Michael Stone.

Mr Stone's book will cover the events of the last 100 years, and he is particularly interested in the early half of the century before World War Two.

Villagers of all ages are contributing their stories and Mr Stone hopes it will become a project the whole community can get involved with.

He said: "It started off with me trying to think of ways to start up a village project.

"Then it came to me that a book about the last century in the village would be ideal.

"A history of the village was written by Louise Kenyon in the 1970s but it concentrated on the middle ages.

"I thought it would be a good way of recording the history and reminiscences of people who are still alive."

To celebrate the project, village artist Michael Cullum has created a 15 foot by 8 foot mural.

It depicts aspects of Great Waldingfield and can be seen at Mr Stone's office at The Street, Great Waldingfield, which is used for meetings to discuss the book.

Mr Stone would like to hear from anyone with information or pictures of the village's history during the last 100 years.

● He can be contacted at his office at The Street, Great Waldingfield on (01787) 882425 or by emailing info@buresbusiness.co.uk.

Suffolk Constabulary - Community Beat Update
Great Waldingfield

03/02/05   Theft of a Silver Magno pedal cycle from Folly Road

19/02/05   Between 17th & 19th unoccupied farm house near to Folly Road was broken into - furniture and toys stolen.

Any problems, we can be contacted on 01284 774340.

PC 270 D Marshall   email: Darren.Marshall@suffolk.pnn.police.uk
PC 216 S Lee-Amies   email: Scott.Lee-Amies@suffolk.pnn.police.uk
Community Police Officers

GLORIOUS sunshine attracted thousands of visitors to a redundant airfield for an annual steam weekend.

Organised by members of the Monks Eleigh Bygone Collectors' Club, the event featured dozens of engines, lovingly restored by their owners.

The weekend, an annual event, was held on the airfield at Great Waldingfield and engines came in all shapes and sizes, from the very large, to model ones.

All the fun of the fair ... Cole's traction engine (right, 0506-

20/10/04	Overnight Ford Sierra stolen later used to commit offences in the Essex area.
29/10/04	Unknown offenders broke into telephone kiosk and stole cash.
23/06/05	Locks forced on a vehicle in Folly Road power tools and fuel stolen.
30/06/05	Overnight a parked and unattended Peugeot 406 colour white was stolen from outside residential dwelling.

COMPETING in their first World Mirror Championships, sisters Emma and Martina Barry from Great Waldingfield finished an excellent 24th, one disqualification costing them nine places.

● Coming ashore after a hard day

Getting to Know You

Angie Jones - Headteacher at Gt Waldingfield Primary School

Married to Maurice (Mogs) and has 3 children.

Lives near Castle Hedingham.

Childhood years in Coggeshall.

Favourite place... cliff tops and South Drakensburg Mountains.

Favourite past time...picking blackberries, browsing in bookshops.

Hobbies... baking, gardening and keeping chickens.

Most admire... my husband and eldest son, Ben.

Historical figure... Jesus.

Pet hate... people pushing in and painfully slow drivers.

Favourite books — John's gospel and Cider with Rosie

Favourite TV... period dramas.

Favourite Music... Debussy and Nichole Nordeman.

Favourite Tree... Bramley apple tree in my garden.

Favourite Colour...green

Favourite Film... Shrek.

Joke...What do you call a lady in the distance?   DOT.

Full Name: Leon Philip Stedman
Party: UK Independence
Age: 61
Marital Status: Married
Children: One, and four stepchildren.
Where do you live? Great Waldingfield.
Occupation: Electrical-mechanical engineer (semi-retired).
Favourite national newspaper: Daily Mail
Likes: My wife's far eastern cookery. Playing bridge badly.
Dislikes: Two-faced bigots.
What makes you laugh: Subtle humour.
What makes you angry: Being asked about my "ethnicity". Such information cannot be used for any legal purpose.
Political history: Joined Tory party age 25, left two years ago. Served as district councillor (Conservative). Did not stand at last election. Joined UKIP within last year.
What is the most important issue that faces your county in the next five years? Repeal of the 1972 Communities Act, to free us from European corruption and bureaucracy. Unless we do this all issues will eventually be decided by unelected officials in the EU.
What do you think are the top five issues for people in your division? Council tax rises, the proposed recycling plant at Waldingfield, road safety and road improvements, personal security and policing, health and pensions.
How do you hope to improve the lives of people in your division, if elected? I hope to ensure that tax money is spent sensibly and wisely to allow people to keep more of their hard-earned cash. Tax rises should be below the rate of inflation.
Summarise yourself politically in three words: Truthful, trustworthy, blunt.

Bryony's the best – at Santa's home

A FORMER Sudbury schoolgirl has found her niche – selling homes in the land of Father Christmas.

Byrony Marsden won a prestigious award for her summer work marketing luxury log cabins in Lapland. The ex-Sudbury Upper School pupil clinched first prize in the marketing category of the Shell and Technology Enterprise Programme.

A law student at Anglia Polytechnic University in Chelmsford now, she also came runner up for Most Enterprising Student in Essex. During her placement, Byrony was flown out to Lapland to meet clients and is now planning exhibitions in London and Dubai for the log cabin company.

Colin Brunt, managing director of Essex-based Trinity Construction, said: "I couldn't be more delighted. I am so pleased she has done well as Byrony has given the business a real boost."

Great Waldingfield Horticultural Show Committee

On Saturday 23rd April, the Show Committee staged the 21st Village Spring Show in the village hall. A lovely spring day attracted 172 exhibits from 31 exhibitors. The number of exhibitors and entries were well up on last year and there were noticeably many new faces, which is encouraging.

On Saturday 10th. September, the show committee staged the 21st Autumn Horticultural Show in the Village Hall. The show attracted 277 exhibits from 85 exhibitors. There were noticeably many new faces, which was encouraging. All sections were well supported - there being only 1 class with no entries. Well done all those who entered!

The new domestic section was well supported with a good standard of entries and the Lillian Haxell Trophy, given by her family for this section, was presented by her grand-daughter Rachael Burnham.

YOUR PARISH TREE WARDEN

I am reintroducing myself in this first edition of the new village newsletter. I have held the voluntary post of tree warden for the last ten years as appointed by the parish council. I am available for advice on matters relating to trees and hedges in the village. I hold details of Tree Protection Orders, and report back to Babergh District Council, which runs training sessions and support for all its parish tree wardens.

CLIFFORD GEORGE LEE

1912 – 2005

Lilian Haxell

8th May 1922—28th February 2004

Lilian was born in Sudbury, the tenth of eleven children. Her family moved to Great Waldingfield when she was a small child and, apart from a few years in Little Waldingfield, she spent 76 years here.

She attended the village school, which at that time was next to the church, and later won a scholarship to the grammar school in Sudbury where she stayed for just three years before having to leave, at the age of 14, to care for her mother.

Lilian joined the church choir and also sang at village concerts accompanied by one of the boys from school—the start of a life-long partnership. She and Ted married in Great Waldingfield church in 1942.

At the start of the war she left her job at the library and joined the National Fire Service and became Sudbury's first firewoman.

Warning others ... Mabel Day was targeted by purse snatchers.

A GREAT-grandmother left shocked and scared after her purse was snatched has warned others to be on their guard against thieves.

Eighty-one-year-old Mabel Day's purse containing £170 was stolen from her bag while she was shopping in Sudbury.

"I want to warn other people to be on their guard. I don't want this to happen to anyone else," she said.

"I think more shops should put up notices saying beware of thieves to remind people to be careful.

"It's so easy to be off your guard and I think it would really help."

In March this year, police reported an alarming rise in the number of similar thefts.

A gang of teenage girls was believed to be targeting town centre charity shops preying on elderly customers.

Mrs Day, from Great Waldingfield, had just collected the cash from Sudbury post office last Wednesday morning when her black leather purse was stolen.

Road closed

A ROAD was closed for more than an hour on Friday following a three-car accident.

The accident happened just after 8am on the B1115 junction with Ten Trees Road, in Great Waldingfield.

The cars involved were a BMW, Ford Courier and Ford Fiesta. There were no reports of any injuries.

Pick of the crop ... Children begin harvesting their own potatoes.

Children grow their own good health

HEALTHY eating in schools has gone a step further at one village primary school, where pupils are growing vegetables in their own allotment.

And this week the Great Waldingfield schoolchilren were celebrating after digging up their first crop of potatoes.

Teacher Angie Jones said: "They have done a great job – the allotments had been overgrown with weeds. They even came down in the summer holidays to make sure the vegetables were coming along.

"We wanted them to learn how to grow vegetables to tie into educating them about healthy eating. It also means they can take home fresh produce from schools for their parents."

Carrots, artichokes, runner beans and radishes have already been picked from the allotment.

NEIGHBOURHOOD WATCH - REVIEW 2004

	L.M.	Glems'fd	Lav'm	Acton	Gt.Wald	Lt.Wald	Newton	Chilton	Lt.Corn'd	Alphet'n
DB	1	1			1					
PO	2									
AP	1	6	2	1	1					
VP	34	15	6	10	5		6		1	5
TP	25	8	14	8	7		3		2	2
TV	10	8	2	5	11		2		1	1
	77	38	24	24	25	Nil	11	Nil	4	8

Key: DB   Distraction Burglary   PO   Public Order offences
AP   Assault on persons   VP   Vandalism-property & vehicles
TP   Theft – property   TV   Theft - vehicles

Gavin Webb (35) of Valley Road, Great Waldingfield. Kept an unlicensed vehicle in Station Road, Sudbury. Proved in absence. Fined £100 with £50 costs and ordered to pay £14.17 back duty.

Shane Raymond Walker (25) of Linshall Road, Great Waldingfield. Knowing a motor vehicle had been taken without the consent of the owner at Bury St Edmunds an accident occurred, damaging a telegraph pole. Committed to prison for two months, concurrent. Disqualified from driving for 12 months and until extended driving test passed.

Donald Victor Slade (72), of Bantocks Road, Great Waldingfield. Used an unlicensed vehicle on the A134 at Bury St Edmunds. Proved in absence. Fined £90, no order for costs. Used an unlicensed vehicle in Northern Road, Sudbury. Fined £120 with £45 costs and ordered to pay £42 back duty.

Nathan Goodwin (19), of Bantocks Road, Great Waldingfield. Kept a vehicle at Hillside, Sudbury, having made a declaration that the vehicle would not be used or kept on a public road during the specified period. Proved in absence. Fined £120 with £50 costs and ordered to pay £36.67 back duty.

Bury St Edmunds Magistrates' Court, August 9

Peter Mark Michael Williams (19) of Brandeston Close, Great Waldingfield. Failed to comply with requirements of curfew order imposed on May 3 for theft, possession of a firearm and a bail offence by compromising part of the electronic monitoring equipment. Fined £50 with £65 costs.

Sudbury Magistrates' Court, August 10

Richard Stuart (44) of Coronation Rise, Great Waldingfield. Failed to provide a specimen of breath at Sudbury police station in the course of an investigation into whether he had committed an offence. Disqualified from driving for three years and fined £300 with £75 costs. Disqualification may be reduced by nine months

Cyril Owen Munson (53) of Folly Road, Great Waldingfield. Drove a Renault Extra van in Tamage Road, Acton, after consuming so much alcohol it exceeded the prescribed limit, namely 79 microgrammes of alcohol in 100 millilitres of breath. The legal limit is 35 mcg. Disqualified from driving for 18 months and fined £240 with £43 costs. Disqualification may be reduced by four months and 14 days if defendant satisfactorily completes a rehabilitation course.

Peter Mark Michael Williams (19) of Brandeston Close, Great Waldingfield. Failed to comply with requirements of curfew order by causing the personal identification device to be compromised. Fined £50 with £65 costs to be paid to Premier Monitoring.

Saved ... common lizard

Nick Oliver (above) is a farmer and wildlife photographer

Flashback... the *Free Press* on March 9

BASKING lizards are not as easy to spot as you might think. They are small and the same colour as the grass and logs they rest on.

But one man who knows a lot about them is George Millins, who captures and relocates lizards when developers move in to their habitat.

Currently employed by Persimmon, he says it's about co-operation between conservationists and developers to save local wildlife.

"I have worked with a lot of developers and Persimmon has been the best. We have to make sure they continue to help, because more houses will be built with the current Government in power."

That is more important than ever, with big developments planned for Great Cornard, where George is currently moving lizards from the Bures Road site.

George is helped by Nick Oliver, a local farmer and wildlife photographer. Nick said: "You have to get on your hands and knees and root around. People often stare at us. I wonder if it's best to tell them I am hunting for lizards or just keep silent. Either way they think you are a bit strange."

George and Nick were carrying out a survey on the outskirts of Great Cornard where they had released lizards.

Looking at specially-placed log

Keeping count at Great Cornard ... wildlife expert George Millins

£4,000 in memory of tragic teenager

THE parents of a teenager who died in a car crash have thanked all those who helped raise £4,000 in his memory.

Angela and Roger Griggs, of Lynns Hall Close, Great Waldingfield, said it was a tribute to son Michael's popularity that so much was raised.

The event on March 25 in the village hall was to raise money for the East Anglian Children's Hospices.

Memories ... (from left) Angela, Katie and Roger Griggs, with a picture of Micheal

THE parents of a teenager who died in a car crash are planning a fund-raising day in his memory.

Angela and Roger Griggs, of Lynns Hall Close, Great Waldingfield, hope the popularity of son Micheal will spur people to support their charity push.

174

Africa waits for Katy, 19

STUDENT Katy Taylor is swapping a Sudbury GPs' surgery for a hospital in Madagascar.

The 19-year-old, who has been working as a receptionist at Siam Surgery, will help build a hospital guesthouse, assist with vaccination programmes and organise sports for children.

Her four-week July visit to Mandritsara is part of a programme run by Christian Relief and charity Tearfund.

Katy, of Whitehall Close, Great Waldingfield, said: "My biggest worry is the injections and anti-malaria tablets."

The University of York student added: "I'm looking forward to seeing a totally different culture, working with children and working as part of a team".

● To sponsor her trip, call 01787 373541.

April 20, 2006

... Katy Taylor is off to help doctors at a hospital in Madagascar   0604-66-48

Wizard reading ... Hary Potter fans Arron and Lewis Lockwood enjoy their books at Great Waldingfield with grandad Albert Darkin.

■ CHILDREN at one primary school pampered their mums with a tasty treat (0603-242-46, above).

The smell of baking wafted through the classrooms at Great Waldingfield Primary School, as pupils made cakes for a special tea party for mums.

Head teacher Angie Jones said: "The tea party is something we do each year

See you ... Rudi Baldwin, Francesca Clark, Ben Armstrong, Sydney Pomroy and school governor Sheila Dunnett enjoy book day at Great Waldingfield Primary School.

PARTY TIME: Great Waldingfield Primary School students Bradley Farthing and Jessica Fry with Jean Misselbrook during their victory party – a tribute to war veterans

2005 July

Photograph: MICHAEL HALL

Victory party tribute to war heroes

SAMPLING stew and dumplings and rabbit pie, pupils turned back time at their Suffolk primary school to pay their own personal tribute to war veterans with a victory party.

Dressed as evacuees, children from Great Waldingfield Primary School, near Sudbury, sat under victory-style bunting, sang wartime songs and sampled typical 1940s food. Yesterday's party was part of a campaign led by the Royal British Legion aimed at commemorating the 60th anniversary of the end of the Second World War.

Headteacher Angie Jones said: "We were delighted to hold a victory thanks party. The children heard about the Second World War from local veterans and they were buzzing with excitement at the prospect of meeting up with them – it was great fun for us all."

The party is part of the Legion's The Nation's Biggest Thank You campaign to give everyone the opportunity to celebrate and remember the men and women who fought for the nation's freedom 60 years ago.

Great Waldingfield

A MODERN take on the traditional Nativity story was told by children at Great Waldingfield Primary School in *Are We Nearly There Yet?* Told through the eyes of a modern-day family on a walking trip, the play featured reception and nursery children as angels and shepherds. Headteacher Angie Jones said: "The children sing so beautifully, the parents were amazed at their singing.

"We had a packed house both evenings with standing room only."

176

Assessing the damage ... old soldier Bill Green's garden wall was attacked during a wrecking spree by vandals, and, inset, Bill as a young man in the Army during the war.

A WAR veteran who spent the past two weeks selling poppies in memory of his fallen comrades was left in despair after vandals attacked his home on Remembrance Day.

But this week 84-year-old Bill Green's faith in human nature was restored when a stranger gave him £50 to help rebuild his wrecked garden wall.

Old soldier Bill, one of the area's most dedicated poppy appeal collectors, was so distressed by the vandalism he almost turned down the chance to take the salute at Sudbury's Armistice ceremony.

But he accepted and on Sunday stood proudly alongside Mayor of Sudbury Lesley Ford-Platt as the parade marched past.

Bill's home in Coronation Rise, Great Waldingfield, was attacked by a gang of vandals who rampaged through the village on Friday night. At least six other properties were also hit.

He found what had happened when he went out on Saturday morning. "They had knocked down the wall and the bricks had fallen all over my roses.

"I didn't have the heart to try and clear anything up. It really upset me, and for a while I just didn't want to know anybody.

"It's so hurtful that young people whose freedom we fought the war to protect can behave in this way.

"Later on the Saturday the people from the British Legion said they had a special job for me – taking the salute.

"I was in such a state I wasn't sure I wanted to do it, but I was so glad I did. It really cheered me up.

"And my neighbours have been so good to me. I don't know what I would have done without them.

"Then, this week, a complete stranger came to my door and gave me £50 towards repairing my wall, which wasn't insured.

"I didn't manage to catch her name and I would love to be able to thank her properly. It has really restored my faith in people."

Bill joined the Army in 1942. His six brothers also served in the forces during the war and his father was a soldier in World War One.

Church vestry searched

A CHURCH in Great Waldingfield was broken into and the vestry searched at the end of January.

It does not appear that anything was taken in the break in at St Lawrence Church, The Street, which happened between 11.30am on January 29 and 11.30am on January 31.

Anyone with information should call Pc Jason Rice at Sudbury Police on 01284 774300 or Crime stoppers on 0800 555 111.

Donald Charles Hooper, 71, of Heath Estate, Great Waldingfield. Drove a Vauxhall Corsa in Waldingfield Road, with 64 microgrammes of alcohol in 100 millilitres of breath. The legal limit is 35mcg. Banned for 16 months, fined £200, £43 costs.

Great Waldingfield

02/05/05   Female offender arrested for criminal damage and assault on police in Bantocks Rd area.

05/05/05   Between 05.00hrs & 06.20hrs offenders broke into telephone cash box outside Post Office.

21/05/05   Unknown offender smashed the front glass on the village notice board situated at Green Acres.

Any problems, we can be contacted on 01284 774340.

● Peter Gostling in training at Sudbury's Kingfisher Pool gym. Sudbury rower Peter is flying back to Philadelphia tomorrow where he is on a sports scholarship at Temple University. Peter, who came home for Christmas, has been training with Leander at Henley. See 'Temple perfect cure for injury', page 60

0601-58-125
Picture: Alex Fairfull

What Contributes To A Sustainable Village?

A shop, a Church, a pub, a community hall, a school and, of course, a village magazine so we all know what's happening! So Good Luck to the new team and it's wonderful to know that every house in the village will be receiving a copy of the magazine.

End of the line ... Councillor Frances Bates at the vandalised Great Waldingfield box 0601_85_28

Fix our phone!

A COUNCILLOR has hit out at vandals who wreck phone kiosks.

And Frances Bates is demanding BT fixes one damaged at Great Waldingfield six months ago.

Mrs Bates, the village's representative on Babergh Council, said: "Phone kiosks are very much needed. Not everyone has a mobile phone and sometimes reception is bad here."

A BT Spokesman said: "We hope to have the one in Great Waldingfield, which has been out of action for an unacceptably long time, back working again soon."

Police said kiosks in Acton and Hadleigh had recently been vandalised.

Two men from Cambridgeshire have been arrested in connection with vandalism of a kiosk in Glemsford and bailed to return to Sudbury police station on March 6.

£40,000 extension

Staff and pupils at Great Waldingfield primary show off their new-look school. 0511-162-50
Picture by Alex Fairfull www.photostoday.co.uk

VISITORS to Great Waldingfield Primary will no longer be faced with a "pokey and dark" first impression of the school, following a £40,000 investment.

The Folly Road school has celebrated the opening of an extension, which includes a revamped reception area and headteacher's office.

Angie Jones, head at the school, said: "The whole place has suddenly opened up and it's welcoming at long last. Before it was always pokey and dark and we couldn't welcome people to the school properly.

"The classrooms are lovely and large - but the first impressions people were getting of the school was that it was pretty dark and squashed.

"Now our reception area is welcoming and friendly to visitors."

The school was built in the 1970s but it is only now thanks to the project, funded by the Local Education Authority (LEA), that the school is finally able to offer parents and visitors somewhere to sit as they

04/11/05	Two sets of number plates stolen from vehicles on private property off Folly Road
05/11/05	Hubcap stolen from vehicle on private driveway in Bantocks Road
07/11/05	Damage caused to one house sign and another was stolen in Folly Road.
	Damage caused to windows of the telephone kiosk in Lavenham Road.
11/11/05	Two youths arrested on suspicion of theft of a road sign. Offence admitted.

Overnight 9 offences of damage and one of theft were committed within the village area. The damage consisted of fence panels being kicked in and brick walls knocked over. The theft related to a house sign that was taken from private property.

On Saturday 7th January some children from Great Waldingfield Primary School went to the village hall. We put a smile on the old people's faces and our Mums' and teachers' faces too because we sang some songs to them all.
Jamie McNicholas

Great Waldingfield Gift Day Update

The total raised for the Gift Day is £1564.15— well done and many thanks!

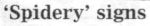

'Spidery' signs

I JUST love the warm red colour and attractive shape of the new Sudbury signs. What a bonus and definite "added value" – if we could actually read that small, spidery writing.

How odd that, in these days of road-safety consciousness, they were allowed in the first place.

The sooner they are down and altered, the better.

But who will pay?
FRANCES BATES,
Rectory Road
Great Waldingfield

Branchlines——Village Community Wood Project

As I am sure none of you are holding your breath to hear the news that we have been allocated land for the wood by the county council you will not be surprised to learn that they are suffering from a 'backlog' and so we are still waiting. However we have decided to think positive. They haven't told us that we can't have it so to keep our spirits up and to keep you interested (you are interested aren't you?) we are asking for your suggestions for a name for our wood. There will be a prize! Send your suggestions to our secretary, Faith Marsden, at the school.

Great Waldingfield CEVCP School 100 Club

Thank you to our regular members who have paid their subscriptions for this year. However, we still need more new members and, you don't have to be associated with the school to join. You get three chances to win £10 a month from January to November and three chances to win £25 in December, left over money goes to the school!

Bug draw winners

GREEN-MINDED youngsters have been helping get the recycling message across through a drawing competition.

Youngsters at Great Waldingfield and Glemsford primary schools were invited by Sudbury's community warden, Andy Nunny, to design posters highlighting the benefits of recycling.

Mr Nunny visited both schools and judged the competition, presenting the winners with book tokens.

Glemsford winners were Jamey Collier, Chloe Ames and Marcus Brooker, with Megan Brett, Amelia Moore and Alisia Hart taking the honours at Great Waldingfield.

Winners ... Great Waldingfield winners Megan Brett, Amelia Moore and Alisia Hart with head teacher Liz Steele and community warden Andy Nunny

March 23, 2006

180

Changes have been made
to the bus timetable.

A new timetable is available
from the Post Office

Proposed Visit to
Romanian Community August 2006
Saturday 18th March
4pm in Acton Church
If you are interested in coming to Romania this
August, come and find out more, also meet
some friends from Mildenhall, who have been
to S.E. Romania and will tell us about their
links there.

John Fieldgate

A GREAT Waldingfield man has
been awarded a crystal decanter
for donating his 100th pint of
blood.

Terry Bacon, of Lavenham
Road, hit the magnificent century just before he retires from
giving blood, at 70, in August.

Mr Bacon began in 1955 during army training.

Although reluctant at first, he
made it part of his routine and
set himself the 100 pint target.

"It's a great way of helping
other people," he said. "It doesn't

Award... Terry Bacon, 69

COMMUNITY ACHIEVEMENT AWARD

On 8th March at a ceremony at Stoke By Nayland Golf Club
Faith Marsden is to be given an award in recognition
Of outstanding work to the community in the Babergh District

Faith works tirelessly in our community to help children and young
people. The award is much deserved and we warmly congratulate he

BRANCHLINES, GREAT WALDINGFIELD COMMUNITY WOOD PROJECT

We have commissioned a valuation on a new 11 acre site. If all goes according to plan, we will raise the necessary finance over the next few months and start planting in the Autumn.
Watch out for further news and a chance to have your say in designing the new wood.

David Taylor

HAIRDRESSING
student Becky Oliver,
from Great Waldingfield,
has taken part in a
national competition to
test her skills in London.

Becky,
who
studies at
West
Suffolk
College,
Bury St
Edmunds,
was
chosen to
represent
the college in the UK
Skills competition after
taking part in the
college's own festival of
hair and beauty.

One big happy
family ... from left
Mia Warburton,
Jaimie
Warburton, Grant
Duff, Therese
Harris, Mabel
Day, Annie Harris
and Harry
Warburton.

www.photos
today.co.uk
0606-52-1

Family brings village pub back to life

A VILLAGE'S only pub is set to
reopen in time for the World
Cup after refurbishment.

The White Horse in Great
Waldingfield closed for several
weeks while new landlords
Therese Harris and Grant Duff
carried out a major refit.

On Friday the pub is set to
reopen, with a newly-installed
widescreen television being put
to good use showing the first

game of the World Cup.

Therese and Grant are no
strangers to the pub trade. As
well as having run several pubs
themselves, Therese is following in mother Mabel Day's footsteps, herself a former landlady.

It will also be a homecoming
for the couple, who lived in
Great Waldingfield before they
took over the Rose and Crown
in Hundon last year. Grant

said: "When we heard the
White Horse was for sale, we
jumped at the chance."

He added: "We want to bring
the village pub back."

They will continue several of
the pub's traditions, including
live music and sponsorship of
the village football team.

They also hope to build a reputation for good pub food.

Smashed

THE windows of a digger
were smashed by
vandals at the Tentree
Road end of Waldingfield
airfield.

Calls about the crime,
which happened between
April 28 and May 2 can
be made to Sudbury
Police, on 01473 613500,
or Crimestoppers, on
0800 555111.

Off to dance for Disney

TWO young dancers are packing their bags for a performance of a lifetime.

Polly Frost, 15, and her 12-year-old friend Emily Wright, who both live in Great Waldingfield, are joining the rest of their dance troupe on a trip to Disneyland Paris.

But meeting Mickey Mouse will have to take a back seat, as the girls will be dancing for holidaymakers after being spotted as they danced in a London show.

Polly said Disneyland Paris representatives were at Her Majesty's Theatre when her troupe, Colchester-based Carole Gale School of Dance, performed.

"We are so excited about going to Disneyland Paris. We can't wait," said Polly, who has been dancing since March last year.

"To be asked to go somewhere like that is brilliant," added Emily.

The girls will be performing modern dance numbers and rock 'n' roll routines.

Exciting trip ... young dancers Polly Frost and Emily Wright.

● Mark Holmes, James Argent, Jo Taylor and Tom Cole with their medals   contributed

Medal winners

TOM Cole and James Argent were among the medal winners when a team from Colchester Phoenix took part in the two-day Reading Cygnets national swimming gala.

Cole, from Great Waldingfield, who has Down Syndrome, had an excellent swim when he competed for the first time in the gruelling 200m breaststroke event, coming in just under his entry time to gain a silver medal position.

In the remainder of his events, including all the team relay events, Cole achieved a total of five silver medal positions.

BRIEF HISTORY OF OUR VILLAGE HALL

Jean Misselbrook

During the early fifties a small group of villagers decided to build a Village Hall. In order to raise the money they held Whist Drives in each other's houses and small fetes and the Hall was built entirely by voluntary labour.

In the sixties a larger committee ran many social events to raise money. Dances, Discos Barbecues etc. were held and the extension was added a new wooden floor was laid throughout and the very muddy car park was resurfaced.

Latterly because a voluntary committee could not be formed the running of the Hall was undertaken by the Parish Council and four Trustees were appointed. Over the years the Hall has been used for Christening Parties, Birthday Parties, Wedding Receptions, Horticultural Shows, Table Sales, Plants Sales, Play Group, Dog Training, Line Dancing, W.I. And many more activities.

What a story the Hall could tell: What a great loss to the Village if this facility was lost.

● THANK you to all those who voted for me. As usual, it was a great pleasure to meet you all, see the wonderful gardens and make friends with your pets, especially the Burmese mountain dog and the American quarter horse!

I have enjoyed being your district councillor for four years.

FRANCES BATES
Rectory Road
Great Waldingfield

I am pleased to report that the new Neighbourhood Watch signs should be in place on the village approach roads in the new year. I would like to thank the Parish Council for their co-operation and for their funding of the project. The work will be carried out by the Highways Department.

Remember, be alert and report incidents you experience or give any information you can about crime to the police.

Brian Rose

Power tools stolen

A HOST of expensive power tools were stolen from a village farm prompting police to issue an urgent appeal for witnesses. Thieves stole an electric saw, sander, router, jigsaw, a twin pack of battery drills and a single drill from an outbuilding on a farm in Lavenham Road, Great Waldingfield.

Anyone with information about the incident - which took place sometime between 5pm on October 20 and 7am on October 21 - should contact Pc Barry Simpson at Sudbury Police Station on 01473 613500.

Thumbnail Sketch on:

Jill Fieldgate—of Yorkshire birth—lived in Nigeria for 8 years, Kenya for 4 years—Worked for UNHCR (United Nations High Commissioner for Refugees). Widowed and worked for a publisher in Bath. Married John after 9 years, enjoys being "Grandma", a game of Bridge, and is described by John as " A full time volunteer".

GREAT WALDINGFIELD CHURCHYARD PROJECT

On Wednesday January 18th, professional contractors will be carrying out tree work in the churchyard. This is in accordance with planning permission from Babergh District Council and the church authorities. We apologise for any inconvenience caused.

Great Waldingfield Bowls and Social Club

UNDER NEW MANAGEMENT

At the annual general meeting held on 15 March, members voted in "Ian" Stares as Chairman. Ian said that he appreciated the efforts of the previous Chairman, Mrs Jean Misselbrook, and proposed that she be made an honorary member of the club. This proposal was accepted unanimously.

40   Free Press, Thursday, February 7, 2008

Wood takes shape

CHILDREN from Great Waldingfield Primary School will plant the first trees of a community woodland tomorrow.

Pupils past and present have been growing trees in the school's nursery for six years.

Now they are ready to be transferred to a plot close to St Lawrence Church.

Campaign group Branchlines has been working on the woodland for six years and secured the site in September.

Old School Wood will become the only woodland in Great Waldingfield.

Villagers are invited to help plant trees between 2pm and 4pm, on Saturday. Tea and cake will be served afterwards at the church.

● GEMMA the guide dog joined in when members of West Suffolk Association for the Blind Sudbury social division staged a fundraising fashion show at Sudbury's Edinburgh Woollen Mill. More than £300 was raised to go towards events for visually impaired people living in and around Sudbury.

For information on the group call Pat Bennett on 01787 310982.

Pictured, left to right: Francesca Davies, Ron Bennnett, Jane Jones, Morley Skipper, Lesley Bannister, Wendy Parker, Mandy Cunnington and her guide-dog, Gemma.

Patrick Proby

Patrick's sudden death shocked and saddened many people in the village. He was a quiet, private person whom I'm sure would have been amazed at the number of people who attended his funeral.

Sadly, we have to report the death of Bill Skinner. After being admitted to Addenbrooks hospital, Bill died on Sunday 19th March 2006.

Suffolk Constabulary - Community Beat Update

Great Waldingfield

27/10/05 During evening of the 27th unknown offenders forced entry into the bowls club off Tentree Rd and stole cash from machine.

04/11/05 Two sets of number plates stolen from vehicles on private property off Folly Road

05/11/05 Hubcap stolen from vehicle on private driveway in Bantocks Road

07/11/05 Damage caused to one house sign and another was stolen in Folly Road.
Damage caused to windows of the telephone kiosk in Lavenham Road.

11/11/05 Two youths arrested on suspicion of theft of a road sign. Offence admitted.
Overnight 9 offences of damage and one of theft were committed within the village area. The damage consisted of fence panels being kicked in and brick walls knocked over. The theft related to a house sign that was taken from private property.

Garage into homes

PLANS to build four new homes on the site of a village garage go before Babergh planners next week.

Great Waldingfield Garage, in Lavenham Road, will be demolished to make way for the semi-detached houses.

In her report to Wednesday's development committee, planner Gemma Pannell has said the current buildings on the site are poor quality.

Great Waldingfield parish councillors have objected to the plan saying the street scene is mainly made up of bungalows and two-storey houses and it would not enhance the area.

Peter James Dagger (39) of Lynns Hall Close, Great Waldingfield. Had in his possession at Ipswich one wrap of amphetamine, a controlled class B drug. Fined £50 with £55 costs. Drugs ordered to be forfeited and destroyed.

Sudbury Court, August 11
Michael Andrew Williams, 53, of Brandeston Close, Great Waldingfield. Exceeded 30 miles per hour speed limit in Bury Road, Lavenham. Fined £60, £35 costs, licence endorsed with three points.

Sudbury, July 10
Sharon Barr, 38, of Bantocks Road, Great Waldingfield. Assaulted Glen Millar in Sudbury. Two counts of assaulting a police officer. Community order for all three offences – supervision for 18 months, curfew at Bantocks Road for six months (10.30pm-7am).

Shaun William Taylor, 44, of Carbonels, Great Waldingfield. Exceeded 30mph limit on the A1141 at Cockfield. Fined £400, £35 costs, licence endorsed with six points.

Raymond King, 56, of Badleys Close, Great Waldingfield. Used a motor van at Heath Way, Great Waldingfield, with no test certificate. Fined £60 with £35 costs.

Plate theft

NUMBER plates were stolen from a red Vauxhall Corsa parked in Alexander Drive, Great Waldingfield, between 10am on Tuesday and 8pm the following day.

Calls about the crime can be made to Sudbury police, on 01473 613500, or Crimestoppers on 08000 555111.

George Barr, 36, of Bantocks Road, Great Waldingfield. Stole two tins of paint value £23.99 belonging to Homebase, Sudbury. Committed to prison for two weeks. Assaulted Neil Dembicki at Sudbury. Committed to prison for two weeks, consecutive.

Ordered to pay £35 compensation. Together with Peter Dagger stole two computer printers and a laundry basket value £219.85 belonging to Tesco Stores Ltd at Ipswich. Committed to prison for eight weeks, consecutive. Twelve weeks imprisonment imposed and suspended by Colchester Magistrates' Court on January 19 to take effect consecutively, period of 25 days on remand to count towards the terms imposed for subsequent offences.

Stole a 15in flat screen TV value £169.97 belonging to Tesco Stores Ltd at Ipswich. Committed to prison for eight weeks, concurrent. Stole two 15in flat screen TVs value £339.94 belonging to Tesco Stores Ltd at Ipswich. Committed to prison for eight weeks, consecutive. Had with him in Copdock retail park a lock knife. No separate penalty, order for knife to be forfeited and destroyed.

G Webb, of Valley Road, Great Waldingfield. Failed to pay Babergh Council £30 excess charge for parking at Magdalen Road without displaying required parking ticket. Proved in absence. Fined £60, £50 costs.

A MAN dressed as Santa Claus featured in a Christmas Eve incident in which a pub customer was wounded by a glass, a court heard.

Shaun Jacobs (24) of Bantocks Road, Great Waldingfield, was jailed for 12 months at Ipswich Crown Court on Thursday after admitting unlawfully wounding Liam Slater.

Donald Victor Slade, 73, of Bantocks Road, Great Waldingfield. Paid for excise licence with dishonoured cheque making licence void. Fined £120, £45 costs, £87 back duty.

Leon Smith, 19, of Alexander Drove, Great Waldingfield. Stole an Apollo mountain bike at Sudbury. Community order for 12 months with supervision. Ordered to pay £200 com-

Harrison Pars 0603-240-88

Jessica Thompson 0603-240-63

Chloe Taylor 0603-240-82

Jamie McNicholas 0603-240-75

Kate Hann 0603-240-76

Aaron Lockwood 0603-240-66

Nicki: What do you think teachers do in the school holidays?
Kate: I think they stay at home and drink tea.
Aaron: They go shopping for lots of food and drink because they haven't got time when they are at school with us.
Harrison: I think they stay at home and have some biscuits and put their feet up.
Chloe: They probably go out to eat and then visit Oxfam and go to parties.
Jessica: They watch telly because they don't at school.
Jamie: Sometimes they play tennis before having a rest.

Nicki: What's best about school holidays? What do you like to do?
Jessica Thompson, seven: I go out to play with my friends and sister. We have lots of fun.
Jamie: I visit granddad in Assington with my bike. I get nice and muddy if it's been raining.
Kate: I normally go to my nan's in Bath. It's lovely there.
Aaron: I stay at home and mess around. I still get up early. Sometimes I'm up at five in the morning in holidays.
Chloe: I go out to the cinema and to the zoo which is fun.
Harrison: I play Sonic Heroes on my Play Station.

Wrong priority

I'VE found it hard over the past few weeks to keep my patience with the people who are moaning about parking tickets. I can't believe the reaction it has provoked.

Perhaps if people put as much effort into campaigning to get harsher penalties for those who speed, drive while using phones or carry an illegal number of passengers, as they do moaning about a traffic warden legally doing his job, we could cut the number of accidents.
L McCARTHY
Bantocks Road
Great Waldingfield

For mummy ... children at First Friends Pre-School in Great Waldingfield sing and dance in a mother's day concert and coffee morning for mums, grannies, aunts and friends.

Steven

STEVEN Chisholm continued his run of form with a high placing in the Kimbolton Festival. Steven, 17, up against some of the country's leading drivers, finishing 18th in the Elite final.

The Sudbury Upper School student, left, from Great Waldingfield, who has been karting for less than three years, knew the event, attracting more than 100 competitors, would be tough.

Kimbolton is his local track, and he was an impressive 11th in his timed practice session, following this up with three excellent heats.

In the first he started 26th on the 34-kart grid, but made steady progress to finish ninth over the eight-lap heat.

Village greets autumn

HUNDREDS of exhibits filled Great Waldingfield village hall for the horticultural society's autumn show.

It attracted 237 entries from 35 exhibitors, including several new faces.

Show secretary John Hughes said: "The handicraft section was particularly well supported. There are some very talented people in the village."

Also popular was the homemade wine section.

But organisers were disappointed by the number of children taking part, with only one entry in the 10 classes available.

Other groups from the village and surrounding area ran stalls outside the hall.

Silver haul... Christine Hutton (above) and Lizzie Anderson
0609-82-1&3

Christmas is a drag!

CHILDREN in Great Waldingfield flexed their muscles to bring a little bit of Christmas back to school.

They collected two Christmas trees from St Lawrence's Church and tried to drag them the half-mile back to the village primary school.

Helpful villagers met them half-way with vans to finish the difficult journey.

Headteacher Angie Jones said: "The trees were very prickly and a bit heavy, but it was a lot of fun."

One is in the playground and one is in the hall, ready to welcome visitors to tonight's Christmas fair, which starts at 6pm.

Father Christmas will be there, as will plenty of stalls.

Police seek ice vandals

POLICE are hunting children spotted throwing lumps of ice at a house before disappearing on their bikes.

They damaged a window in Chapel Close, Great Waldingfield, between 3pm and 4pm on Sunday, March 23.

They were eight to 12 years old. One was wearing a grey hoodie, dark trousers and white trainers and riding a white bike. The second had a dark jacket, trousers and dark bike.

Anyone with information should call Pc David Murphy on 01284 774100.

Sisters in top ten

AFTER three days of competition, Emma and Martina Barry, from Great Waldingfield, were lying tenth in a fleet of 79 at the Mirror World sailing championships at Port Elizabeth, South Africa. Their best placing was a third on the second day. The championships finish today.

Sisters take on world

EMMA and Martina Barry launch their bid for the World Mirror Championships at Port Elizabeth tomorrow, the first day of a week-long regatta at Nelson Mandela Bay, described as the watersport capital of South Africa.

The sisters, from Great Waldingfield, qualified for the championships early last year, and spent time in the autumn training with European champion Hector Cisneros tuning their boat.

The pre-Worlds were sailed earlier this week, which sorted out the final qualifiers, and 100 crews will line up tomorrow for day one.

There are five days of racing, excluding Sunday and Tuesday, with the final day on Thursday next week, and the closing ceremony and prize-giving on Friday.

by Ken Watkins

EMMA and Martina Barry are off to the Irish national sailing championships in Cork next week, getting in some starting practice as part of their build-up to the World Mirror Championships in January.

The sisters, from Great Waldingfield, competed in the UK and European Championships at Poole, coming seventh and 13th, missing out on a higher finish in the latter as some slow starts left them playing catch-up.

Once under way, their excellent boat speed saw them surging through the rest of the fleet, but in a sport where a good start is crucial, they often left themselves too much to do.

The girls' potential and boat speed have been noted by the National and European champion, Hector Cisneros, and they have been selected to do some boat tuning with him, and the recently introduced new mast, prior to the World championships.

Emma, 16, and Martina, 10, were up against 108 other Mirror dinghies in the 12-race open European Championship. Competitors were allowed two discards, and one was their first race, where they rounded the first mark in 76th place, but steadily worked their way up through the fleet to finish 45th.

They had a slightly better start in the next race, rounding the first mark in 25th, again working hard to improve their position and finishing an excellent seventh.

● Emma and Martina Barry with RYA national squad coach Peter Aitken and their trophies from the Nationals at Poole
contributed

Bikes stolen

TWO girls' mountain bikes were stolen from a front garden in Bantocks Road, Great Waldingfield, between 9.30am and 2.30pm on March 8.

Bird scarers... pupils at Great Waldingfield Primary School have made model scarecrows for the school garden 8hw2702011
Right: William Champkin with his new friend 8hw2702013
Pictures Helen Whitcombe

Cub Scouts from Acton and Great Waldingfield get ready for some conservation work   Picture submitt

by Jonathan Schofield

APPLAUSE and cries of victory rang out as controversial plans for quarry by a dangerous stretch of road were rejected by councillors after claims it would make a major road "suicidal".

Drivers of 60 vehicles join protest

Quarry decision today

March 13, 2008

VIPs ... Lewis Lockwood, seven, and Kaye Gooderham eight, on The Terrace at the House of Commons, where they represented Great Waldingfield Primary School at environmental day   Contributed pi

21st November 1933 - 9th February 2008

RONALD JAMES LEEKS

Denise Caron Byford, 42, of Badleys Close, Great Waldingfield. Failed to provide specimen of breath for analysis. Banned from driving for 12 months, fined £220, £60 costs. Ban may be reduced by three months if defendant completes rehabilitation course.

Before ... Charlie Steed takes a fortifying swig before his fundraisng makeover in aid of Great Waldingfield Primary School.

The money poured in from regulars at the pub – raising £300 for the school. Contributed picture

The night farmer Charlie turned into James Bond

Landlord Grant Duff said Mr Steed, 40, a former pupil at Great Waldingfield Primary School, was a willing volunteer for the Trinny and Suzannah-style makeover.

A HAIRY farmer has transformed his appearance to raise cash for a school.

When the licensees of the White Horse in Great Waldingfield set out to raise money for the village school, they decided to give one of their regulars a full fundraising makeover.

And they looked no further than fuzzy-faced farmer and lifelong village resident, Charlie Steed.

Flower beds damaged by drivers

POLICE are seeking more information about drivers who damaged flower beds and grass on the Heath in the centre of Great Waldingfield by driving over them. The incident took place between 8pm on Sunday March 30 and 8am the next morning. Calls in relation to this incident should be made to PCSO Lucy Rout at the West Babergh Safer Neighbourhood Team on 01284 774100.

● Tom with his medals and T-shirt
0611-196-1
Picture: Alex Fairfull

TOM Cole is bidding to emulate Olympic swimmer and Commonwealth Games 200m backstroke gold medallist Adam Ruckwood, and, after winning five medals at this year's world championships, he's well on the way.

Tom, 17, from Great Waldingfield, picked up two golds, two silvers and one bronze medal in Limerick swimming for the GB team in the Down's Syndrome championships.

But Tom's Olympic dream is on hold. At present he is unable to compete as there is no separate category for Down's in the Paralympics.

Don't ask... Janet Baldwin waits at the bus stop – with her birth certificate

JANET Baldwin loves her local bus service. It's regular and reliable and ideal for shopping trips to town.

But she often reaches her destination feeling distinctly depressed because well-meaning drivers keep asking to see her bus pass... and Janet is only 58.

EMMA and Martina Barry had a successful World Mirror championship at Port Elizabeth, South Africa, finishing a creditable 13th.

Emma, 16, and Martina, at 11 one of just five competitors in South Africa under 12, now have their sights set on the UK Mirror championships at their home club of Brightlingsea in August, and the next World event at Pwllheli, North Wales in 2009.

The sisters, from Great Waldingfield, will be working with current champion Hector Cisneros in the run up to the UK championships.

WALDINGFIELD – Did you know that aerial photographs of the village were taken during the Second World War by the Luftwaffe, and Harry Theobald, a Waldingfield villager, was the most decorated man in the village for his feats during that war? Mike Stones of Bures Business Centre explained these and other interesting facts in his talk about our village's past and some amusing tales. Mike is preparing a book on the 20th-century history of the village and would welcome any information from WI members and others on events during this period. Edna Allen showed us an album of photographs and news cuttings of Waldingfield from the 1940s to the present day.

● Taking in the sights. Emma and Martina relaxing before competition starts
Picture: Paula Barry

BRANCHLINES—Gt. Waldingfield Commu

● Emma and Martina, with the green and yellow spinnaker, at the heart of the fleet as it leaves harbour
Picture courtesy Hugo Studio

THE OLD SCHOOL WOOD

I really enjoyed typing that! Is there anyone in the village who doesn't know that the first planting took place on February 8th with village schoolchildren planting trees some of which they had grown? Then on February 9th, 127 people, including 33 children, planted about 500 trees in two hours. All this was done in glorious sunny weather. We were delighted with the support we had, and the lovely community spirit that was evident. All our past problems faded away and we could really believe in the reality of a village woodland. We thank you all and hope for your continued support.

BRANCHING OUT: An unused field has been obtained by community group Branchlines for a woodland in Great Waldingfield, near Sudbury. Left to right: Brian Rose, Lyn Humphries and Shirley Rose

Shaun Anthony Jacobs, 29, c/o address in Bantocks Road, Great Waldingfield. Failed to comply with community requirements of a suspended sentence order by failing to attend unpaid work appointments. Original offence of assaulting a female re-sentenced. Suspended sentence of 12 weeks imprisonment suspended for one year implemented as a sentence of four weeks. Damaged front door of council house in Hawthorn Road, Great Cornard, also re-sentenced. Suspended sentence of 12 weeks imprisonment suspended for one year implemented as a sentence of two weeks. Overall length of sentence four weeks.

Hermitage Ensemble

Professional ensemble of soloists from St Petersburg, Russia.

Present a concert of Russian Sacred Hymns & Folk Songs   a cappella.

At
St Lawrence Churc
Great Waldingfiel
On Friday 4th April at 7.0

Bill 'escapes' hospital

OLD soldier Bill Green "escaped" hospital to play his part in the cermeony at Sudbury town hall.

Mr Green, 86, of Great Waldingfield was hit by a car while selling poppies outside Tesco two Sundays ago. He has been in West Suffolk Hospital with an injured knee since.

But he turned out in medals – and a wheelchair – for Saturday's event.

Mr Green (pictured) has been selling poppies for more than 30 years.

Sudbury and District Royal British Legion's poppy appeal organiser, Stuart Hume, said Mr Green was back in hospital this week.

Mr Green joined the Army in 1942 and served in North Africa – surviving when his troop ship was torpoedoed.

He moved to Great Waldingfield more than 30 years ago to run the village shop with wife Elsie.

CLASS series turing on pupils schools

New faces... the latest in our line-ups of new kids on the block are the reception c Waldingfield Primary School, with teacher Julia Arthurs   0610-141-1 available at www.p

A Tribute to Iris Fisher

It is with great regret we announce the death of Iris, a dear friend and neighbour. Moving to the village from London in the late 1970's with her late husband Roy affectionately known as Fish, they soon became a part of the community and to love their country home.

A lover of music and complete devotion to animals saw Iris caring for her family of geese and dogs along with many others that needed looking after. Very soon she became renowned near and far, giving home from home attention to all in her care. There were often as many as eight canine friends in her home and so many have said how their faithful friends looked forward to their holidays with Iris.

We give thanks for her, for her deep faith and humble self giving. Her sense of humour and cheerful personality has been a gift to this village and to all who had the privilege to make her acquaintance.   Name supplied

Garden lights stolen

Police are appealing for witnesses after 10 solar lights were stolen from a front garden in Great Waldingfield, near Sudbury.

Anyone with information about the incident - which took place sometime between 6pm and 10.30pm on Sunday 11th March in Coronation Rise - should contact Pc Darren Marshall at Sudbury Police Station on 01473 613500 or Crimestoppers on 0800 555 111.

FAMILY OCCASION: Rhona Damant's husband David and children Kristopher and Francesca with the posthumous Babergh Community Achievement award in Rhona's name at last Wednesday's ceremony at Stoke-by-Nayland Golf Club and inset Rhona with husband David at the Extravaganza Ball
Photograph: OWEN HINES

NEIGHBOURHOOD WATCH

Crime Memo extract for Gt.Waldingfield   January 2007

07/01/07   Overnight damage to a parked and unattended car on a private driveway.
14/01/07   Overnight damage caused to the Bowls Club in Ten Tree Rd.
14/01/07   Overnight damage caused to a parked and unattended car in Heathway.

As you may be aware the Village Hall will be out of commission for th foreseeable future.

The Church is available as a venue for suitable functions such as com mittee meeting/talks and exhibitions i.e. art/craft and others.

The cost will be £10 per hour.
For further details please contact
Chris Francis on 01787 370734

March 2009

4 Mar	'The Way of Faith' course
6 Mar	Women's World Day of Praye
7 Mar	Bowls Club 'Spoon Drive'
7 Mar	Churchyard Work Party
9 Mar	Parish Council meeting
13 Mar	Acton Primary Quiz Night
20 Mar	First Friends Quiz Night
21 Mar	Antiques Fair
28 Mar	40's Dance
29 Mar	Bowls Club Whist Drive
29 Mar	Table Top Sales

April 2009

| 2 Apr | Russian Concert |
| 25 Apr | Horticultural Show |

On February 22nd, we said our final farewell to a very dear friend Muriel Turner, who was 99 years old. She was the last of four sisters who lived together on 'Greenacre' for nearly thirty years.

Husband of cancer sufferer receives award on her behalf

COLUMNIST Rhona Damant, whose brave battle with cancer touched the hearts of thousands, was honoured last Wednesday for her inspirational charity work with a posthumous community award.

The mother-of-two, from Great Waldingfield, near Sudbury, raised thousands of pounds for breast cancer charities before her death in November.

She also inspired countless people through her frank and uplifting column in the Mercury's sister paper, the East Anglian Daily Times, portraying life with terminal cancer.

Her work was last night acknowledged with an achievement award from Babergh District Council.

Rhona's devoted husband, David, who collected the award at a ceremony at Stoke-by-Nayland Golf Club, said: "It is wonderful to receive an award and Rhona would have been very happy to receive such marvellous recognition.

"I would have preferred it if she could have collected it herself but it wasn't a sad occasion. The award is a celebration of what she achieved and her effect on people."

Close friend Laini White, who wrote Rhona's column when she was too ill to do so herself, said: "I think she would have been thrilled and in view of what has hap-

pened it is a fitting tribute to her and all she has achieved.

"I am proud of her but I had mixed emotions at the ceremony because it was the first event I have been to without her.

"It has been a traumatic time – I can't tell you how much I miss her."

Laini helped Rhona arrange charity events, including her pink themed balls, until she died of breast cancer at the age of 45, the same age her own mother died of the disease.

In a submission to Babergh, Rhona's nominee, who has not been named, said: "Rhona gave so much and over the last few years has inspired and encouraged the local community to understand more about life and death.

"Rhona wanted everyone in her situation to do as much as possible and I believe she has succeeded."

Rhona was among 25 winners of the council's community achievement awards for 2007.

Council corporate support officer Jill Barton paid tribute to all the winners.

She said: "The number of people who go out of their way to help others is humbling and proves that everyone can play a part in Babergh's success."

NEW DISTRICT COUNCILLOR—JENNY ANTILL
www.jennyantillsblog.blogspot.com

Ballroom & Latin Dancing Success
for Leila Silva & Stephen Daw

Congratulations to Leila and her dance partner (and boyfriend) Stephen, who lives in Newton. Both competed in the Imperial Society of Teachers of Dance Medallist Festival on Sunday 23rd September held in Haverhill Sports Centre. They were in the under 40 years pre-bronze group and being 17 and 19 years old respectively were some of the youngest in this group of very experienced dancers .

Information received from Leila's Mum, Angelina Silva of Bantocks Road.

ARMED police swooped on a quiet village street to seize a suspect after a man was attacked and injured.

A firearms response unit and police helicopter crew were called in after the victim suffered wounds to his leg and neck.

The dramatic scenes in Folly Road, Great Waldingfield took place around two hours after the assault in Blackfriars, Sudbury on Thursday evening.

The road was closed off by police as officers moved in to arrest 40-year-old Stephen Oliver.

He was later charged with causing grievous bodily harm, criminal damage, and failing to provide a specimen of breath.

Oliver was granted bail with a string of conditions when he appeared before magistrates in Bury St Edmunds on Monday.

The conditions include not entering Suffolk except for solicitors or court appointments, living at an address in Swansea, Wales, surrendering his passport, and not contacting a list of seven named people.

He is due to appear at Ipswich Crown Court on August 14.

David J. Floyd
Retirement from Parish Council

Great Waldingfield Parish Councillors past and present got together in May to wish David Floyd a happy retirement after 37 years on the Parish Council, for 19 of which he was Chairman.

The 2003 Community Achievement Award winners at a ceremony to celebrate their contributions

THE colour and exuberance of visit-inf Anglican bishops dazzled and enthralled schoolchildren.

Bishops from Melanesia and Tanzania, on route to the Lambeth Conference, took the time to visit children in Sudbury, Cavendish and Great Waldingfield last week.

The Right Rev Jackton Lugumira, Bishop of Lweru, Tanzania, and his wife Josephine spent time with youngsters at Tudor Primary School before enjoying lunch at Great Waldingfield primary.

Angie Jones, headteacher at Waldingfield, said: "The children were quite overawed by his presence and were asking him lots of questions. He told them how he would love his children to come to a school like this."

Friendly welcome... Great Waldingfield Primary School pupils with Bishop Jackton Lugumira and his wi Josephine, of Lweru, Tanzania.   8vs1407003 Pictures available at www.photostoday.co

Hymn book creator had career of note

A NEW book celebrates a rector whose own writings once outsold everything except the Bible and prayer book – yet he remains almost unknown.

John Hopkins, of Great Waldingfield, was co-author, with Thomas Sternhold, of the first English national hymn book, published in 1562.

The book has been written by a former Great Waldingfield resident and chorister, Susan Ranson, who now lives in Norwich.

She took over the job from former Clare headmaster and Great Waldingfield choirmaster Tom Wells, who passed on his research when he

became too old to carry on.

She said: "It was very interesting, but also very difficult.

"I didn't know anything about the life of John Hopkins, but I had an interest in 16th century church music thanks to singing in choirs since I was at college."

Mrs Ranson, a freelance proof-reader, published the book herself.

Sternhold and Hopkins rewrote the psalms as musical hymns for the first time, when the newly formed Church of England needed music for its services.

Many of the hymns are still sung today, in-

cluding *All People That on Earth Do Dwell* – the oldest hymn in the English language still sung to its original tune.

The book, *John Hopkins, Metrical Psalmist and Rector of Great Waldingfield*, will be launched this weekend during the Great Waldingfield flower festival.

It costs £7.50 and profits will go towards the upkeep of Great Waldingfield Church.

● **Copies will be available at the launch, and from Border Editions, 5 Albemarle House, Norwich, NR2 2HP. For more information phone (01603) 454366.**

Garden theft

A WATER butt was stolen from a garden in Bantocks Road, Great Waldingfield.

Bury St Edmunds Magistrates' Court, July 10

Christopher Smart, 18, of Lynns Hall Close, Great Waldingfield. Used a car in Waldingfield Road, Sudbury, with no insurance. Fined £150, £45 costs, six points. No test certificate, fined £60. Drove a vehicle otherwise than in accordance with licence, fined £60.

Hopes grow for boxes

HOPES are rising that almost 30 rural phone boxes threatened with closure might be saved.

Babergh District Council, which has put forward a list of strong reasons for keeping them open, is now waiting to hear BT's final decision.

A MAN arrested when police swooped in Folly Road, Great Waldingfield, on July 31, has appeared at Ipswich Crown Court.

Stephen Oliver, 40, of Great Waldingfield, did not enter a plea to a charge of wounding with intent.

Oliver was bailed with the conditions that he does not contact prosecution witnesses or enter Suffolk except for solicitors or court appointments.

He is currently living in Swansea.

Oliver is due to appear again at Ipswich on October 10.

His arrest followed an alleged assault in Blackfriars, Sudbury.

December 2:

David Robert John Porter, 40, of Heath Estate, Great Waldingfield. Assaulted a man by beating at Sudbury. Community order made for 12 months with requirement to carry out unpaid work for 60 hours. Ordered to pay £100 compensation to victim.

On board... (clockwise from above) Jodi Rogers, Maxwell Scott, Louis Lockwood, Dean Pullen and Aaron Lockwood; Cody Ennis-Hadley; Cody, Poppi and Kelsie Ennis-Hadley and Tom Robinson   8wo1108011,12&13 Pictures by Will Oliver

Skaters get safety message

YOUNGSTERS got the chance to try skateboarding for the first time or learn new tricks during a free taster session.

Around 60 children and 20 parents went to a mobile skatepark at Great Waldingfield Primary School.

Babergh Community Safety Partnership staff organised the event and handed out information on drinking, drugs, personal safety, domestic abuse and home security.

Ann Scott, Babergh community safety officer, said: "The mobile skateparks combine a fun, healthy activity with a chance to learn more about community safety and issues affecting young people.

"Even some of the parents had a go in the skatepark.

"We gave out lots of advice and taught some of the children new board skills."

● Sailing to success. Sisters Emma and Martina Barry, from Great Waldingfield, in action at Poole where they clinched the national Mirror championships.

The sisters had to battle with difficult conditions at both Llandudno and Poole to take the honours.

Only four races were sailed because of strong winds, with Emma, 18, and Martina, 12, taking two firsts, a second and an eighth.

They became the first all-female crew to win the nationals in the 45 years Mirrors have been sailed.

Read Emma's account of the

● Emma and Martina with Olympic gold medallist Reg White   Pictures: Paula Barry

...am: Martina and Emma with their trophies

Village joins WI's big day

GREAT Waldingfield WI celebrates its 90th anniversary with a "Midsummer Madness" day at the village's St Lawrence Church on Saturday, June 21.

The event, which starts at 10.30am, will include organ music, songs by "the noise" youth group, guitar and violin music, bell-ringing and history displays.

Admission is £2 with children under 14 free.

The day ends with a performance in the church by the Selion Jazz Band, starting at 7.30pm.

Tickets are £6 for adults and £3 for children under 14, from Great Waldingfield Post Office, WI members or Sheila Dunnett, on 01787 466859.

All money raised will go towards the St Lawrence Church refurbishment fund.

Night at church proves peaceful

TWO friends got their heads down in the unlikely setting of Great Waldingfield's St Lawrence Church to raise money for restoration work.

Margaret Shannon, from Great Waldingfield and Lesley Mitchell, from Sudbury, spent a night at the church and raised £600 for its funds through sponsorship.

They spent 12 hours at the church, from 7pm to 7am, sleeping in the chancel and the lady chapel.

Mrs Shannon, who is also lay elder of the church, said: "I am 72 and too old to do a sponsored cycle and can't walk that far, so I got the idea to do a sleep-in. If I can't cycle and walk, I can certainly sleep!

"Lesley agreed that it was a great idea and asked to join me and that was that."

And despite the bats and unfamiliar surroundings, the pair had much more fun than they imagined.

"It was fun," said Mrs Shannon. "And we both slept a lot better than either of us thought we would. It was really, really peaceful."

Churchgoers trying to raise £47,000 to repair and decorate the interior of St Lawrence's, as the walls are crumbling and in a bad state of decoration.

The church hosts a harvest and flower festival and gift aid days on Saturday, September 29 and Sunday, September 30.

Getting comfy... Margaret Shannon at St Lawrence's

Jason Jacobs, 9, with Trevor Donovan and Jay Meekings, 9, with Jeff Meekings get to grips with an albino python at Great Waldingfield Primary School.

6-20-

New start ... and guests at the official opening of First Friends Pre-School in Great Waldingfield

Opening day at pre-school

FIRST Friends Pre-school staff and guests celebrated the successful relocation of the Great Waldingfield-based facility with a special opening ceremony.

Babergh District councillor Jenny Antill cut the ribbon on the new building, which has been built in the grounds of the village primary school.

The pre-school, which had been based in Great Waldingfield Primary School, had seven months to find a new home when the school announced it would need its classroom back in February.

Pre-school leader Ann Stone and chairman Mandy Branch secured funding from Suffolk County Council Early Years and the new facility opened its doors to children on September 14.

Ann said: "It has been quite an achievement really.

"The building is brand new and very light and airy.

"We have an all-weather play area as well as space to grow vegetables and flowers.

"We have also got a wildlife area where we are growing wildflowers."

The pre-school, which is open from 9am to 3.30pm five days a week, caters for children from two-years-old to school age.

Call 01787 882473 for more details.

Gardening show at hall

A SILVER anniversary horticultural show will take place in Great Waldingfield Village Hall on Saturday.

The event celebrates 25 years since the formation of the village's show committee.

Village gets £75,000 boost

A GRAND opening ceremony of a village's new £75,000 play area will take place this weekend.

The new play area in Great Waldingfield was built thanks to grants from Suffolk County Council, Babergh District Council, the Suffolk Environmental Trust, the Corporate Regeneration Trust and Great Waldingfield Parish Council.

Harry Taylor, who helped the project become a reality, said: "After a period of almost three years with many challenges, this project illustrates what can be achieved when organisations, young people and the community come together with a common goal as the aim."

The new play area, which is on the village's playing field, replaced a 25-year-old timber trail.

A HEADTEACHER has come in for a storm of criticism for taking children on to a frozen pond during a recent cold snap.

Youngsters from years one and two at Great Waldingfield Primary School were led out on to the ice last month by head teacher Angie Jones as part of a lesson on the weather.

Some parents are now insisting she leaves the school saying she is unfit to be in charge of children.

One parent, who did not want to be named, claimed Mrs Jones's action had almost resulted in a tragedy.

"This led to one of the children thinking it was all right to do this at home and he took his three-year-old brother on to the pond and he fell through."

She said his mother had to get in the water to save him.

"Obviously, Mrs Jones is not fit to be in charge of our children," she added.

Kirsty Swain, 29, whose daughter attends the pre-school said: "If it had been my child who was led out on to the ice I would have taken

● Angie Jones

"No matter what the circumstances are no child should be taken out on to the ice. In fact no adults should be on there in the first place. I'm extremely concerned that my child will soon be in the primary school with that type of irresponsible leader-ship."

PARENTS have rallied round a head teacher after she was criticised for allowing children on to a frozen pond during a lesson on the weather.

Angie Jones, headteacher of Great Waldingfield School, took pupils from years one and two out to the school pond while studying winter conditions.

Parents unhappy with her decision during the cold snap on January 9 felt the action was irresponsible and dangerous.

But following publication of the story in last week's *Free Press* dozens of parents have written letters and voiced their support for the "wonderful job" Mrs Jones does at the school.

Kind gesture ... Great Waldingfield Horticultural Society donates the chairs to the Old School Wood.

Benches mark 25th birthday

TWO seats have been presented to a community woodland by the Great Waldingfield Horticultural Society to mark its 25th anniversary.

The presentation, on Saturday, was made to the Old School Wood in the village.

Shirley Rose, a member of the woodland's committee, Branchlines, said the seats were a good addition to the area.

She said: "The seats have been restored beautifully and we are very pleased to have them because for years they sat outside St Peter's Church in Sudbury.

"They have been put at the top of the hill in the wood on a special site that we have created and you get a really good view."

"It's good to think of them being used again and in such a pleasant setting."

Around 40 people turned out to watch the presentation ceremony and then there was a village picnic and games including a treasure hunt.

Hold on tight ... More than 100 people attended the official opening of a new £75,000 play area in Great Waldingfield.   MSFP-10-04-10 HW025

196

2010

Prize giving proves a great success

GREAT Waldingfield Bowls and
Social Club held their annual prize
giving.

The event was a great success with
more than 40 members and guests
attending.

Pictured are some of the trophy
winners. From left: club chairman
Ian Stares, Noel Game, Margaret
Parmenter, Mick Fosker, May Knock,
Joce Mallett, Mary Jackson, Geoff

Stares, Eddie Harris, Roger Stearn,
Celia Dixon-Wright.

● Anyone interested in joining the
club, either beginners or experienced
bowlers, should contact chairman Ian
tares on 01787 370590.

Toast of the community ... Babergh's awards winners gather at the Stoke-by-Nayland Club

Here's to unsung heroes

Jean
Misselbrook and Shirley Rose

(both Great Waldingfield),

DINNER LADIES DO A TURN

Working party ... members and helpers of Acton and Waldingfield Cubs stop for a team picture as they tackle some tidying up on the meadows near Brundon Lane

Christmas story

Great Waldingfield Primary School Nativity complete with donkey.

Samantha Hays RN, Bill Green, Army and Geoff Braybrooke RAF receive the specially commissioned flag.

Forces day celebrated

CROWDS gathered around the region on Saturday for special ceremonies to celebrate the first Armed Forces Day.

It was the first time that a day has been dedicated to all those who have served in the Army, Navy and Air Force.

In Sudbury, town officials lowered the specially-commissioned flag that had been flown throughout the week and presented it to three veterans,

one from each service.

Second World War veteran Bill Green was also celebrating his 88th birthday and was presented with a rose for his garden.

Town clerk, Sue Brotherwood said: "People stopped and gathered because it was a busy market day and it was a very pleasant occasion.

"We all sang happy birthday to Bill and you could see that he was really taken aback by it all."

Bill Green, whose 88th birthday was Saturday

Bags of help ... Great Waldingfield CEVCP junior school students with shopping bags recycled from the old school hall curtains. Left to right: Jordan King, Kaye Gooderhan, Connor Sparkes and Caitlin Moulton.   Picture: 8wo2901007 www.photostoday.co.uk

History lesson ... Pupils at Great Waldingfield Primary School shared a roast dinner and lessons about Suffolk's past with visiting grandparents.   MSFP-13-05-10 HW 006

A 30-YEAR-old man from Great Waldingfield has died from his injuries following a car crash in Sussex.

Chris Alderton, of Green Acre, suffered serious head injuries in the crash, which happened near Horsham on the night of Friday, January 14.

A WHITE Mercedes Sprinter van was stolen from the street in Barrow Hill, Acton, while its driver was making a delivery between 2.30pm and 2.45pm on Wednesday afternoon.

The van was later found abandoned at Upsher Green, Great Waldingfield, with items for delivery missing. Empty boxes and personal items were also found in Badley Road, Great Waldingfield.

Bronwen Elizabeth Griffiths, 55, of Holbrook Close, Great Waldingfield. Drove a Vauxhall Corsa in Great Waldingfield Road, Sudbury, after consuming excess alcohol: 64 microgrammes in 100 millilitres of breath. Legal limit is 35 mcg. Committed to prison for 12 weeks suspended for 18 months. Offence so serious, had flouted court orders. Defendant must comply with following requirements within 18 month supervision period: have treatment for alcohol dependency under direction of supervisor for six months and attend appointments with probation service. Banned from driving for 36 months. Ban may be reduced by six months if defendant completes an approved course. Drove while disqualified, suspended sentence order. Used vehicle without third party insurance. No separate penalty. Ordered to pay £85 costs.

GREAT WALDINGFIELD: 30-year-old driver dies

By Jonathan Schofield

A SUFFOLK village has been left in shock after a 30-year-old man died from injuries he suffered in a crash nearly three weeks ago.

Christopher Alderton, from Great Waldingfield, near Sudbury, was driving along the A24 at Dial Post in Haywards Heath, Sussex, on Friday, January 14.

He was travelling in a northbound direction when his blue Nissan Micra collided with a Renault recovery truck waiting to turn right into the Old Barn Nurseries at about 6.40pm.

Mr Alderton, of Green Acre, was taken to the Royal Sussex County Hospital in Brighton with serious head injuries and was later trans-

ferred to Hurstwood Park Neurological Centre in Haywards Heath for further treatment.

He remained at the specialist centre until his death, which was announced by Sussex Police last week.

The 48-year-old man driving the recovery truck was unhurt in the collision.

The Reverend Caroline Hallet, from the Church of St Lawrence, in Great Waldingfield, said his death was a tragedy for the entire family and all Christopher's friends and had come as a great shock to the village.

She said: "Everyone's thoughts and prayers are with the family at this terrible time."

Sussex Police are still investigating the collision and appealing for witnesses to the incident to contact them.

jonathan.schofield@eadt.co.uk

FIRST FRIENDS Pre - School Nursery

Pre School is an established Pre School Nursery in Folly Road, Gt Waldingfield.

based in Great Waldingfield,

We are opening a new bright, spacious, stimulating pre school nursery on **Monday September 14** for children from 2 years

We are a non profit making Pre School offering affordable childcare with fully qualified childcare s

OPENING HOURS
Monday - Friday 9.00am - 3.30pm

Funded and unfunded spaces available

Contact: Ann Stone

Picturedabove: Ann Stone (third from left)and the team at First Friends

GREAT WALDINGFIELD: Learner's national award

COLIN SPENCE (Conservative, Sudbury East and Waldingfield division): Mr Spence, who is the council's portfolio holder for public protection said:

"When you see that we have had to find £43million of savings from the budget this year, with £50 million to find next year, and £30 million the year after, it makes you realise how much further we have to go.

"We have listened to many people voicing their concerns and, bearing in mind the pressures we face in terms of funding cuts, we have worked very hard to do the very best we can."

He said he voted against all the budget amendments and supported the budget.

By Jonathan Schofield

A DETERMINED student from west Suffolk has been nominated for a national award after turning her life around through education.

Gill Camilleri, 45, from Great Waldingfield, was forced to give up work due to ill health and had been unemployed for six months when she was advised to join an IT training programme at West Suffolk College, in Bury St Edmunds, last May.

After sailing through a series of computer classes at the college's Sudbury Centre, she is now up for the national Adult Learner of the Year Award, which will take place in May.

Alan Fraser, who died suddenly

STIFANI ANTONY PETER After a long battle with cancer, sadly died on Sunday 23rd January 2011 at the St Nicholas Hospice aged 54. Loving husband to Faye, devoted father to Emma and James and crazy grandad to Max & Kitty. The funeral service will take place at the Holy Trinity Church, Long Melford on Friday 11th February 2011 at 11.00am followed by burial in the cemetery. Family flowers only but donations if desired, made payable to the Macmillan Unit, West Suffolk Hospital, may be sent care of Hunnaball of Sudbury, New House, 62a North Street, Sudbury CO10 1RE.

ACHIEVER: Gill Camilleri outside the Sudbury Centre in Cornard Road.

Photograph: CONTRIBUTED

A taste of native American dance

DONNING feathers and facepaint, children aged seven to nine at Great Waldingfield Primary School were taught some authentic dances as part of this term's study of North American Indians.

Head of dance at Sudbury Upper School Tania Verow visited the school on Thursday to hold a special lesson on native American dance, giving pupils the chance to incorporate their own ideas.

They wore jewellery they had made themselves, painted their faces and used feathers brought along by Miss Verow.

Class teacher Katherine Hart said the North American Indian project was very popular.

"It's the second time we have done it and the children love all the different aspects. They are building a totem pole and have made tepees and jewellery.

"It is cross-curricular and covers six subjects including PE and art."

Tomorrow pupils will be painting their faces again and wearing their jewellery for a native American Indian assembly.

Fun lesson ... Great Waldingfield pupils have been learning about native American culture. 9HW2901023 www.photostoday.co.uk

You are warmly invited to TEA

to say

Farewell

to Margaret Shannon
on Sunday 20 February
at 4pm at Acton Vicarage

Jury fails to reach verdict

A GREAT Waldingfield man is to face a retrial after a jury failed to reach a verdict.

George Browning, 51, of Lavenham Road, had denied charges of possession of cannabis and possession of criminal property.

He stood trial at Ipswich Crown Court but on Friday, the jury was discharged after being unable to reach a verdict on either charge.

GREAT WALDINGFIELD
WOMEN'S INSTITUTE
(Founded June 1918)

PROGRAMME 2011

President: RACHEL SWAN
280280

Vice-President: MAISIE ROOT
377088

Secretary: MARY JACKSON
371068

Treasurer: PRISCILLA BACKHOUSE
319073

Hall Hostess: MARION BOWES
312846

**MEETINGS on first Wednesday of the month
2 p.m. AT AFTERNOONS THROUGHOUT THE YEAR**

Subscription £30.00

Facing closure ... Great Waldingfield's First Friends pre-school is a victim of its own success.

PARENTS and staff at a village pre-school have described their shock and anger after being told their school is facing closure.

Great Waldingfield's First Friends pre-school is currently housed in one of the classrooms at the village primary school.

Staff have been told the primary school needed the room due to increased numbers and the 40 toddlers that attend would have to leave by July 15.

Devastated staff were left to tell parents the bad news.

Kirsty Swain, a pre-school committee member, said: "This has upset so many people. The parents of the village who see this as a lifeline in juggling jobs and childcare; the children who are very settled here and the staff that have worked so hard to make the pre-school so successful."

School scores highly in latest inspection

A PRIMARY school in west Suffolk has been recognised for its strong sense of community in its latest Ofsted inspection.

Inspectors visited Great Waldingfield Primary last term and awarded the school high accolades in almost every category.

Headteacher Angie Jones said she was thrilled with the recognition which she said was down to the hard work of both staff and pupils and the support of parents.

Alan Geoffrey Sagon
16th August 1928 – 3rd March 2011

Ethel's 100th a delight

FIVE generations of a family gathered in Suffolk to make sure a 100th birthday was a memorable occasion.

Ethel Hampshire got two surprises in one day when her Sudbury retirement home staged a tea party for her after the extended family gathering.

A great great grandmother to eight and a great grandmother to nine, she was able to mark her special day in the company of the living lineage of her family spanning five generations.

The former Waldingfield WI member also received a bouquet from the club she formerly attended as well as a card from the Queen.

"My mother was just delighted to see all her extended family there together. She was really pleased," said daughter Jean Willings.

Family members made donations to the upkeep of the Red House retirement home's garden, which Mrs Hampshire still enjoys walking around.

A widow for 56 years, Mrs Hampshire is originally from Lancashire. She moved to Suffolk with her husband who was a slaughterman in Bures.

Her nine grandchildren were represented at the family occasion, held in All Saint's Hall, by family members from Cornwall and Somerset.

ref tmo 09 ethel hampshire 5

HAPPY BIRTHDAY: Ethel Hampshire celebrates her 100th birthday with daughter Jean Willings, granddaughter Judy Arscott, great grandson Gavin Helyar and great great granddaughter Millie Helyar

Photo: TUDOR MORGAN-OWEN

Widow's loving tribute to Alan

by Anne Wise
anne.wise@
suffolkfreepress.co.uk

A SUDBURY law firm closed for business on Tuesday afternoon as a mark of respect to attend the funeral of its hugely popular retired conveyancer Alan Fraser, who died suddenly two weeks ago.

Staff from Bates Wells & Braithwaite, in Friars Street, attended the 63-year-old's funeral at Holy Trinity Church in Long Melford.

He had worked for the firm for more than 30 years, and was well-known in the town, retiring three years ago after suffering ill-health.

Mark Heselden, a senior partner at the firm, said: "Alan was a hugely popular member of the firm and was sorely missed when he retired.

"We have received countless calls from former members of staff, clients and other professionals in the town wishing to pass on their sympathy."

This week, his widow, Barbara, of The Street, Great Waldingfield, paid tribute to her husband of 39 years.

They met when she was a temporary secretary and they worked together at a law firm in Romford, Essex, before moving to Suffolk.

Born in Chigwell, he started his conveyancing career at a firm in London. After a spell working in Dorset, the couple moved to live in a cottage in Friars Street, Sudbury, so Alan could be close to his new job at Bates Wells & Braithwaite.

She said: "Alan really loved living here, and Suffolk has been very kind to us over the years.

"He was a man with a huge sense of humour and love of life and people. Everybody talks about his smiling face.

"He had high blood pressure and retired from his job and during this time, we had a wonderful three years together.

"He loved anything to do with the sea and we had a favourite walk every day with the dog. He became interested in woodwork and got himself a router.

"He also worked in Waitrose doing a part-time job and he loved it. The staff there were incredibly fond of him.

"For me, he was the warmest, kindest, most loving man I could ever have known and I feel privileged to be able to say he was my husband.

"He wouldn't want us to be sad so I will certainly be trying to learn from the wonderful memories that I have of him."

She said people described him as a real character with a great sense of humour.

"He would put people at ease, and he never regarded what he did as a conveyancer as just a job," she said.

"He always tried to help people get the house they wanted, and make them happy – it was always about the people."

Mr Fraser died on January 13 after a heart attack. His brothers, nieces and nephews travelled from Bristol and Kent to attend his funeral.

Sam Thornton, from Thornton's, in Friars Street, paid tribute to him. He said: "I will miss his friendly face and smile whenever we met.

"If every solicitor were half as caring and concerned for clients, the world would be a better place.

"His values almost seemed old-fashioned, but in truth it should be what we all strive for."

On February 28th a much-respected Great Waldingfield farmer died, following a battle with cancer. Owen Kiddy was a great character with a huge sense of humour and always a ready joke. He and his wife Judith and their four children had lived at Brandeston Hall for over forty years. Owen loved the land and was at his happiest when on a tractor. He had a long association with our local church and at one time was church warden. The affection in which he was held was reflected by an overflowing church for his funeral. This was a beautiful service with some of Owen's favourite hymns. He will be sadly and greatly missed.

OWEN KIDDY

18th November 1928 - 28th February 2011

203

Hats off to mums as children say thanks

MOTHERS got special VIP treatment at Great Waldingfield Primary School on Friday when they were invited into the school by their children for a pre-Mother's Day treat.

Children held an assembly where they read out their tributes to mums, grans and aunts. The school even had boxes of tissues on hand in case of tears and later on, there was a tea party with children helping to serve cakes and gingerbread biscuits they had made especially for the occasion. Mums wore hats made at home, using recycled materials such as carrier bags and even a lampshade.

Head teacher Angie Jones said: "It was a wonderful day. We had 70 mums, grans and aunts who came along. We like to do the same for the dads, too, for Father's Day.

Head start ... Mums got a big thankyou at Great Waldingfield primary school children when their children made hats for a Mother's Day treat. Pictured are Debbie Rogers and her son Joe Harris, six, and Jennie Bonner with her son Archie, seven.

Love blossoms ... Joy and Vic Abbott, who celebrate 60 years of marriage today, and, right, on their wedding day in 1951. **MSFP-10-03-11 MM 004** **Picture by Mecha Morton**

Couple toast anniversary

MAKING the most of what you have is the secret to marital bliss, according to a couple celebrating their diamond wedding.

Joy and Vic Abbott, from Rectory Road in Great Waldingfield, mark 60 years of marriage today.

The pair, who are both members of the Sudbury branch of the Salvation Army, say they have had their ups and downs since tying the knot but have always been happy.

Joy, 78, said: "We had very little money when we first got together and didn't expect too much.

"Our house was a real mess when we moved in and that tested our patience and love for one another, but I think if you have things easy you can become dissatisfied."

Joy, a former nurse maid, said she could still remember everything about her wedding day in 1951. The couple spent their honeymoon in London.

"We look on reaching 60 years of marriage as normal," she said.

"We realise how blessed we've been. We've had some rough times when we didn't know where our next pennies were coming from but we've just made the most of everything we've had."

The couple have three children, Jeff, Faith and Sharon, six grandchildren, three step-grandchildren and two great grandchildren.

Joy added: "We're very much a family and have always been very close.

"We love spending time with all our grandchildren."

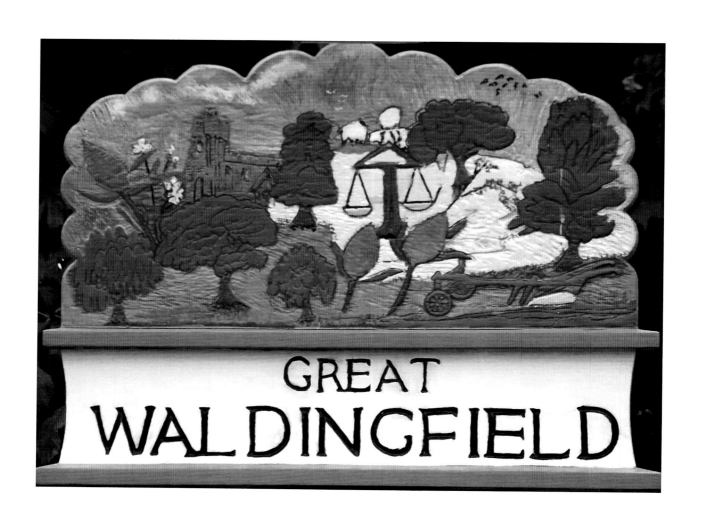

GREAT
WALDINGFIELD

GREAT WALDINGFIELD

VILLAGE SCRAP BOOK

Presented by the Members of

GREAT WALDINGFIELD
"WOMEN'S INSTITUTE"

December 5th, 1951

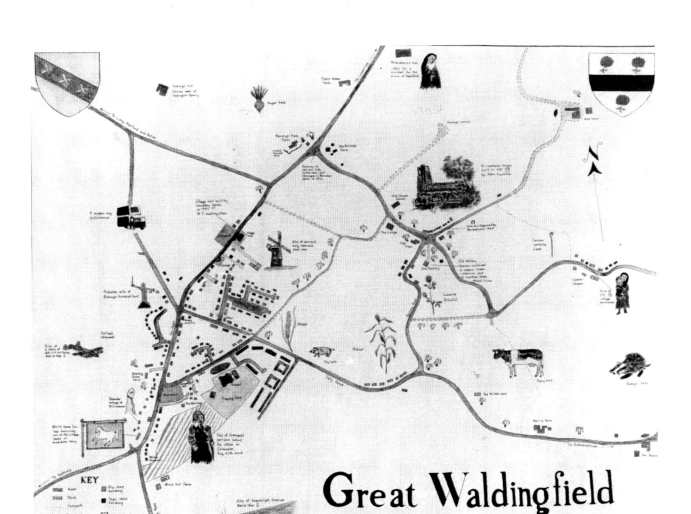

Great Waldingfield

The village scrapbook is contained within a single leather-bound volume with a brass clasp presented to the village by the members of the Women's Institute on 5th December 1951. A committee was formed to maintain the book and they made various notes, prefacing many of the sections which in themselves provide an interesting insight into village life.

The main celebration in 1951 was the 'Festival of Britain' and we understand that all Women's Institutes were invited to produce a book of historical interest for their villages. We can only imagine that this was the background to the commencement of the scrapbook, although we have not been able to confirm this. Subsequently, pages were added to record the events of the Coronation but this was not until 1953.

The Village sign (above left), situated on our village green, was erected in about 1970 and we believe it originated from a banner made by the WI which also formed the basis for the map (above). The map was hand-embroided with various symbols identifying activities and points of interest in the village. Only a photo now exists of this. The sign incorporates various trees present in the village with symbols indicating the commercial and agricultural activities in the village.

From a population of under 1,000, over the centuries since the Second World War Great Waldingfield has mushroomed to around 2,000 inhabitants. There are a small number of businesses in the village, which is mainly residential but with many rural and historical aspects; a significant number of villagers can trace their origins back several generations.

207

First published in 2011
by
DESERT ISLAND BOOKS LIMITED
16 Imperial Park, Rawreth Lane, Rayleigh, Essex SS6 9RS
United Kingdom
www.desertislandbooks.com

© 2011 Edna Allen

British Library Cataloguing-in-Publication Data
A catalogue record for this book is available from the British Library

ISBN 978-1-905328-91-8

Printed in Great Britain

LIST OF FIRST EDITION SUBSCRIBERS:

Joy & Vick Abbott, Christine & John Anderson, Jenny & Nick Antill, Priscilla Backhouse, Janet Baldwin, Julie Barber, Michael & Madeline Barker, Gary & Hazel Barnard, Molly Blackwell, Ian & Shirley Black, Sally & Brian Brinton, Betty Bullard, Jos Butcher, Alison Butcher, Norma & David Chambers, Jo & Peter Chapman, Eileen Coleman, Leslie & Audrey Cremer, Lyn & Mick Culham, Cliff & Tracey Dark, Pauline East, Sarah & John Fensom, Rose & Alf Finch, David & Anne Floyd, Patrick Friend, Margaret & David Graves, Glenda & Ron Griffiths, Trevor Groome, Jackie, Charles, Will, Bethan & Kate Hann, Katherine & Colin Hart, David & Karen Hayward, Martin & Shirley Hewett, Michael & Margaret Hills, Lyn & Vince Humphries, Claire & Mike Kiely, Michael Lang, Sid & Pat Leathers, Colin & Linda Lutz, Charles & Joce Mallett, Faith & Frank Marsden, Kathy & Richard May, Mandy, Colin & Kate McCallum, Jean & John Misselbrook, Jackie Morden, Fred Nice, Helen Page, Andrea Parkinson, Jean Pearson, Patricia Proby, Doris Ratcliffe, Shirley & Brian Rose, Bernard & Linda Rushton, Valerie & John Saberton, Margaret Shannon, Paul & Aileen Smeathers, Michael & Ann Stone, Deanna & Gregory Stow, Hilary & David Taylor, Betty Tegg, Derek & Suzanne Thompson, William Vowles, Linda Ward, Amy & Saul Ward, Ruth Warren, Katherine Whitelodge, Shirley Whittaker, Mary Wright (formerly Nice), Tony Smith & Carol Marney.